FIRSTBORN SONS,
THEIR
RIGHTS & RISKS

An Inquiry as to the Privileges and
Perils of the Members of the Church
of God.

G. H. LANG

SCHOETTLE PUBLISHING CO., INC.
P.O. BOX 1246
HAYESVILLE, N.C. 28904
1997

PRINTED IN THE UNITED STATES OF AMERICA

ISBN 1-56453-106-6

PUBLISHERS COMMENTS

The works of George Henry Lang have long been treasured by the better Bible students. They have been loaned and borrowed since the early part of this century with great value in Bible study.

Their value has increased to the point that the Lord has burdened the Publisher to once again make available this searching exposition of G.H. Lang. Prayerfully, we continue the task of reprinting the long list of valuable books, pamphlets, and studies that emanated from the talented and God-blessed pen of Mr. Lang.

It is entirely possible that our collection of all of Mr. Lang's works is not complete. We are trying to compile all of his articles and especially his letters, and it may be, that you can loan us your copy for insertion in these future works. Your participation is invited in this worthy venture.

It was said of Mr. Lang by M. Collier that . . . "Two courageous men were born in 1874; Churchill and G.H. Lang. He was never called before kings or judges, but he was that rarity – a man who taught what he really believed, and lived by what he taught regardless of consequences. This simple courage was to him but simple common sense. God was his father, and father's wisdom is always good. I commend the idea to us all. It saves a lot of heartaches if you refuse to look at the hazards, and look simply to God . . ."

SCHOETTLE PUBLISHING CO. INC.

PREFACE

This volume is the first in a proposed series of reprints of the works of G.H. Lang by Messrs. Conley & Schoettle in the U.S.A. The series will embrace not only prophetic matters, but also the vast range of divine truth which came from Lang's pen such as Church order, finance, the Christian role in society, the present world order and its end, the judgment of both Christians as well as the ungodly at the Bema and the Great White Throne respectively.

The larger works, long out-of-print, will come first, followed by smaller books and pamphlets bound-up in larger volumes. Finally, it is hoped hitherto unpublished material, especially his Magnum Opus, left in manuscript for, **PREVAILING TO ESCAPE** being a definitive treatment of the Partial Rapture doctrine from the author's standpoint.

G.H. Lang was a teacher whose oral ministery had great lucidity and weight: his written work shared these qualities. Just as his holy walk gave weight to all he said, so every page of written work breathes devotion to Christ as he seeks to bring before the Christian public the mind of the Eternal. Above all, Lang was master, as his Puritan forebears, at **application** of Scripture to the life and walk of God's people.

However, being an independent thinker, it was in the realm of **interpretation** of Scripture, especially prophecy, that caused him to become the most controversial figure among Brethren among whom he mostly moved, since J.N. Darby. In the words of a relative by marriage, Douglas Brealey, himself a much used servant of Christ, his study of prophecy "led him into avenues where some of us could not follow" - exactly the position of the publishers and of the present writer. Nevertheless, for mature students to have such vital, scholarly and thought provoking writings before them must be a great service to the Church of God at large. Whilst rejecting the Partial Rapture and its concomitants, they acknowledge much to warm the heart, inform the mind, and direct the feet of the Saints in the writings of G.H. Lang.

May all who know the benefits of these works join in prayer, wishing all involved in the God speed.

Hemsworth, England   Jack Green
23 October 82

CONTENTS.

George Henry Lang

Born November 20, 1874 in London, England. With the Lord at Wimbourne, Dorset, England on October 20, 1958.

FOREWORD.

Is it worth while to follow Christ ? Does not being His disciple involve so great loss and so much persecution and other trouble as to cause reasonable men to ask if it is worth while ? Did He not Himself say to His disciples, " In the world ye have tribulation?" and is it not written that "all that would live godly in Christ Jesus shall suffer persecution ?" (John xvi, 33; II Tim. iii, 12). Is there adequate compensation for such sacrifice and endurance ?

The following pages give part of the answer to such questions. Only part, however ; for there are other recompenses to be allowed weight in giving a complete answer. But the line of thought here followed is one least often enlarged upon, and yet one that is very largely set forth in God's Book. The writer has himself felt the stimulus of the prospects and warnings here opened up, and he prays that by these pages others may be enlightened and strengthened, and so be encouraged to " follow the Lamb whithersoever He goeth."

This book was written in Egypt in 1914. More than twenty years further reflection having confirmed the writer's convictions, it is now sent forth with the prayer that it may be used to provoke others to love and to good works.

Quotations are usually from the Revised Version.

Son of God ! Thou now art seated
   High upon Thy Father's throne,
All Thy gracious work completed,
   All Thy mighty victory won.
Every knee in heaven is bending
   To the Lamb for sinners slain :
Every voice and heart is swelling,
   "Worthy is the Lamb to reign."

Lord, in all Thy power and glory
   Still Thy thoughts and eyes are here ;
Watching o'er Thy ransomed people
   To thy gracious heart so dear,
Thou for us art interceding,
   Everlasting is Thy love ;
And a blessed rest preparing
   In our Father's house above.

Jesus, Lord ! Thy faithful promise
   Says "Behold I quickly come " ;
And our hearts, to Thine responsive,
   Cry, " Come, Lord, and take us home."
Oh ! the rapture that awaits us,
   When we meet Thee in the air,
And with Thee ascend in triumph,
   All Thy deepest joys to share.

Lamb of God ! when Thou in glory
   Shalt to this sad earth return ;
All Thy foes shall quake before Thee,
   All who now despise Thee mourn ;
Then shall we at Thine appearing,
   With Thee in Thy kingdom reign,
Thine the praise, and Thine the glory,
   Lamb of God, for sinners slain.

CHAPTER I.

THE COMING KING.

"For the Son of Man shall come in the glory of His Father with His angels ; and then shall He render unto every man according to his doing."—(Matt. xvi, 27).

Things will not for ever go on as they are. Sin and sorrow crushing mankind, and death daily hurrying multitudes to its gloomy depths, are not to be permanent conditions on this old earth. The ancient poets used to sing of a golden age far back in times remote beginnings; but they had no sure prospect of things becoming in the future better than they are. The nations were without God and without hope (Eph. ii, 12). But the prophets of God exhausted the possibilities of language in describing to the Jewish race a golden age that is to be. And this prospect is not for that nation only, but is God's purpose for the whole world.

A few of these declarations of the prophetic Scriptures are given, beginning with the first covenant with Abram, which constitutes the initial step taken by God to reveal to man His method of fulfilling through Abram His gracious purpose and promise to bless all the race.

"Now Jehovah said unto Abram, Get thee out of thy _{Genesis xii, 1-3 (1921, B.C.)} country, and from thy kindred, and from thy father's house, unto the land that I will shew thee : and I will make of thee a great nation, and I will bless thee, and make thy name great ; and be thou a blessing : and I will bless them that bless thee, and him that curseth thee will I curse : and in thee shall all the families of the earth be blessed.

Deut. xxxii, 43. (1451 B.C.) Rejoice, O ye nations, *with* his people :

For he will avenge the blood of his servants,

And will render vengeance to his adversaries,

And will make expiation for his land, for his people.

15

16 THE GOD OF JACOB SHALL REIGN.

Psalm lxvii (about 1000 B.C.) God be merciful unto us, and bless us,
And cause his face to shine upon us ;
That thy way may be known upon earth,
Thy saving health among all nations.
Let the peoples praise thee, O God ;
Let all the peoples praise thee.
O let the nations be glad and sing for joy :
For thou shalt judge the peoples with equity,
And govern the nations upon earth.
Let the peoples praise thee, O God ;
Let all the peoples praise thee.
The earth hath yielded her increase :
God, even our own God, shall bless us.
God shall bless us ;
And all the ends of the earth shall fear him.

Isaiah ii, 1-4, (750 B C.) "The word that Isaiah the son of Amoz saw
[This and the following dates concerning Judah and Jerusalem.
are given in round numbers]. "And it shall come to pass in the latter days, that
the mountain of Jehovah's house shall be
established in the top of the mountains, and shall be exalted
above the hills; and all nations shall flow unto it. And many
peoples shall go and say, Come ye, and let us go up to the
mountain of Jehovah, to the house of the God of Jacob; and
he will teach us of his ways, and we will walk in his paths ;
for out of Zion shall go forth the law, and the word of Jehovah
from Jerusalem. And he shall judge between the nations,
and shall reprove many peoples: and they shall beat their
swords into plowshares, and their spears into pruninghooks :
nation shall not lift up sword against nation, neither shall they
learn war any more.

Isaiah ix, 6, 7 "For unto us a child is born, unto us a son is given :
and the government shall be upon his shoulder: and his
name shall be called Wonderful, Counsellor, Mighty God,
Everlasting Father, Prince of Peace. Of the increase of his
government and of peace there shall be no end, upon the throne
of David, and upon his kingdom, to establish it, and to uphold
it with judgement and with righteousness from henceforth even
for ever. The zeal of Jehovah of hosts shall perform this.

"And there shall come forth a shoot out of the stock of
^{Isaiah xi,} Jesse, and a branch out of his roots shall bear fruit; and
₁₋₁₀
the spirit of Jehovah shall rest upon him, the spirit of wisdom
and understanding, the spirit of counsel and might, the spirit
of knowledge and of the fear of Jehovah; and his delight shall
be in the fear of Jehovah: and he shall not judge after the
sight of his eyes, neither reprove after the hearing of his ears:
but with righteousness shall he judge the poor, and reprove
with equity for the meek of the earth: and he shall smite the
earth with the rod of his mouth, and with the breath of his
lips shall he slay the wicked. And righteousness shall be the
girdle of his loins, and faithfulness the girdle of his reins.
And the wolf shall dwell with the lamb, and the leopard shall
lie down with the kid; and the calf and the young lion and the
fatling together; and a little child shall lead them. And the
cow and the bear shall feed; their young ones shall lie down
together: and the lion shall eat straw like the ox. And the
sucking child shall play on the hole of the asp, and the weaned
child shall put his hand on the basilisk's den. They shall not
hurt nor destroy in all my holy mountain: for the earth shall
be full of the knowledge of Jehovah, as the waters cover the sea.

" And it shall come to pass in that day, that the root of Jesse,
which standeth for an ensign of the peoples, unto him shall
the nations seek; and his resting place shall be glorious.

"Ho, every one that thirsteth, come ye to the waters, and
^{Isaiah lv,} he that hath no money; come ye, buy and eat; yea,
₁₋₅
come, buy wine and milk without money and without price.
Wherefore do ye spend money for that which is not bread?
and your labour for that which satisfieth not? hearken diligently
unto me, and eat ye that which is good, and let your soul delight
itself in fatness. Incline your ear, and come unto me; hear,
and your soul shall live: and I will make an everlasting
covenant with you, even the sure mercies of David. Behold, I
have given him for a witness to the peoples, a leader and
commander to the peoples. Behold, thou shalt call a nation
that thou knowest not, and a nation that knew not thee shall
run unto thee, because of Jehovah thy God, and for the Holy
One of Israel; for he hath glorified thee.

Daniel ii,
44.
(600 B.C.)
"And in the days of those kings shall the God of heaven set up a kingdom which shall never be destroyed, nor shall the sovereignty thereof be left to another people; but it shall break in pieces and consume all these kingdoms, and it shall stand for ever.

Daniel vii,
13, 14
(355 B.C.)
"I saw in the night visions, and, behold, there came with the clouds of heaven one like unto a son of man, and he came even to the ancient of days, and they brought him near before him. And there was given him dominion, and glory, and a kingdom, that all the peoples, nations, and languages should serve him: his dominion is an everlasting dominion, which shall not pass away, and his kingdom that which shall not be destroyed.

Joel ii.
28-32.
(800 B.C.)
"And it shall come to pass afterward, that I will pour out my spirit upon all flesh; and your sons and your daughters shall prophesy, your old men shall dream dreams, your young men shall see visions: and also upon the servants and upon the handmaids in those days will I pour out my spirit. And I will shew wonders in the heavens and in the earth, blood, and fire, and pillars of smoke. The sun shall be turned into darkness, and the moon into blood, before the great and terrible day of Jehovah come. And it shall come to pass, that whosoever shall call on the name of Jehovah shall be delivered: for in mount Zion and in Jerusalem there shall be those that escape, as Jehovah hath said, and among the remnant those whom Jehovah doth call.

Zech. vi,
12, 13,
(510 B.C.)
"Thus speaketh Jehovah of hosts, saying, Behold, the man whose name is the Branch; and he shall grow up out of his place, and he shall build the temple of Jehovah; even he shall build the temple of Jehovah; and he shall bear the glory, and shall sit and rule upon his throne; and he shall be a priest upon his throne.

Malachi ii., 17
iii., 1-6 and ch.
iv., 1-3
(400 B.C.)
"Ye have wearied Jehovah with your words. Yet ye say, Wherein have we wearied him? In that ye say, Every one that doeth evil is good in the sight of Jehovah, and he delighteth in them; or where is the God of judgement? Behold, I send my messenger and he shall prepare

"the way before me : and the Lord, whom ye seek, shall suddenly come to his temple; and the messenger of the covenant, whom ye delight in, behold he cometh, saith Jehovah of hosts. But who may abide the day of his coming? and who shall stand when he appeareth? for he is like a refiner's fire, and like fuller's soap : and he shall sit as a refiner and purifier of silver, and he shall purify the sons of Levi, and purge them as gold and silver ; and they shall offer unto Jehovah offerings in righteousness. Then shall the offering of Judah and Jerusalem be pleasant unto Jehovah, as in the days of old, and as in ancient years. And I will come near to you to judgement; and I will be a swift witness against the sorcerers, and against the adulterers, and against false swearers; and against those that oppress the hireling in his wages, the widow, and the fatherless, and that turn aside the stranger from his right, and fear not me, saith Jehovah of hosts. For I Jehovah change not ; therefore ye, O sons of Jacob, are not consumed.

"For behold, the day cometh, it burneth as a furness; and all the proud, and all that work wickedness, shall be stubble: and the day that cometh shall burn them up, saith Jehovah of hosts, and it shall leave them neither root nor branch. But unto you that fear my name shall the sun of righteousness arise with healing in his wings; and ye shall go forth, and gambol as calves of the stall. And ye shall tread down the wicked; for they shall be ashes under the soles of your feet in the day that I do make, saith Jehovah of hosts."

Thus by a succession of messengers, covering a period of no less than fifteen centuries, did God foretell to men the glorious things that He is working out for this earth in conjunction with the heavenly world.

Then shall Satan and his hosts be bound in the abyss under the earth (Rev. xx, 1-3), and thus there will be no temptation from without to incite to evil. Then shall God's own spirit of unity, love and peace be poured out upon all (Joel ii, 28) and all men shall know God and love one another (Hab. ii, 13, 14). The perverse and rebellious shall be destroyed from amongst men, that the virtuous may receive unhindered blessing. The beasts will lose their ferocity, and the fields be exceeding fruitful. The very mountain tops shall wave with ripened corn (Psalm lxxii, 16), and all creation "shall be delivered from the bondage of corruption into the liberty of the glory of the children of God" (Romans viii, 21).

But every kingdom requires a king; and who is the sovereign wise enough and strong enough to produce such a kingdom over the whole wide world, or to maintain it when set up?

The prophets long since declared that no one but God would be equal to this great task, and so announced that One should be born Who should be none less than "Emmanuel" (God with us), the mighty God, the Father of eternity. He, thus become man, would be the Prince of Peace, of whose kingdom there should be no end (Isa. vii, 14 and ix, 6, 7).

Suitable to the greatness of His Person should be the uniqueness of His entrance into humanity, for a virgin should be His mother. Thus begotten by the direct action of the Holy Spirit He should be without that taint and entail of an inherited sinful nature which effectually forbade that any other could save the world, since each other himself needed to be saved.

The country and the town where He should be born were also named several centuries before He was to come (Micah v, 2).

But the prophets of God foretold that the Messiah would come to earth twice. The first time He would be "lowly," and be "despised and rejected of men, a man of sorrows, and acquainted with grief" (Zech. ix, 9; Isa. liii, 3).

Then He would be violently killed by enemies: yet this as part of God's counsel concerning Him; for thus dying He would provide for men healing from the fatal disease of sin, and freedom from dread of judgment, for, says the prophet, "He was wounded for our transgressions, He was bruised for our iniquities: the chastisement of our peace was upon Him, and with His stripes we are healed" (Isa. liii, 5). "It is impossible that the blood of bulls and goats should take away sins" (Hebrews x, 4), for the life of an animal is not of equal moral value to that of a man. Therefore such a sacrifice could not satisfy justice, so that the right to live, forfeited by man through sin, should be restored to him and be made sure to him for ever. But the life of "God manifest in the flesh" was more than worthy to make propitiation for the whole world (I John ii, 2). He bore our sins in His body on the tree (I Peter ii, 24); yea, He bore away the sin of the world (John i, 29), as well as the guilt of men's actual sins. Thus in Him God was reconciling the world unto Himself (II Cor. v, 19), and thus He made it just that the repenting, believer sinner should be forgiven. If we walk in the light, the blood of Jesus God's son cleanseth us from all sin (I John i, 7), "for the life of all flesh is the blood thereof" (Lev. xvii, 14), and the shedding of blood means the taking of life, means death, means, that is, that the just penalty of sin has been paid. But as the penalty has been paid the sinner who repents and has faith need no more dread lest he be called upon to pay it, his Redeemer having done this for him, and done it once for all (Heb. x, 12-14; I Peter iii, 18).

God had duly revealed through the prophets the resurrection of His Son from among the dead, as also that He should ascend to heaven, there to intercede for His people, so securing for them the full benefit of His saving work on the cross; and that He should there sit at the right hand of the Father until the time should come for all His foes to be suppressed by force (Isa. liii, 12; "maketh intercession"; Heb. i, 13; Psa. cx, 1).

The same voice that declared that Messiah should be "cut off out of the land of the living" immediately added that "He shall prolong His days, and the pleasure of Jehovah shall prosper in His hand" (Isa. liii, 8-10), and that He shall receive a great reward. The psalmist, one thousand years before He should come, put into his mouth this song:—

Psalm xvi.
8-11

> I have set Jehovah always before me.
> Because he is at my right hand, I shall not be moved.
> Therefore my heart is glad, and my glory rejoiceth:
> My flesh also shall dwell in safety.
> For thou wilt not leave my soul to Sheol;
> Neither wilt thou suffer thine holy one to see corruption.
> Thou wilt shew me the path of life:
> In thy presence is fulness of joy;
> In thy right hand there are pleasures for evermore.

Thus He would go into death, but would not be left there, nor would His body be suffered to go to corruption (a most astounding miracle in a hot climate) ; but along the path of resurrection life He would ascend to the presence of God in fulness of joy.

All these details the Messiah *must* fulfil, for they were settled and foretold by God, and His word cannot be broken. He only to Whom all these things came true can be the Saviour and King. The Messiah when He should be present would be known to all having sight by His fulfilling these and many more such predictions. Now all of these more than three hundred events of which God's prophets had spoken were literally fulfilled in Jesus; which the diligent and honest may see for themselves by comparing the statements of the prophets with the histories of Christ Jesus given in the four Gospels.

These considerations establish the following truths :—

1. That the words of the prophets were the words of God, since He only can certainly foresee and accurately foretell the future.

2. That Jesus is the Messiah, for in Him only have the words of the prophets (that is, of God) been fulfilled.

3. That Jesus is God become man. For the same prophets that showed themselves to be speaking from God by truly foretelling His life, wove into their God-given utterances statements such as these : She " shall call His name Immanuel (God with us) ; "His name shall be called . . . . Mighty God " (Isa. vii, 14; ix, 6) ; "Awake, O sword, against My shepherd, against *the man* that is *My fellow*, saith Jehovah of hosts " (Zech. xiii, 7).

4. That it was necessary for the Saviour of the world actually to die, and afterwards to rise again and ascend to the throne of God.

5. That in due time Christ must come again to the earth, and establish by force the kingdom of God, and so be the cause of blessing to the whole world.

It is to this last subject that we now turn as our special theme.

CHAPTER II.

THE COMING KINGDOM

*" The kingdom of the world is become the kingdom of
our Lord and of His Messiah ; and he shall reign unto
the ages of the ages."—(Rev. xi., 15).*

Twenty-four centuries before the time of Christ mankind
had so corrupted his way upon the earth, that God destroyed
the race by a flood of waters, sparing only Noah and his family.
Unawed by so dread a judgment, man, upon once more
increasing in numbers, quickly turned again to evil, and very
especially to the worship of idols. Thus the knowledge of the
true God, Who demands holiness from His creatures, was
willingly given up, in order that man might gratify unholy
passions (Romans i). In a few centuries there were left but
very few who worshipped God. Yet God had His purpose to
save this world from the power of Satan and from the grip of
sin and death ; and He had already announced in the hearing
of our first parents that the seed of the women should fulfil this
His merciful design (Gen. iii, 15).

It was therefore necessary that a godly race should be
preserved on earth among whom the promised Saviour should
be born. For this purpose God visited a man named Abram,
living in the great city of Ur in Chaldea, and then an idolater.
The God of glory appeared to this man (Acts vii, 2), and called
him to leave his home and kindred and country, and to follow
His leading to a distant land of which he then knew nothing. To
him this promise was given : " I will make of thee a great nation,
and I will bless thee, and make thy name great; and be thou a
blessing: and I will bless them that bless thee, and him that
curseth thee will I curse; and in thee shall all the families of
the earth be blessed " (Gen. xii, 2, 3). In these words is given
the foundation fact of all true study of the philosophy of the
history of nations.

Abram responded to this revelation and call, forsook everything, and went off on the long journey to the land of Canaan.
He found it already occupied by some of the most wicked peoples
then on earth; but on his arriving Jehovah appeared to him
again, and repeated the promise that the land should belong to
his seed.   Seven times over did God renew to Abraham these
promises; once He confirmed them to his son, Isaac; and four
times did He renew the covenant to Isaac's son Jacob.   No less
than ten times did God mention the land of Canaan as being
the everlasting possession of the sons of Abraham.

Moreover, God being most graciously willing to establish the
confidence of those to whom the promise was given, not only
gave a simple promise (though that were enough from GOD),
but He presently turned the promise into a formal covenant;
and then, as if to make assurance doubly sure, He ratified the
covenant by an oath (Gen. xxii, 16), saying, "By Myself
have I sworn, saith Jehovah."   Now sometimes, though indeed
rarely, circumstances may arise which make it right not to
fulfil a promise; and it is lawful for the parties to a covenant
to alter the terms of their arrangement; but an oath none may
vary or ignore.   And thus God has put it beyond even His own
power to alter or dispense with His covenant with Abraham
and His seed.   Therefore the land of Canaan is theirs; and
their ultimate supremacy over their enemies is guaranteed; and
also, only through that race can the final blessing of the whole
world be brought about.

In pursuance of the assurance of national supremacy, God
spoke to David, the king of Israel about nine hundred years
after the time of Abraham (say 1000 B.C.), and made to him
this promise:—

II Samuel "Now therefore thus shalt thou say unto my servant
vii, 8-17 David, Thus saith Jehovah of hosts, I took thee from
the sheepcote, from following the sheep, that thou shouldest
be prince over my people, over Israel: and I have been with
thee withersoever thou wentest, and have cut off all thine
enemies from before thee; and I will make thee a great name,
like unto the name of the great ones that are in the earth.

"And I will appoint a place for my people Israel, and will plant them, that they may dwell in their own place, and be moved no more; neither shall the children of wickedness afflict them any more, as at the first, and as from the day that I commanded judges to be over my people Israel; and I will cause thee to rest from all thine enemies. Moreover Jehovah telleth thee that Jehovah will make thee an house. When thy days be fulfilled, and thou shalt sleep with thy fathers, I will set up thy seed after thee, which shall proceed out of thy bowels, and I will establish his kingdom. He shall build an house for my name, and I will establish the throne of his kingdom for ever. I will be his father, and he shall be my son: if he commit iniquity, I will chasten him with the rod of men, and with the stripes of the children of men; but my mercy shall not depart from him, as I took it from Saul, whom I put away before thee. And thine house and thy kingdom shall be made sure for ever before thee: thy throne shall be established for ever. According to all these words, and according to all this vision, so did Nathan speak unto David."

This covenant also God confirmed with an oath, as these words witness :—

Psalm lxxxix, 3, 4.

I have made a covenant with my chosen,
I have sworn unto David my servant;
Thy seed will I establish for ever,
And build up thy throne to all generations.

It is to be observed that God declared that when the time should come for the complete fulfilment of these covenants, then the Jewish nation shall be fixed in their own land as a planted tree that is not to be removed to another spot, and they shall "be moved no more"; and then, too, neither shall "the children of wickedness afflict them any more, as at the first." Neither of these promises has yet been fulfilled. Again and again Israel has been driven from the land of promise; still they are the people of the wandering foot and weary breast; still they are the most persecuted and oppressed of all peoples. But God's promise cannot fail, nor His solemn oath be broken; and so there must come a time when these covenants shall be fulfilled.

Anything less or other than a national future for Israel in their land would leave unfulfilled covenant and sworn promises of God. This is impossible.

The sons of David that ruled after him, nearly all went after strange gods, and worshipped idols; and so evil was their way before God that some six hundred years B.C. He suffered Israel to be conquered by the king of Babylon, Nebuchadnezzar.

Thus the sovereignty of the earth which had been given to the house of David, passed into the hands of a non-Jewish ruler, and in such hands it has ever since remained. But long though the delay seems, yet the oath to David must be fulfilled, and so the period of Gentile sovereignty of the earth cannot be permanent.

God took very special pains to impress this point upon the first Gentile monarch who ruled the whole world. To Nebuchadnezzar was given the following dream : and this was later supernaturally revealed to the prophet Daniel without the king having hinted to him the nature of the vision. This most remarkable thing, of a second man being made aware of what another had previously dreamed, was plainly intended to inspire absolute confidence in the interpretation which should be given by the prophet. The dream, then, as related by Daniel to the king, was as follows :—

Daniel ii, "Thou, O king, sawest, and behold a great image. This
31-35 image, which was mighty, and whose brightness was excellent, stood before thee ; and the aspect thereof was terrible. As for this image, his head was of fine gold, his breast and his arms of silver, his belly and his thighs of brass, his legs of iron, his feet part of iron, and part of clay. Thou sawest till that a stone was cut out without hands, which smote the image upon his feet that were of iron and clay, and brake them in pieces. Then was the iron, the clay, the brass, the silver, and the gold, broken in pieces together, and became like the chaff of the summer threshing-floors; and the wind carried them away, that no place was found for them : and the stone that smote the image became a great mountain, and filled the whole earth."

The following is the interpretation of the dream which the God-instructed prophet gave to the great monarch :

_{Daniel ii,
37-47} " Thou, O king, art king of kings, unto whom the God of heaven hath given the kingdom, the power, and the strength, and the glory ; and wheresoever the children of men dwell, the beasts of the field and the fowls of the heaven hath he given into thine hand, and hath made thee to rule over them all : thou art the head of gold.   And after thee shall arise another kingdom inferior to thee ; and another third kingdom of brass, which shall bear rule over all the earth.   And the fourth kingdom shall be strong as iron : forasmuch as iron breaketh in pieces and subdueth all things : and as iron that crusheth all these, shall it break in pieces and crush.   And whereas thou sawest the feet and toes, part of potters' clay, and part of iron, it shall be a divided kingdom ; but there shall be in it of the strength of the iron, forasmuch as thou sawest the iron mixed with miry clay.   And as the toes of the feet were part of iron, and part of clay, so the kingdom shall be partly strong, and partly broken.   And whereas thou sawest the iron mixed with miry clay, they shall mingle themselves with the seed of men ; but they shall not cleave one to another, even as iron doth not mingle with clay.   And in the days of those kings shall the God of heaven set up a kingdom, which shall never be destroyed, nor shall the sovereignty thereof be left to another people ; but it shall break in pieces and consume all these kingdoms, and it shall stand for ever, forasmuch as thou sawest that a stone was cut out of the mountain without hands, and that it brake in pieces the iron, the brass, the clay, the silver, and the gold ; the great God hath made known to the king what shall come to pass hereafter : and the dream is certain, and the interpretation thereof sure.   Then the king Nebuchadnezzer fell upon his face, and worshipped Daniel, and commanded that they should offer an oblation and sweet odours unto him.   The king answered unto Daniel, and said, Of a truth your God is the God of gods, and the Lord of kings, and a revealer of secrets, seeing thou hast been able to reveal this secret."

All this forecast, given five and a half centuries, before Christ, and when the first of the empires was at its commencement only, the subsequent history of the nations of the earth has accurately fulfilled almost to the end.

The empire of the Medes and Persians followed that of Babylon (B.C. 538-333) ; the Grecian monarchy, established by Alexander the Great, overthrew and absorbed the Persian (B.C. 333-31, the year of the battle of Actium) ; and then the mighty empire founded at Rome was built upon the ruins of the three that had preceded it. This last empire (never in Scripture called "Roman," and to centre at last in Babylon rebuilt), God regards as still continuing, inasmuch as it is seen in the vision as lasting on to the hour when a kingdom that God will set up takes its place by violently destroying all the empires. The variations in its component countries, chief centres, and forms of rule are not material from the prophetic point of view.

And as the head of gold was a symbol of the absolute monarchy of Nebuchadnezzar, so the silver was a picture of the partly limited government of the Persians, in which the king was a good deal dependent upon his great nobles, and could not do altogether as he might like, as Nebuchadnezzar had done (Dan. vi). The Grecian rulers were still more largely dependent upon their princes and soldiers ; whilst the fourth empire was mainly ruled by a senate of the chief citizens, and even the later emperors were but little able to rule as autocratically as Nebuchadnezzar. In our own days we see how that the will of the people is more and more consulted by rulers; and the discerning can perceive that on this account weakness and variableness in governing are conspicuous features of the times.

The gold has given place to iron and clay, mixed indeed, but which cannot blend into a strong whole. And thus it will be till the One comes to Whom alone can be safely entrusted that absolute, unlimited monarchy which is God's ideal and is the best for the governed, provided the Ruler be perfect, as the Son of Man will be.

That Daniel should have thus minutely foretold the past two thousand five hundred years of national history is convincing

proof that we have in his writings a divine revelation, and it
demands that we expect the due fulfilment of the rest of his
forecast.   That is to say, we are bound to expect the sudden
and violent breaking up of the world kingdoms by a heaven-
sent power—the "stone cut out without hands," which shall
itself increase and fill the whole earth.   It is not reasonable
that so sudden and crushing an event as this boulder smashing
up the image and grinding it to a powder that the wind drives
away, should represent the very slow, very gradual and peaceful
conversion to God of all mankind by the persuasive and
gracious influences of the gospel message now being preached.
The necessary rapidity of the fall of such a block of stone, and
the violence with which it would strike, and the immediateness
of the destruction resulting, render the picture most entirely
unsuitable for carrying such a meaning.   This moreover is
clear from the distinct statement that it is in days when ten
kings are reigning that the stone falls, which condition yet waits
realization.   These kings are as plainly the final rulers of the
empires as the ten toes are the bottom members of the image.

The fulfilment of this sudden descent of the stone is vividly
pictured in a prophecy which is at the close of the Book of
God, and which reads thus :—

Rev. xix.
11-21.
"And I saw the heaven opened; and behold, a white
horse, and he that sat thereon, called Faithful and True ;
and in righteousness he doth judge and make war.   And his
eyes are a flame of fire, and upon his head are many diadems ;
and he hath a name written, which no one knoweth but he
himself.   And he is arrayed in a garment sprinkled with blood :
and his name is called The Word of God.   And the armies
which are in heaven followed him upon white horses, clothed
in fine linen, white and pure.   And out of his mouth
proceedeth a sharp sword, that with it he should smite the
nations: and he shall rule them with a rod of iron: and he
treadeth the winepress of the fierceness of the wrath of
Almighty God.   And he hath on his garment and on his thigh
a name written, KING OF KINGS, AND LORD OF LORDS.

"And I saw an angel standing in the sun ; and he cried with a loud voice, saying to all the birds that fly in mid heaven, Come and be gathered together unto the great supper of God ; that ye may eat the flesh of kings, and the flesh of captains, and the flesh of mighty men, and the flesh of horses and of them that sit thereon, and the flesh of all men, both free and bond, and small and great.

"And I saw the beast, and the kings of the earth, and their armies, gathered together to make war against him that sat upon the horse, and against his army. And the beast was taken, and with him the false prophet that wrought the signs in his sight, wherewith he deceived them that had received the mark of the beast, and them that worshipped his image : they twain were cast alive into the lake of fire that burneth with brimstone : and the rest were killed with the sword of him that sat upon the horse, even the sword which came forth out of his mouth : and all the birds were filled with their flesh."

Further descriptions of this mighty intervention of the Word of God are given in such scriptures as Isa. lxiii, 1-6 and Joel iii, 11-17. That such an event has never taken place does not require proof, for Jehovah, the God of Israel is not yet dwelling in Zion, the hill of David in Jerusalem ; and hence we are bound still to look for these things. Reader, at that day will you, if alive, be found amongst those who wait longingly for Christ, or will you be amongst His enemies ?

Look, ye saints, the sight is glorious:
See the Man of Sorrows now!
From the fight returned victorious
Every knee to Him shall bow:
Crown Him, crown Him!
Crowns become the Victor's brow.

Crown the Saviour! angels, crown Him!
Rich the trophies Jesus brings:
In the seat of power enthrone Him,
While the vault of heaven rings:
Crown Him, crown Him!
Crown the Saviour King of kings.

Sinners in derision crowned Him,
Mocking thus the Saviour's claim;
Saints and angels crowd around Him,
Own His title, praise His name:
Crown Him, crown Him!
Spread abroad the Victor's fame.

Hark! those bursts of acclamation;
Hark! those loud triumphant chords;
Jesus takes the highest station:
Oh, what joy the sight affords!
Crown Him, crown Him!
King of kings and Lord of lords!

(T. Kelly).

CHAPTER III.

ISRAEL'S PLACE IN THE KINGDOM.

"He shall reign over the house of Jacob unto the ages." (Luke i, 33)

Let us now remember that the King Who will thus come in glory is, as to His earthly birth, a Jew, a son of Abraham. That He should be the cause of blessing to all the families of the earth will therefore be the fulfilment of the covenant with Abraham. Christ, moreover, is of David's house; and the covenant with David that his seed should rule the world will thus be fulfilled in Christ, for "the Lord God shall give unto Him the throne of His father David: and He shall reign over the house of Jacob for ever; and of His kingdom there shall be no end," as the angel declared when announcing His coming birth (Luke i, 32-33). Nor is there any other descendant of David known to be now alive; a fact which the Jew who is looking for the hope of Israel will do well to ponder, as apart from Jesus his hope is impossible of fulfilment. Had Christ not been of the house of David, His priestly enemies, having access to the temple genealogies, would have had no difficulty in showing that He was not so, and then all further claims by Him to be the Messiah would have been frustrated, and the twentieth century would probably never have heard of Him.

Thus Christ will wrest from the Gentiles the sceptre of the world; and in His reigning, and the glory of Israel with Him, will at last be fulfilled the promise that Abraham's seed shall finally triumph. It will follow necessarily from their relationship to Him that His own people will rise with Him to the supreme place amongst the nations of the earth. For Israel, who formerly rejected Messiah in wilful ignorance, will be made to know that the crucified Nazarene was indeed their Saviour-God. A touching description of their sorrow and surprise is given by the prophet Zechariah as he pictures them face to face with Christ returned to glory:—

^{Zech. xii,} "And it shall come to pass in that day, that I will seek
^{9-10;}
^{xiii, 6.} to destroy all the nations that come against Jerusalem.
And I will pour upon the house of David, and upon the
inhabitants of Jerusalem, the spirit of grace and of supplication ;
and they shall look unto me whom they have pierced: and
they shall mourn for him, as one mourneth for his only son,
and shall be in bitterness for him, as one that is in bitterness
for his firstborn. And one shall say unto him, What are these
wounds between thine hands ? Then he shall answer, Those
with which I was wounded in the house of my friends."

It was to this day that Christ looked forward with comfort in
the sad hour when it became evident that His own people were
determined to cast Him out. Leaving the temple for the last
time He lamented in these words :

^{Matt.xxiii.} "O Jerusalem, Jerusalem, which killeth the prophets,
³⁷⁻³⁹ and stoneth them that are sent unto her ! how often
would I have gathered thy children together, even as a hen
gathereth her chickens under her wings, and ye would not !
Behold, your house is left unto you desolate. For I say unto
you, Ye shall not see me henceforth, till ye shall say, Blessed
is he that cometh in the name of the Lord."

That the day when Israel shall thus welcome Him may be
hastened let us pray and work.

The apostle Paul felt it to be of much importance that non-
Jewish christians should understand that God had not finally
cast away His people Israel. He argues the matter at much
length in writing to the believers in Rome, the then metropolis
of the Gentile world (chs. ix-xi). He shows that God has not
changed His mind in regard to Israel (xi, 28-29). He takes for
granted that the Old Testament promises will be literally
fulfilled to the literal Israel, and quotes several of these in the
literal sense. Therefore he certainly expects that a " Deliverer
will come out of Zion," and that thus all Israel left at that time
shall be saved (xi, 26), for this is God's covenant unto them
(xi, 27). It is impossible to suppose that by " Israel " he meant
the " church," as some seem to wish it to mean, for he was
writing *to* the " church " *about* " Israel," and members of the

latter nation were dwelling in the same city by the side of members of the former company, and could not be confused with these. And he reasons that if, whilst the covenant people are out of fellowship with God, some Gentiles receive blessing, through the gospel reaching them, the Jews nationally having rejected the good news, much more abundantly will the world be blessed when its chief people, Israel, return to God and are in His favour (xi, 11-12).

It is thus seen that both the rule of the world by Gentile powers, and the preaching of the good news to Gentile sinners, are interim arrangements ordered by God till Israel be repentant, and fit for her high destiny, according to the covenants sworn to the fathers of that race. When the Gentile powers shall have filled up the measure of their sins, the "times of the Gentiles," foretold by Daniel, will have been fulfilled (Luke xxi, 24). At the same period Israel, moved by God's good Spirit, will be humbled by His chastisements, and be ready to fill their place in God's counsel; and just then also "the fulness of the Gentiles will have come in"; and the way thus be prepared for the coming of God's King and kingdom.

If not decisive it would be at least interesting could we ask, say, Isaiah how he himself understood his prophecies concerning his people, land, and city; whether, firstly, he took his words to predict as literal a restoration as his accompanying words predicted a literal destruction; whether, secondly, he anticipated for his people as actual a supremacy over the rest of the nations as they were for a time to be actually subject to them; or whether thirdly, when restored they are to be only one among many other nations as to rank; or whether, fourthly, the only future for them is, that such of them as come at the end of the age to faith in Christ will simply be merged into the spiritual privileges of the church of God, and have no racial or national existence at all. In short, whether his words meant, as history proved, just what they said as to destruction, but mean something quite different to what they seem to say as to restoration.

That Israel as a people is to have a national future, and to be the ruling nation on earth, is the consentient testimony of the prophets, their words being taken in their plain sense. And the difficulty with some esteemed people is that they do not take the plain sense, but argue it away on what they suppose to be spiritual considerations. As if God's spiritual principles ever conflicted with His plain statements.

From among countless passages one may be taken, and the case be almost left to turn upon it alone. In Isaiah lx, 5, it is said of Zion, " the wealth of the nations shall come unto thee," and in verse 11 that " men (shall) bring unto thee the wealth of the nations, and their kings led with them," and in verse 12, " For that nation and kingdom that will not serve thee shall perish, yea, those nations shall be utterly wasted."

By no fair dealing can there be applied to these statements the much-abused process mis-called " spiritualizing." For (1) the " nations " are not the " church " (I Cor. x, 32 ; Rev. xxi, 24) ; and (2), in the church there are no special kings to be singled out for mention, for though all its final members are to reign they are not to be kings of particular Gentile kingdoms, or there would need to be as many nations as there will be members of the church. Thus here is no picture of the merging of Israel and the church.

Further (3), while believing Gentiles enter into a share of the spiritual wealth of Israel (Rom. xi, 13-21 ; xv, 27 ; Gal. iii, 6-14), saved Israelites receive no spiritual wealth from the nations, for these have no spiritual riches.

Therefore the kings of this passage must be actual Gentile rulers, and the wealth be material riches ; which demands that Zion here must be the literal city, the centre of the literal Israel. Exgetical theories aside, is not this the obvious sense of the words, as of all the prophetic statements on these themes ? Consider e.g., Haggai ii, 6-9, the first of which verses shows that the passage still awaits fulfilment, and in a house at Jerusalem as literal as the former building with which it is in terms identified, " for this house " then in building is regarded by God as one with that house to come into being at the time of the shaking of heaven and earth.

And if verse 12 of Isaiah lx does not teach the political subjection of all other peoples to Israel we may despair of finding any settled meaning in language : "the nation and kingdom that will not serve thee shall perish, yea, those nations shall be utterly wasted." What did the same statements mean when a prophet of the same period said in the same language to the same people of Israel (Jer. xxvii, 8), "the nation and the kingdom which will not serve the same Nebuchadnezzar king of Babylon . . . that nation will I punish until I have consumed them ? "

The root divergence between the differing views on this subject is : Have the prophecies a literal meaning, even when it is expressed under oriental imagery, or do they *mean* something *quite different* to what they *say* ?

"FOR YET A LITTLE WHILE," Heb. x 37.

———

"A little while"— the Lord shall come,
And we shall wander here no more ;
He'll take us to His Father's home,
Where He for us is gone before,
To dwell with Him, to see His face,
And sing the glories of His grace.

"A little while "—He'll come again,
Let us the precious hours redeem ;
Our only grief to give Him pain,
Our joy to serve and follow Him,
Watching and ready may we be,
As those that wait their Lord to see.

"A little while "—'twill soon be past,
Why should we shun the promised cross ?
Oh, let us in His footsteps haste,
Counting for Him all else but loss !
For how will recompense His smile,
The sufferings of this "little while."

"A little while "—come, Saviour, come !
For Thee Thy bride has tarried long :
Take Thy poor waiting pilgrims home,
To sing the new eternal song,
To see Thy glory, and to be
In everything conformed to Thee !

(J. G. Deck).

CHAPTER IV.

THE CHURCH OF GOD.

"We must not adhere to those systems of doctrine which never can bear an infringement of a view that is held popularly. For instance, perhaps we have all been brought up in the notion that all the children of God, in all ages, compose the Church of God. Now it will be found on closer research that this is not supported by the word of God." (William Kelly, "Occasional Lectures." Lec. 7. 19).

It is very important to distinquish clearly between the two phrases which have been just quoted. "The times of the Gentiles being fulfilled" means that the period foreseen and determined by God during which He would allow Gentile powers to control the world, will have come to its end. "The fulness of the Gentiles shall have come in" means that all those individuals who are to become members of the heavenly church will have been gathered from the nations and prepared for their special duties and glories in the coming kingdom. The suggestion that this phrase indicates the salvation of all the nations, as nations, is inadmissible. The passage makes the national conversion of Israel to follow the coming in of the fulness of the Gentiles: " and so all Israel shall be saved." But numerous scriptures declare that the turning of the Gentiles as a whole to the Lord will *follow* that of Israel. (see Ch. VI).

The matter of this company called "the church of God" is so extremely important that it must receive special attention.

Down to the time of Christ, God saw all mankind as divided into two visible classes: (1) The Jews, His chosen people, and (2) the rest of the world. The former had many vast privileges, and, firstly, this one, that to them were intrusted the " oracles of God " (Rom. iii, 2); they had His written Word. To them also belonged the honour of the true God having adopted them from among the other nations to be His special people ; the glory of God was seen in their temple ; the covenants and the law were theirs ; they were taught the true way to worship the living God; and the rich promises of which we have before spoken belonged to them. The Gentile nations were left without these advantages, to find out by sad and long experience that man without God is in darkness and misery (Jeremiah ii, 19), and that not by his own wisdom can he find out God (I Cor. i, 21).

But God always kept in mind His purpose to bless the whole race, and often spoke to Israel about this ; and when His Son came to earth it was as " a minister of the circumcision for the truth of God, that he might confirm the promises *given* unto the fathers, and that the Gentiles might glorify God for his mercy; as it is written,

Therefore will I give praise unto thee among the Gentiles,
And sing unto thy name.
And again he saith,
Rejoice, ye Gentiles, with His people.
And again,
Praise the Lord, all ye Gentiles;
And let all the peoples praise Him.
And again, Isaiah saith,
There shall be the root of Jesse,
And he that ariseth to rule over the Gentiles;
On him shall the Gentiles hope. " (Rom. xv, 8-12)

When therefore Christ, after His resurrection, sent forth His servants to tell the good news of salvation through Himself, He sent them to the whole world, bidding them to make disciples from among all the nations (Matt. xxviii, 19), by being His witnesses (Acts i, 8). For the time had come for the last and highest purpose of God to be fulfilled. Much of His mind as God had formerly made known, there remained one great secret of His plans of which He had given hints but had not openly revealed it, but which the apostles were taught by the Holy Spirit. This secret (" mystery " it is called in the New Testament, which does not mean something " mysterious," but only something hitherto kept secret, but which may be in itself quite simple to understand once it is explained)—this secret introduces us to some new and marvellous thoughts of God, of which we specially notice these :—

1. That there was a third division of mankind to be established—the church of God, in addition to the already existing Jewish nation and the other peoples (I Cor. x, 32). In the times of the apostles there would have been found in many a town of the empire, but prior to a christian preacher having visited the place, two very distinct centres of worship— the heathen temple and the Jewish synagogue. But after the successful preaching of the good news of salvation through Christ, a third centre of worship arose—the christian assembly. This centre drew from both the others, but was sharply divided from both and hated by both. When therefore the Scriptures, the Old Testament or the New, were read by persons then living, it was quite impossible that the reader should be misled into any such confusing notion as that the terms Jew or Israel meant the christian assembly. It will be well also to notice that in the picture of the future and final state, the eternal world (Rev. xxi, 22), there are these same three classes of the saved—"the bride, the wife of the Lamb"; Israel, the names of the twelve tribes being on the gates of the city; and the nations entering by the gates. (See Ch. IX). For there is to be a new eternal earth, as well as new heavens, and so there will be earthly saints for ever as well as heavenly. This shuts out the suggestion that all the saved of all ages will form ultimately one universal and unseparated company. There will be one *family* of God, but it will be distributed as to residence (" in My Father's house are *many* abiding places "), (John xiv, 2) and its members will vary in glory and service. The "family" is only one picture of those ages, and does not give the whole conception. The very word "church" forbids the notion of one universal company ; for *ecclesia* signifies a limited number called out from amongst a larger company.

2. That this new company, thus gathered from both Jews and Gentiles, should be united into " one *new* man," by their

equal privileges in Christ Jesus (Eph. ii, 11-iii, 13). So that the members of this church are no longer regarded by God as either Jews or Gentiles, but are viewed only as related to Christ.

3. That into these the very Spirit of Christ is sent, so that they become actually united to Him, in a vital spiritual union. This oneness is set forth under the figure of Christ being the living Head, and His church being to Him a body, of which each individual believer is a separate member (I Cor. xii; Eph. iv, 11-16). As a man uses his body to perform those works which he desires to do, so Christ, being not Himself on earth in His own person, uses the members of this " body " to do those things which he wishes done. For example, Christ desired that the news of salvation should be spoken to an Ethiopian officer who was seeking light; to accomplish which end He, by an angel and by His Spirit, directed His servant Philip to go to a point of road on a desert, and to arrive at so quiet and retired a spot just when he should meet the man in question.

4. Further—and this is of first importance—because the Head is no longer on earth, nor earthly, so neither does God consider His body to belong to the earth. God looks on the body as belonging to heaven, because the Head is of and in heaven. By His Spirit the heavenly character of Christ is being reproduced in His members; and let it never for one hour be forgotten that " if any man have not the spirit of Christ he is none of His " (Rom. viii, 9).

5. Consistently with this heavenly relationship and standing before God in Christ, God has graciously appointed a heavenly future for this company. Israel and the saved nations are promised a sphere of rich blessing on earth, as we have seen ; but the church of God is called to a nobler inheritance in God's own region of His universe, the heavens (I Pet. i, 3-5).

Christians are accustomed to speak of the life hereafter as " going to heaven," but it is to be feared that few have any clear idea of what is meant.

It should be noted first of all that man does not properly belong to the heavenly regions. He was made to rule the earth, and was made, as to his body, of the earth. Had he not sinned he would not have died, but would, for ought that we are told, have continued to live on the earth. The heavens are not a realm of material things, but of that kind of substance which is called spiritual; and because man is partly material by constitution, part of him being a material body, therefore he is not fitted to live in a purely spiritual realm, as says the Scripture, "flesh and blood cannot (is not able, *ou dunatai*) to inherit the kingdom of God" (I. Cor., xv, 50). Therefore it is a very remarkable thought that he should be taken from the region to which he belongs by creation and be made to live in another, and very different realm. Nor do we know of any other instance of God thus altering the station in the universe of any of His creatures. Each is expected to abide in that realm and state in which the Creator set him (Jude 6, 7, etc.).

It follows of necessity that man's being, because it is unsuited to the spiritual world, must be changed by the power of God, and be fitted to live in the heavens. A bird would need a mighty change to be able to live under the water, or a fish to live in the air; but the Lord promises a much more striking change to the members of His church (I. Cor., xv, 35-58; Phil. iii, 20-21; I. Thessa iv, 13-18; I. John iii, 1). Such a change of state and locality the body of Christ went through at His resurrection and ascension; and His case is the proof that such a thing can be, and is the solid basis for the hope of His people that thus it shall be with them also. For the God Who promised it to His Son has promised it to Christ's members also. The glorifying of His Son, the lifting Him from the grave to the throne, is the standard of God's power, and it is "to us-ward who believe" (Eph. i, 19-23); that is, this same power is working on our behalf to bring us where Christ is, and to make us like Him. "Now He Who wrought us for this very thing is God, Who gave unto us the *earnest* of the Spirit" (2 Cor. v, 5). The "earnest" is the interest on capital paid in advance, and thus the proof that there is an estate; the grapes of Eshcol were this to the Israelites who had never seen the land for themselves. Thus the true hope of the christian is the "appearing of the glory of our great God and Saviour Jesus

Christ " (Titus, ii, 13), at which event the dead in Christ will be raised in glory, and the living at that moment will be changed into His likeness, and all together will be caught up to meet the Lord in the air, thenceforth to be for ever with Him. Well did the poet sing :

> And is it so, we shall be like Thy Son ?
> Is this the grace that He for us has won ?
> Father of glory, thought beyond all thought,
> In glory, to His own blest likenes brought !

Father, Thy sovereign love has sought,
　Captives to sin, gone far from Thee;
The work that Thine own Son hath wrought,
　Has brought us back in peace and free.

And now as sons before Thy face,
　With joyful steps the path we tread,
Which leads us on to that blest place
　Prepared for us by Christ our Head.

Thou gav'st us, in eternal love,
　To Him to bring us home to Thee,
Suited to Thine own thoughts above,
　As sons, like Him, with Him to be

In Thine own house.　There love divine
　Fills the bright courts with cloudless joy;
But 'tis the love that made us Thine,
　Fills all that house without alloy.

O boundless grace! what fills with joy
　Unmingled all that enter there—
God's nature, love without alloy—
　Our hearts are given e'en now to share.

God's righteousness with glory bright,
　Which with its radiance fills that sphere,
E'en Christ—of God the power and light—
　Our title is that light to share.

O Mind divine! so must it be
　That glory all belongs to God:
O Love divine! that did decree
　We should be part, through Jesus' blood.

O keep us, Love divine, near Thee,
　That we our nothingness may know,
And ever to Thy glory be,
　Walking in faith while here below.

　　　　　　　　　　(J. N. *Darby*).

CHAPTER V.

THE PURPOSE OF GOD IN THE CHURCH.

"God's purpose in calling us to be labourers together with Him during this present age is not simply that the apparent work which He sets before us may be accomplished. It is rather, that, in the accomplishment of this work, we may be prepared for our chief and ultimate service in the age to come."—Dr. F. L. Chapell.

Let us now enquire what are the purposes that God has in view by this marvellous and unique scheme.

1. In Eph. iii, 10, God tells us that this astonishing dealing with man is intended to teach the heavenly beings something of God's great wisdom. The church is a school in which angelic beings see object lessons of God's greatness and goodness. Well therefore may the child of God cheerfully submit to whatever is ordered or allowed for him by His God and Father, for He knows not what high end in heaven itself is being served. It is as when our Lord took a little child into his arms, and used it as a means of teaching the disciples some salutary lessons, the child meanwhile being all unconscious of the dignity that was thus put upon it as the lesson-book used by the Lord of glory.

2. In Eph. ii, 7, we further learn that God deals thus with guilty, rebellious, and defiled sinners of the earth in order that "in the ages to come He might shew the exceeding riches of His grace in kindness towards us in Christ Jesus." This plural term "the ages to come," as well as the oft-used phrase "the ages of the ages" (for ever and ever), forbid the assertion that the gospel age now in progress is the final age of man's history. It is evident that finite beings, because they cannot encompass the idea of absolute eternity, will be for ever necessitated to think in limited periods. For us eternity must for evermore

be composed of "ages," that is, periods of some limit. God alone can think eternally, without time measurements. When the saints are then seen radiant with the glory of God, how richly will God's grace be revealed, in that sinners, who might justly have been sent to the lake of fire, have been not only pardoned, but raised to the highest place of glory and happiness. It is as if a prince should see in the slave market a miserable slave girl, and, taking pity upon her, should pay the price required, and set her free ; and then, because of an astonishing and all undeserved love to her, should cleanse and clothe and educate her, and take her to himself as his queen. How greatly would his grace be revealed as she appeared at his court in his own glory, the special object of his love, and fitted for her exalted position. And thus " Christ also loved the church, and gave Himself up for it, that He might sanctify it, having cleansed it by the laver of the water in (the) word, that He might present the church to Himself a glorious church, not having spot or wrinkle or any such thing; but that it should be holy and without blemish" (Eph. v, 25-27).

3. But there is a further object in the purpose of God in thus glorifying the saints. It is as if a king, having to deal with a serious rebellion, not only pardoned those rebels who submitted to his authority, but went on to choose some from among them to appoint these as chief ministers of state and high officers in the kingdom.

Is not this the true sphere in which the fact and doctrine of election and foreordination have place ? Note that we are said to be chosen " before the foundation of the world, that we should be holy and without blemish before Him " (Eph. i, 4). In chapter 5, 26-27 this term " without blemish " is plainly set in reference, not to our present state, but to the day of visible glory, and so it is in Jude 24. We are foreordained " unto adoption as sons " (Eph. i, 5), which is a far higher thought than deliverance from hell, and again has reference to the day of glory, as may be seen in Rom. viii, 19, 23, where we learn that the " earnest expectation of the creation waiteth for the revealing of the sons of God," and that we also are " waiting for our

adoption, the redemption of our body." A king may pardon
a rebel without going on to treat him as a prince of the royal
house. "Whom He foreknew, He also foreordained to be
conformed to the image of His Son" (Rom. viii, 29). Here again
it is the destiny and dignity of the saved that is the subject of
God's sovereign decision. We also read of God being willing
"to make known the riches of His glory upon vessels of mercy
which He afore-prepared unto glory" (Rom. ix, 23), not simply
unto escaping punishment due.

The emphasis of all the leading passages is upon the *glorifying*
of the saints being the matter of foreordination, rather than
their escape from eternal death. Once we read in English of
men being "ordained unto eternal life" (Ac. xiii, 48); but many
expositors of weight do not see in the verb as used here (τάθθω)
any reference to eternal predestination, but understand the
sense that as many of the hearers as were found disposed to
receive the message of eternal life believed it, in contrast to
those mentioned who rejected it. So Alford, Whitby, Mede,
Rotherham, Du Veil, Wordsworth, and Bloomfield. The full
and impartial note of the last-named is worthy of study. That
this favourable disposition to the message heard is produced by
the work of the gracious Spirit, by means of the truth, is
assuredly true; but this does not demand eternal predestination.
That same blessed working of the Spirit brings many to a good
disposition to be saved who later recede therefrom and at last
reject the truth (Matt. xiii, 20, 21), showing they were not
predestined unto salvation.

Some others conceive that there are two divine elections, one
unto eternal life, another to share the kingdom of Christ; but
this seems unwarranted by the Word, with all theories which
suppose that only some are elect of God unto eternal life, and
others must be lost.

A king issues to a rebel army a general offer of pardon, which
in the king's intention is *bona fide* open to every man of them.
But he secretly determines that of those who may submit he
will appoint certain individuals that he in his own mind selects,
to certain offices in his state and house.

Similarly God's offer of salvation through Christ is open for universal acceptance, and is made without any mental reserve on His part. When Scripture says that God loved the world, it means the *world*, not the world of the elect. To the assertion that "world" in such a passage, *e.g.*, as I John ii, 2, "He is the propitiation . . . for the whole world," means the world of the elect, it suffices to reply by enquiring what the identical phrase means later in the same epistle (v, 19), "the whole world lieth in the evil one." In both verses there is the same emphatic contrast between the circle of believers and the rest of mankind. So when it is stated that Christ gave Himself a ransom for all (I Tim. ii, 6), it means *all*, not some only. And, on the other hand, when God tells us of His electing grace and foreordination He connects these with the high destiny for which He has selected some from amongst the vast total of those who will accept His mercy. It were much that the sovereign should freely pardon rebels. If clemency prompted this it did not demand that any of them should be exalted to share in the government against which they had fought. And not being bound thus to favour any of them, it is perfectly legitimate for the king to give these honours to such individuals as it pleases him to choose. The conditions upon which they must qualify for these dignities we shall consider later.

Returning to the main subject, if we would understand God's plan we must gain some idea of the scope of His kingdom and the scheme of its organization and government.

There are two principal regions in the kingdom, the heavens and the earth. The centre of government is, of course, where the king dwells, that is, in the heavenly portion of the kingdom. There is a true sense in which God is everywhere: "behold, heaven and the heaven of heavens cannot contain Thee" (I Kings viii, 27; and see Psalm 139, etc). But there is a place in the heavens where the glory of God is, as it were, concentrated, and from which it radiates; and this "throne of His glory" (Jer. xiv, 21) is the centre of government. Upon that throne, at the right hand of the Father, sits His Son, Jesus Christ our

Lord, in whom since His ascension "dwelleth all the fulness of the Godhead bodily" (Col. ii, 9).

God carries on the government of the universe by the agency of numerous heavenly beings, and these are of different grades and have differing degrees of dignity and glory. In God's revelation we read of "thrones" (Col. i, 16 ; Rev. iv, 4 ; Dan. vii, 9), of dominions, principalities, authorities, of an archangel with a multitude of angels (that is, messengers) under him, and of seraphim and cherubim. Into the detail of their duties and workings we need not now enter, though much is revealed concerning this. It is enough that we get before the mind the thought that God's kingdom is thus well organized.

Upon earth, for the well-being of society, there is a similar arrangement. For the offices of kings and of subordinate rulers are of divine sanction (Rom. xiii, 1-7), though, of course, rulers may misuse their powers and act contrary to God's intentions and commands. Still, the office is of God, part of His scheme of government, and co-ordinate with that in the heavenly realm.

But what is of first importance to be observed is that the heavenly government dominates the earthly, that is, that the powers of earth are under the control of those of the heavens. The unwelcome fact that the first, and very proud, universal monarch, Nebuchadnezzar, had to learn was that "the heavens do rule" (Dan. iv., 25, 26, 34, 35), and a severe lesson was needed to convince him.

Consistent with this are those passages which speak of the earth kingdoms being secretly guided by angelic "princes." Israel, Persia, Greece and Tyre, each in their time, were invisibly directed by such a spiritual ruler (Dan. xii, 1 ; x, 13, 20, 21 ; xi, 1 ; Ezk. xxviii, 12, 14).

Proportionately to their higher rank and authority so is the glory of these angelic rulers greater than human glory. Angels are greater than men in power and might (II Pet. ii, 11 : Psa. 103, 20). So impressive is their majesty that by the sight of even one of them prophets and saints have been overcome (Dan. x, 7,8 ; Matt. xxviii, 1-4 ; Rev. xxii, 8, 9). And so great is the respect due to them from men that to "rail" against them, even though it be against sinning angels, is a grievous offence before God (Jude 8).

But the terrible, yet plainly revealed, truth is that not a small portion of these heavenly rulers and workers are in rebellion against God, and these use their great opportunities to encourage and protect the wicked, and to corrupt or injure the godly. "His tail draweth a third part of the stars of heaven" (Gen. iii; vi, 2-4; Psa. 82; Rev. xii, 3, 4). These evil spirits are led by Satan, the first and chief sinner (I John iii, 8), and loyally do his hosts serve him, and skilfully do they corrupt the thoughts, blind the hearts, and promote the wickedness of men. Their main object is to maintain the kingship of Satan, so as to rob God of His rights in mankind. Thus at present, as our Lord Himself allowed, (John xiv, 30; xvi, 11), Satan is the "prince of this world," as he is also the "god of this age" (II Cor. iv, 4), thus being at once its ruler and its religious head.

God has indeed not allowed these rebels to have their own way entirely, but neither has His time yet come for completely overthrowing their system and dispossessing them from their place and power in government. Already He ofttimes thwarts and disappoints them: He gives holy and faithful angels power to check them (Dan. x, 13); He knows how to deliver the godly from their malign influence; and He is working steadily to defeat them all, so as ultimately to have "a new heavens and a new earth wherein dwelleth righteousness" (Isa. lxv, 17; II Pet. iii, 13).

The incarnation of the Son of God was the chief step towards this end. For the first time there was on earth a Man Who could fully defeat the devil. Satan had met his Conqueror, and was routed in the fight: "to this end was the Son of God manifested, that He might destroy the works of the devil" (I John iii, 8). And ever since then, by filling with His own Spirit the faithful of His followers, Christ has made these also to be more than conquerors by His power (I John iv, 4). They, like their Lord, have often proved unconquerable, no matter what sufferings were inflicted upon them. And by means of their witness and toils Christ is defeating Satan in the further fact of a great multitude of His captives being freed from his cruel grasp in the dungeons of error and sin, so as to become the willing happy slaves of their Liberator. "God hath delivered us out of the authority of darkness, and translated us into the kingdom of the Son of His love " (Col. i, 13).

Satan, moreover, carries the war against God and His people into the heavenly world by his work as the diligent "accuser of the brethren" (Rev. xii, 10, and Job i, ii). But before God also he is defeated when the accused plead that the death of Christ having already satisfied justice concerning their sins, there is left no just ground of complaint against them. This plea cannot be defeated, endorsed as it is by the advocacy of their cause by the exalted Saviour Himself, Who, having provided redemption, now acts as the Priest, the Advocate, of all who avail themselves of that redemption, and "draw nigh unto God through Him" (Heb. vii, 25).

Further, a little before the appearing of Christ on earth to establish visibly the kingdom of God, Satan will be driven down from the heavens to the earth, and his angels with him, and will be thus limited to this world as his sphere of activity (Rev. xii, 7-12). And not long thereafter, at the season of Christ's descent, he will be driven from the surface of the earth, and will be shut up in the "abyss," which is in the "lower parts of the earth" (Rev. xx, 1-3; Rom. x, 7; Eph. iv, 9). Thus he will not be able to tempt man during the thousand years of Christ's reign. After that period he will be allowed a short season of liberty, and will promote a last rebellion against God, thus proving himself to be beyond repentance and man to be unable to stand faithful to God without Christ (Rev. xx, 7-10). Taken in this awful climax of wickedness the once glorious cherub will be confined for ever in the lake of fire, together with all his angels, and with those of mankind who have persisted in following him in rebellion (Rev. xx, 15; Mat. xxv, 41-46).

Now it will at once be seen that the driving out of the heavens of so large a section of the powers that had there ruled will necessitate an entire reconstruction of that heavenly government. And it is at this point that we see the supreme wisdom and rich grace of our God.

CHAPTER VI.

CHRIST AND THE CHURCH TO RULE.

In Acts xv, 14-18, there is this brief and remarkably clear outline of the Lord's program.

"And after they had held their peace, James answered, saying,

"Brethren, hearken unto me : Symeon hath rehearsed how first God did visit the Gentiles, to take out of them a people for his name. And to this agree the words of the prophets ; as it is written.

"After these things I will return,

"And I will build again the tabernacle of David, which is fallen ;

"And I will build again the ruins thereof,

"And I will set it up :

"That the residue of men may seek after the Lord,

"And all the Gentiles, upon whom my name is called,

"Saith the Lord, who maketh these things known from the beginning of the world."

Here are stated four great stages as follows :—

1. "God is visiting the Gentiles *to take out of them a people* for his name."—The present gospel work.

2. "After these things," that is, after the outgathering of this people, "*I will return.*"—Christ's second coming to the earth.

3. "I will build again the tabernacle of David which is fallen."—The restoring of the kingdom to the house of David, according to all scriptures. The "building the tent" is an oriental figure of re-establishing the family in honour.

4. "That the residue of men may seek after the Lord, and all the Gentiles."—The conversion of the rest of the world.

For this order of the conversion of first Israel and then the Gentile nations, see Psalm lxvii, "God shall bless us (Israel) ; and all the ends of the earth shall fear Him." Also the same sequence in Psalm xxii, which connects the sufferings of the

Messiah with the glories that will yet follow them. Heb. ii, 12, shows that the "brethren" of v. 22 of that psalm are the out-gathered church. Next, in v. 23, Israel is called to join in the praise for their Redeemer's triumph; whilst in v. 27 "all the ends of the earth" are seen turning to and worshipping the Lord.

Chapters liii, liv, and lv of Isaiah's prophecy shew precisely the same order. Chapter liii is the pathetic and minutely accurate portrait of Messiah in the rejection that issues in exaltation. Chaper liv, shews Israel restored to fellowship with their covenant-keeping God; and chapter lv calls the nations everywhere to come to the freely flowing blessings and to partake in the covenant and mercies of "David," that is Messiah.

But why is God thus deferring the restoration of Israel, and the consequent saving of the world at large, until after a separate and limited company of mankind, the church of God, has been gathered out from all the nations? We have seen that it is (1) for the purpose of teaching heavenly beings His wisdom; (2) that the greatness of His grace may be for ever exhibited; and (3) that His Son may have the delight of a circle of His blood-bought ones being as near to Himself as is a bride to her bridegroom. And now (4) we are to learn that it is the plan of God that Christ and His church should take the place, yea, a still larger place, in the governing of the heavens and the earth which Satan and his servants have so long misused.

"All authority," said Christ, "hath been given unto Me in heaven and upon earth" (Matt. xxviii, 18). "For neither doth the Father judge any man, but He hath given all judgment unto the Son; that all may honour the Son even as they honour the Father," (John v, 22, 23). And with the authority is given the glory suitable thereto: "The Son of man shall come in the glory of His Father, with His angels"; "the Son of man . . . cometh in His own glory, and the glory of the Father, and of the holy angels"; "when the Son of man shall come in His glory, and all the angels with Him, then shall He sit on the throne of His glory," (Matt. xvi, 27; Luke ix, 26; Matt. xxv, 31).

That Christ Himself should be thus honoured by His Father is easy to be understood by one to whose heart there has been given any sense of His incomparable worth ; but what wondrous words are these that we now read? The Son of God is speaking to His Father concerning His disciples, and He says, "The glory which thou hast given Me I have given unto them" (John xvii, 22); and one who heard those words was afterwards moved by the Holy Spirit to add these : "Beloved, now are we children of God, and it is not yet made manifest what we shall be. We know that, if He shall be manifested, we shall be like Him ; for we shall see Him even as He is" (I John iii, 2).

Another scripture declares that, "When Christ, Who is our life, shall be manifested, then shall ye also with Him be manifested in glory" (Col. iii, 4) ; and yet another proclaims that "our citizenship is in heaven; whence also we wait for a saviour, the Lord Jesus Christ: who shall fashion anew the body of our humiliation, that it may be conformed to the body of his glory, according to the working whereby he is able even to subject all things unto himself," (Phil. iii, 20-21).

Our Lord Himself had promised that He would come again to receive His followers to Himself, and take them to one of the many regions of the heavenly world which He would go and prepare for them (John xiv, 2). That "abiding place" was not then ready, since (presumably) Satan's hosts were occupying it. But when they should have been cast out, and those heavenly places should have been cleansed by the blood of Christ (Heb. ix, 23) from the defilement of their sin, then should the saints be taken there, clothed in bodies spiritual and heavenly, and so be suited to their new home, and robed in glory like that of their Lord. Thus shall they be presented before the glory of the Father with exceeding joy, and shall see God, Whom no man on earth, in man's earthly condition, can see (Exod. xxxiii, 20 ; I Tim. vi, 16). That is the hour when there is heard in heaven "as it were the voice of a great multitude, and as the voice of many waters, and as the voice of mighty thunders, saying, Hallelujah : for the Lord our God, the Almighty reigneth. Let us rejoice and be exceeding glad, and let us give the glory unto him: for the marriage of the Lamb is come, and his wife hath made herself ready (Rev. xix, 6, 7).

That too is the hour when judgment shall be given to the saints of the Most High (or of the high places), and the time have come for the saints to possess the kingdom (Dan. vii, 22); for God "calleth (us) into His own kingdom and glory" (1 Thess. ii, 12). And if the trembling heart says, "it is high; I cannot attain unto it," then for our encouragement we are assured that what we indeed cannot do, God can do, and that "the God of all grace Who called you unto His eternal glory in Christ, after that ye have suffered a little while, shall Himself perfect, stablish, strengthen you" (1 Peter v, 10); for "the things which are impossible with men are possible with God" (Luke xviii, 27).

Just what is meant by being called to the kingdom is shown by the case of the Jewish maiden, Esther, being chosen by the Persian monarch to be his queen, for it is said that she had "come to the kingdom" (Esth. iv., 14).

Our Lord spake a most illuminating parable just before reaching Jerusalem for the last time, and thought the teaching of such importance that He repeated it a few days later (Luke xix, 11-27 and Matt. xxv, 14-30). The former scripture reads thus :

"And as they heard these things, he added and spake a parable, because he was nigh to Jerusalem, and because they supposed that the kingdom of God was immediately to appear. He said therefore, A certain nobleman went into a far country, to receive for himself a kingdom, and to return. And he called ten servants of his, and gave them ten pounds, and said unto them, Trade ye herewith till I come. But his citizens hated him, and sent an ambassage after him, saying, We will not that this man reign over us. And it came to pass, when he was come back again, having received the kingdom, that he commanded these servants, unto whom he had given the money, to be called to him, that he might know what they had gained by trading. And the first came before him, saying, Lord, thy pound hath made ten pounds more. And he said unto him, Well done, thou good servant: because thou "wast found faithful in a very little, have thou authority over ten cities. And the second came, saying, Thy pound, Lord, hath made five pounds. And he said unto him also, Be thou also over five cities. And another came, saying, Lord, behold, here is thy pound, which I kept laid up in a napkin : for I feared thee, because thou art an austere man : thou takest up that thou layedst not down, and reapedst that thou didst not sow. He saith unto him, Out of thine own mouth will I judge thee, thou wicked servant. Thou knewest that I am an austere man, taking up that I laid not down, and reaping that I did not sow ; then wherefore gavest thou not my money into the bank, and I at my coming should have required it with interest ? And he said unto them that stood by, Take away from him the pound, and give it unto him that hath the ten pounds. And they said unto him, Lord, he hath ten pounds. I say unto you, that unto every one that hath shall be given ; but from him that hath not, even that which he hath shall be taken away from him. Howbeit these mine enemies, which would not that I should reign over them, bring hither, and slay them before me.

"And when he had thus spoken, he went on before, going up to Jerusalem."

The points of this lesson which are to be specially noted are :—

1. A long absence of the Lord from the earth. "A far country" meant a long journey ; and it was only "after a long time" that the lord of the servants returned (Matt. xxv, 19). This negatives the idea that Christ taught the apostles to expect His early return.

2. Upon the return of the nobleman he richly rewarded those servants who had been diligent and successful during his absence. And the special reward indicated is that "*authority over cities*" was given in proportion to their fidelity ; that is, they were appointed to high places in the kingdom of their lord. And thus both the governmental authority and personal glory of our Lord He will most graciously and royally share with such as are accounted worthy of these dignities. And the degree of

our faithfulness now will be the measure of our worthiness then.

These things the apostles laboured to impress upon the disciples, and taught them to order their daily life by such hopes. For example, to deter christians from submitting their disputes with one another to the decision of worldly judges, Paul exclaims "Know ye not that the saints shall judge the world? and if the world is judged by you, are ye unworthy to judge the smallest matters? Know ye not that we shall judge angels? how much more, things that pertain to this life? (I. Cor. vi, 2-3)." A truly wondrous prospect, and certainly a powerful argument where there are those who have understanding of these things. Yet to how few believers could such reasoning appeal today, seeing that the more part *are* ignorant of these revealed purposes of God. But would the Lord's people thus be uninformed if the *teachers* of the church first understood what were evidently regular themes of the apostles, since otherwise they could not have taken for granted that such appeals would have weight?

The Head that once was crowned with thorns
  Is crowned with glory now ;
A royal diadem adorns
  The mighty Victor's brow.

The highest place that heaven affords
  Is His by sovereign right :
The King of kings and Lord of lords,
  He reigns in glory bright.

The joy of all who dwell above,
  The joy of all below
To whom He manifests His love
  And grants His name to know :

To them the Cross with all its shame,
  With all its grace is given ;
Their name an everlasting name,
  Their joy the joy of heaven.

They suffer with their Lord below,
  They reign with Him above,
Their profit and their joy to know
  The mystery of His love.

The Cross He bore is life and health,
  Though shame and death to Him :
His people's hope, His people's wealth,
  Their everlasting theme.

                             (T. Kelly).

"Jesus became man to remain man for evermore ; and when Jesus was living on earth His great object, the great task set before Him, was to get back again where He was before. He had left His position, never again to have it as He had before, never again to divest Himself of His humanity. He had, as it were, cut off the bridge behind Him, by identifying Himself with our nature, with all our load of sin, on the cross . . . . Because He died and rose again, He could take His place on high, as the first-born of many brethren, as the Saviour of His people. Jesus knew that through suffering alone could He get back again into that glory, which He had with the Father before the world was."

                (Adolph Saphir. *Memoir* 353).

CHAPTER VII.

GLORY THE REWARD OF SUFFERING.

*" Behoved it not the Messiah to suffer these things,
and to enter into His glory ?"   (Luke xxiv, 26).*

It is now needful that we observe very specially the ground upon which Christ *as man* is exalted to the supreme rule of heavens and earth. As the eternal Son of God it is his position by right. But man has no right to the heavenly world and its government : and the Son of God, in order to become man, "emptied Himself," and took the "form of a bondservant," not that of a king (Phil. ii, 6, 7). By what right, then, does He now as man hold this position and glory ? For the Scripture takes pains to emphasize that it is as man that He does so hold these glories. When Daniel the prophet saw beforehand the coming King, he describes Him as "One like unto a son of man" (ch. vii, 13) ; and Christ Himself intimated that the Father had appointed Him to be the sovereign judge because of His being "a Son of man" (John v, 27.)

The answer to this question is that the Lord Jesus is thus exalted as His Father's recompense to Him for His fidelity and sufferings on earth. At infinite cost, even of death itself, He made possible the display of God's mercy and the salvation of the sinner, overcoming Satan and death, and completely solving all the dread problems that sin had caused in heaven and earth. And proportionate to his toils shall be His reward. Because He shall reduce to order the kingdom of God, thrown into disorder by rebellion, therefore shall He be its sovereign Ruler.

By weakness and defeat
He won the meed and crown :
Trod all His foes beneath His feet
By being trodden down.

The following passages declare and emphasize this connection between Messiah's humiliation and exaltation :

61

Isa. liii, 12. "*Therefore* will I divide Him a portion with (among) the great, and He shall divide the spoil with the strong (or, as Luther, Lowth, Wordsworth, "the mighty people shall he share as his spoil," as Psalm 2, 8); *because He poured out His soul unto death,* and was numbered with the transgressors."

Phil. ii, 8, 9. "He humbled Himself, becoming obedient unto death, yea, the death of the cross. *Wherefore* also God highly exalted Him, and gave unto Him the name that is above every name."

Heb. ii, 9. "We behold Him Who hath been made a little lower than the angels, even Jesus, *because of the suffering of death* crowned with glory and honour."

Luke xxiv, 26, I Peter i, 11. In view of the plan of God, and of the revelation of that plan through the prophets, our Lord Himself, reviewing from resurrection ground the but lately endured agony of the cross, enquired of perplexed disciples whether it "behoved not the Messiah to suffer these things, and to enter into his glory?" And later on Peter gave this as a summary of the message of the Spirit of Christ through the prophets, that He had "testified beforehand the sufferings (which should come) unto Messiah, and the glories which should *follow* them," not precede nor be independent thereof.

Rev. v. In the visions of the actual and official recognition of the Lamb in the heavens as the Governor, the praise is rendered to Him because of His conquest (v. 5 "hath overcome"); and because He had been slain (vv. 9, 13).

Whoever should wrest the sceptre from the hands of the rebel prince, Satan, should himself wield it; and this Christ alone did, and did it as man. Faint pictures of His thus winning His bride and His authority are seen in such incidents in the Old Testament as Othniel winning Caleb's daughter by conquering the town of Hebron (Judges i, 13), and Joab securing the office of commander-in-chief of David's armies by attacking and entering the hitherto impregnable Jebusite fortress of Zion (1 Chron. xi, 4-6). The satanically and monstrously wicked nations of Canaan, whom Israel found in possession of the land of promise, are the old-time type of the wicked spirits who are as yet in possession of the heavenly places and powers which the church are to occupy. And for those spheres we must fight; and we secure only as much as we win at the sword's point. Perhaps the words, "the iniquity of the Amorite is not yet full" (Gen. 15, 16), which were God's explanation as to why Abram's seed could not for a long while after have possession of the land, are a hint to the spiritual mind as to one reason for the long delay in the glorifying of the church. Angels as well as men are shown full leniency and given full probation.

Two truths unite in this exaltation of God's Son. First, on God's side, it was of old true that the Father had appointed His Son to be heir of all things (Heb. i, 2). But then, on the outward side of things, Christ must vindicate this appointment by showing Himself as man worthy of it by victoriously suffering; "for it became Him (the Father) for Whom are all things, and through Whom are all things, in bringing many sons unto glory, to make the Author of their salvation (the Son) perfect through sufferings," perfect that is, not as to His nature or character, but in his experimental fitness for the work in view (Heb ii, 10).

And it is upon precisely the same double condition that Christ's people will share with Him His honours. In the first place, it is the choice of God, and the call of God, that create even the possibility thereof, and it is the effectual working of God, by His Spirit, that alone can make actual this purpose of God. Thus it is wholly of grace, and by the power that grace supplies, that any will be glorified, and their glory will be to "the praise of the glory of His grace, which He freely bestowed on us in the Beloved" (Eph. i, 6).

Yet, on the other hand, it is plainly set forth in Scripture that these honours must be reached through fidelity and suffering during our earthly course. Forgiveness of sins, and the possession of eternal life and salvation, are indeed free gifts (Rom. iii, 24 ; vi. 23), but the inheriting the kingdom requires that we prove our fitness and worthiness by sharing our Leader's toils whilst pressing on after Him along His path in life.

Gracious indeed it is of God that pardon and life eternal, the irreducible minimum for us if we are to escape perdition, should be secured to faith solely upon the ground of the merits of Christ.   Indeed, as the pardon of a rebel is a matter that must be determined with regard to the strict requirements of God's justice, it is obvious that no efforts of man could meet the case, since only a sinless man can be personally acceptable, and no rebel is this.   Hence, the merit of the only perfect One is necessarily the ground upon which that pardon can be extended and secured.   But it is as gracious as wise, and as wise as gracious, that the kingdom and its honours are presented to us as a goal to be reached by strenuous endeavour, as a prize to be gained by earnest toil, as a reward to be earned by faithful service, as a crown to be won by keen fighting.

Of the many who heard Christ's teaching, and who appear to have believed on Him as the Messiah, only a few followed Him wholly; but to these the Lord said, ' But ye are they who have continued with me in my temptations : and I appoint unto you a kingdom, even as my Father appointed unto me, that ye may eat and drink at my table in my kingdom ; and ye shall sit on thrones judging the twelve tribes of Israel." (Luke xxii, 28-30).

Thus authority in the kingdom, and the honour of sitting at His own, the chief, table in the day of His royal feasting, are plainly promised as superior rewards for superior devotion. And having thus set aglow their hearts by so bright a prospect, Christ immediately gave warning that straight before them was severe conflict with Satan.   This is the normal experience of those who aim to supersede the powers of darkness in the places of heavenly authority ; the latter hate the more those who will succeed them, and attack them the more fiercely, as witness the fierce but futile endeavour of the dragon to devour the man child (Rev. xii, 4, 5).   And this opposition is wisely permitted of God so that those whom He has chosen for His kingdom may become thoroughly qualified for their duties in that age.   The sons of royal and noble houses are by their birth entitled to expect riches to use, honours to bear, and high offices to fill.   But though their birth is their title to such great things, the training, educating and disciplining of such must be as thorough as their future is exalted. If we are God's children, we are therefore His heirs; heirs indeed (men) of God, but (de) joint heirs with Christ, if so be that we suffer with Him that we may be also glorified with Him (Rom. viii, 17). It has been well said that "the path of sorrow is not indeed the meriting, but the capacitating, preparation" for being glorified with Christ (Moule, Rom. viii, 17).

David, Christ's kingly ancestor, is in this himself a type of his Lord. For chosen by God to succeed the lawfully appointed but rejected king (Saul), he was yet for many years allowed to be hunted and persecuted by the doomed monarch whom he was to follow. During these wanderings over the mountains and wilds his faithful followers shared his hardships, and he and they together learned to endure and to fight; and thus when God's time of preparation was over, and their training had been completed, David and his men were found equal to the great task of freeing God's people from all bondage to their foes. And of course, those brave men who had shared their leader's path, with its dangers and distresses, were rewarded with the chief positions of glory in the kingdom. Surely everyone can see the fitness of this, and can appreciate how worth while it finally proved to have shared their king's rejection and persecution. And thus in intenser measure will it be in the day of Christ, "for the Son of Man shall come in the glory of His Father with His angels; and then shall He render unto every man according to his doing"; and again, "Behold," is our Lord's final message to His people, "I come quickly, and my wages with me, to render to each man according as his work is" (Matt. xvi, 27; Rev. xxii, 12).

We again remark that so thoroughly did the apostles of our Lord enter into this teaching that they heavily emphasized it for both the warning and encouraging of disciples. To the ungodly they said: "Be it known unto you therefore, brethren, that through this man is proclaimed unto you remission of sins: and by him every one that believeth is justified from all

things, from which ye could not be justified by the law of
Moses." (Acts xiii, 38, 39) ; but so as to confirm the souls of the
same hearers, who through believing had become disciples, and
when exhorting them to continue in the faith, they add, that
"*through many tribulations we must enter into the kingdom* of
God" (xiv, 22). Again, we find the apostle saying to the
Thessalonians, "we ourselves glory in you in the churches of
God for your patience and faith in all your persecutions and in
the afflictions which ye endure ; which is a manifest token of the
righteous judgement of God ; to the end that ye may be counted
worthy of the kingdom of God, for which ye also suffer"
(II Ep. i, 4, 5).   He further assures slaves that if they but
cheerfully and faithfully conduct themselves in their socially
degraded and ofttimes cruel lot, they shall receive from the
Lord the heavenly inheritance as His recompense to them for
serving Himself (Col. iii, 24).   The word "recompense" holds
the picture of making the scales even.   A touching yet stupen-
dous thought is this : the Lord of glory is taking minute notice
of the behaviour of the meanest of men, whom the great and
worldly hold in contempt, and is preparing a noble compensation in return for fidelity to His cause and Person.

> "O happy band of pilgrims,
>   Look upward to the skies,
>   Where such a light affliction
>   Shall win so great a prize."

Looking on to that wondrous time, Abram was strengthened
to forsake his home in a grand earthly city, for "he looked for
the city that hath the foundations (Rev. xxi, 14), whose
Architect and Master-builder is God" (Heb. xi., 10).   And thus
he continued as a pilgrim for no less than one hundred and five
years, patiently pressing on towards the goal ; not indeed perfect
in all his ways as a pilgrim, but yet never turning back from
the hope of that glorious day.   Thus Moses, though sharing
the glory and power of Egypt when it was the greatest kingdom
on earth, was enabled to give up all, and to choose "rather to
be evil entreated with the people of God, than to enjoy the
pleasures of sin for a season ; accounting the reproach of the

Messiah greater riches than the treasures of Egypt: for he looked unto the recompense of reward" (Heb. xi, 25, 26). And by the same vision multiudes since have been nerved to dare, to suffer, to die, enjoying the spiritual fellowship of Christ while suffering for His sake, and kept firm to the end because of the hope set before them in the gospel.

And we also shall find strength to endure if we too welcome to our hearts these promises, as they of old did (Heb. xi, 13), and fix our eye on the prize of our high calling of God in Christ Jesus (Phil. iii, 14). We too shall so run as to attain, and so strive in the contest as to receive the incorruptible crown, if we "set our hope perfectly on the grace that is being brought unto us at the revelation of Jesus Christ" (I Cor. ix, 24, 25 ; I Peter i, 13). In our case also shall become true this word : "our light affliction, which is for the moment, worketh for us more and more exceedingly an eternal weight of glory, while (on the condition that, see Alford) "we look not at the things which are seen, but at the things which are not seen ; for the things which are seen are temporal ; but the things which are not seen are eternal" (II Cor. iv, 17, 18).

Thus to us and our throne and sceptre, as to our Lord and Leader, apply the words, "Thou hast loved righteousness, and hated iniquity (lawlessness) ; therefore God, thy God, hath annointed Thee with the oil of gladness above Thy fellows (Heb. i, 8, 9).

That true saint and rare expositor quoted at the beginning of this chapter, Adolph Saphir, wrote further as follows: "I often pray that you may have much inward peace, and that the Lord may remove all that causes anxiety. And yet, as the Germans say, das liebe Kreuz, the dear cross. No doubt our afflictions and trials are signs that God has not forgotten us, but is educating us in Fatherly love (Heb. xii). I have felt of late years constantly drawn to those passages of Scripture which teach the mystery of our fellowship with Christ in suffering, or rather fellowship of His sufferings, and sometimes hope that I am beginning really to rejoice in Christ, though I am often ashamed of being so depressed and feeling so disappointed. The return of the Lord

" Jesus, and our being glorified together with Him (if so be that we suffer with Him), this true and lively hope seems to me like a star, which is not seen in the garish light of prosperity and a smooth course, but only in the stillness of sorrow, or at least of a chastened, crucified condition. I think this is one reason why the church lost this hope, after the first ages of martyrdom, and why now-a-days it so often degenerates into a mere sentimental speculation." (*Memoir* 216).

CHAPTER VIII.

THE FIRST RESURRECTION—A PRIZE.

"I press on toward the goal unto the prize."
—*(Phil. iii, 14).*

Am I a soldier of the cross,
  A follower of the Lamb?
And shall I fear to own His cause,
  Or blush to speak His name?

Must I be carried to the skies
  On flowery beds of ease,
Whilst others fought to win the prize,
  And sailed through bloody seas?

Are there no foes for me to face?
  Must I not stem the flood?
Is this vile world a friend to grace,
  To help me on to God?

Since I must fight if I would reign,
  Increase my courage, Lord!
I'll bear the toil, endure the pain,
  Supported by Thy word.

(Isaac Watts).

From Jeremy Taylor's *Holy Living and Dying*, ch. iv, sec. 2:
Of the Hope of a Christian.

" Faith differs from hope in the extension of its object, and in
the intention of degree. St. Austin [Anselm] thus accounts their
differences (Euchirid, ch. 8). Faith is of all things revealed, good
and bad, rewards and punishments, of things that concern us
and of things that concern us not : but hope hath for its object
things only that are good, and fit to be hoped for, future, and

concerning ourselves; and because these things are offered to us upon conditions of which we may so fail as we may change our will, therefore our certainty is less than the certainty of faith; which (because faith relies only upon one proposition, that is, the truth of the Word of God) cannot be made uncertain in themselves, though the object of our hope may become uncertain to us, and to our possession. For it is infallibly certain that there is heaven for all the godly, and for me amongst them all, if I do my duty. But that I shall enter into heaven* is the object of my hope, not of my faith; and is so sure as it is certain that I shall persevere in the ways of God."

The connection between sharing the sufferings of our Lord and sharing His glory was never more distinctly stated than by Himself when answering the two disciples who requested to be assured that they should sit on His right hand and left hand in His glory. To these aspirants for chief honours Christ most significantly replied, "Ye know not what ye ask"; and the context shows that their ignorance lay, not in their not having some sense of the greatness of the desired honour, but in their not appreciating the price to be paid in suffering with Him if such dignity was to be attained; for, He added, "Are ye able to drink the cup that I drink? or to be baptized with the baptism with which I am baptized?" And our Lord strikingly showed that in such matters there is to be no favouritism by adding that "to sit on My right hand or on my left hand is not Mine to give, but to them for whom it hath been prepared" (Mark x, 37-40).

It is in line with this that authority over the nations, and sharing the regal glories of the Lord, are promised to "conquerers," as in Rev. ii, 26, 27; and iii, 21. This latter verse reads: "He that overcometh, I will give to him to sit down with me in my throne, as I also overcame, and sat down with my Father in his throne"; and the words "even as I also conquered" firmly establish the parallel between Christ and His people in the matter of the condition upon which they, as He, must

---

*Probably Taylor uses this expression as equivalent to " being saved " : we take it in the stricter sense of a privilege additional to salvation.

attain to the throne. Alas, that these words of an old writer should still be true of so many: "Jesus has now many lovers of His heavenly kingdom, but few bearers of His cross. He finds many companions of His table, but few of His fasting. Many follow Jesus as far as the breaking of bread, but few to the drinking of the chalice of His passion."

It was Paul's yearning to follow the Lamb whithersoever He went. Writing to the Philippians he states very powerfully the distinction between the righteousness which justifies before God, in which no works of ours have the slightest part, and that full knowledge of the Lord by the justified one which will ensure a full reward. He says, "Howbeit what things were gain to me, these have I counted loss for Christ. Yea verily, and I count all things to be loss for the excellency of the knowlege of Christ Jesus my Lord: for whom I suffered the loss of all things, and do count them but dung, that I may gain Christ and be found in him, not having a righteousness of mine own, even that which is of the law, but that which is through faith in Christ, the righteousness which is of God by faith: that I may know him, and the power of his resurrection, and the fellow-ship of his sufferings, becoming conformed unto his death; if by any means I may attain unto the resurrection from the dead. Not that I have already obtained, or am already made perfect: but I press on, if so be that I may apprehend that for which also I was apprehended by Christ Jesus. Brethren, I count not myself yet to have apprehended: but one thing I do, forgetting the things which are behind, and stretching forward to the things which are before, I press on toward the goal unto the prize of the high calling of God in Christ Jesus. Let us therefore, as many as be perfect, be thus minded: and if in anything ye are otherwise minded, even this shall God reveal unto you: only, whereunto we have already attained, by that same rule let us walk. (Phil. iii, 7-16).

The being raised in the first resurrection assures a place in the kingdom, and honour therein; and such as are not then raised will miss that kingly glory, since the second and last resurrection is not to take place till after the millenial period

(Rev. xx, 4-6). On the other hand, those who attain to that kingship will retain it for ever, and not cease to reign at the end of the thousand years, for it is written concerning such that "they shall reign for ever and ever" (Rev. xxii, 5). From which it would appear that those who enter the kingdom at the close of the millenial period will not attain to kingly dignity therein, since that is stated only of those who had reached the bridal glory, the members of the Jerusalem which is above. It thus becomes a matter of everlasting consequence to be of those who participate in the first resurrection.

The phrase "the out resurrection from among the dead" (*teen exanastasin teen ek nekrōn*) is an emphasized repetition of words previously used by Christ. Asked by some concerning the resurrection He spoke of such as should be "accounted worthy to attain to that age and the resurrection out of (from among) the dead"—*tees anastaseōs tees ek nekrōn*. (Luke xx, 35). The expression "that age" must mean the millenial; for reaching the *eternal* ages is not a matter of our, but of our Saviour's, worthiness. And Scripture speaks of eternity as "ages" not as an "age." Moreover, "the coming age" (Mark x, 30; Luke xviii, 30) is the period "when the Son of man shall sit on the throne of His glory" and the apostles shall rule over Israel, *i.e.*, the millenial age. See the parallel passage Matt. xix, 28. The translation "world" is a darkening of the divine counsel by a word that is inaccurate. The R.V. gives "age" in the margin. Darby translates by "the coming age."

In the same line is a statement of the Lord in connection with the rich young ruler who enquired as to gaining life eternal (Matt. xix, 16-20; Mark x, 17-31; Luke xviii, 18-30). The question was indefinite as to when in the future this life might be gained, and the Lord left that point, simply directing him to the commandments, which "if a man do he shall live" (Lev. xviii, 5). When the rich man showed the grip his possessions had on his heart the Lord remarked on the great difficulty riches are to "entering the kingdom of God." The disciples took this "entering" as equivalent to being "saved," and rightly so, for he who is saved will be in the kingdom of

God, and they who are not at last in the kingdom will be unsaved.

So far all has been said on the ground of what was the then expectation of men, as expressed later by Martha: "I know that my brother shall rise again in the resurrection *at the last day*" (Jo. xi, 24); which was what the Lord had promised to such as came to Him in faith, saying once and again, "I will raise him up *at the last day*" (Jo. vi, 40, 44). That resurrection will bring to the saved entrance into the kingdom, with eternal life, but it will be after the millenial era of the kingdom.

Peter then reminded the Lord that he and the other apostles had fulfilled the condition that the ruler had shunned, and had left all to follow Him. What would be their recompense for this sacrifice? Christ answered that all such would receive in this life much more of the same class of possessions than they had given up, accompanied by persecutions; of which Peter had due fulfilment in the numberless friends and homes that he found as a wanderer for the sake of the gospel, as many other persecuted and hunted souls have done.

But to the promise of this present recompense the Lord added that such should receive life eternal "in the age the coming," which age is shown in Matthew's account to be "the regeneration, when the Son of man shall sit on the throne of His glory" and the twelve apostles shall sit on thrones judging the twelve tribes of Israel (Matt. xix, 28). This promise implies of necessity sharing in the first resurrection, not in that of "the last day"; the one being before the thousand years reign and the other at its close, according to Rev. xx.

Now this inheriting of eternal life in "the coming age" is distinctly stated by Christ to be part of the reward of suffering for His sake in this present age. This agrees with all other passages to the effect that one must be accounted worthy of that coming age and of the resurrection from among the dead.

It is in evident spiritual harmony with this that the three histories all relate next that Christ then pressed on the apostles the severe tests that shortly awaited Him and them on reaching Jerusalem at the end of that journey; and that two of the accounts introduce at once the request of James and John for

the chief places in the kingdom, with the answer of the Lord
that such positions involved a sharing in His baptism of death
and His cup of grief.

To be so accounted worthy was Paul's set determination, and
he knew that to attain to such a state of fitness it was imperative
that he, like his Lord, should be "dead" to the godless age
which Christ has rejected, seeing that it has rejected Him. He
knew too that if such moral conformity to His death is to be
attained, the sufferings that bring death must be shared. To
suffer with Christ, either by toil or need incurred in furthering
His ends, or at the hands of the world, for His sake and for
righteousness, or otherwise as He may appoint for our perfecting,
is a simple and sure way of growing like Him in holiness, "for
he that hath suffered in the flesh hath ceased from sin" (I Peter
iv, 1). A man cannot at once live in daily fellowship with the
cross of Christ and go on in the sin for which Christ there
suffered, nor easily continue in fellowship with the world that
so treated his Lord.

Therefore also Paul said to the Thessalonian saints, "To
which end we also pray always for you, that our God may count
you worthy of your calling, and fulfil every desire of goodness
and every work of faith, with power; that the name of our Lord
Jesus may be glorified in you, and ye in him, according to the
grace of our God and the Lord Jesus Christ" (II Ep. i, 11, 12).
He desired, as he had said in ver. 5, that they might so live and
suffer "to the end that ye may be counted worthy of the
kingdom of God, for which also ye suffer." And, of course,
as Bishop Lightfoot has said, "the conformity with the
sufferings of Christ implies not only the endurance of
persecution for His name, but all pangs and all afflictions
undergone in the struggle against sin either within or without."

Sharing the kingdom, to which we are called, is thus
repeatedly declared to be the portion of those who are
"accounted worthy," and their worthiness is shown to depend
upon their conduct as disciples. Speaking to disciples (Matt.
x, 37, 38), and of disciples (ver. 24), the Lord plainly said, "He
that loveth father or mother more than me is not worthy of

"me ; and he that loveth son or daughter more than me is not worthy of me. And he that doth not take his cross and follow after me, is not worthy of me." And this He said in full view of and because of the trials that must needs befall any faithful follower of Himself. And on another occasion, and still addressing such as were expressing not merely faith in Him the Saviour sent by God, but a readiness to follow Him as disciples, but who wished to give the first place to certain natural, and in themselves proper, things, Christ uttered these searching words: "No man, having put his hand to the plough, and looking back, is *fit for the kingdom* of God " (Luke ix, 62). He did not say that such could not be saved from hell, or that if one who had commenced gospel service [1] retired therefrom because of its laborious nature, he would forfeit eternal life ; but that such a one is not "fit for the kingdom." For officers of state, whether civil or military, must be prepared to give their monarch and their high duties a place of priority over all other persons and affairs, or they are not fit for such posts.

Thus also must a betrothed damsel honour her future bride-groom, or she is unfit to be his consort. And with this in mind it will be profitable to study Paul's words to the Corinthians whom he had led to the Lord. He says (II Ep., xi, 1-3) : "Would ye that ye could bear with me in a little foolishness : nay indeed, bear with me. For I am jealous over you with a godly jealousy : for I espoused you to one husband, that I might present you as a pure virgin to Christ. But I fear, least by any means, as the serpent beguiled Eve in his craftiness, your minds should be corrupted from the simplicity and the purity that is toward Christ."

"I am jealous over you with a jealousy of God." God is jealous that the affections of His people should be all His own and should not be bestowed upon His enemies, the self-nature, Satan, or the world : "thou shalt love the Lord thy God with *all* thy heart," "For I espoused you to one husband, that I might present you as a pure virgin to Christ." In eastern lands it ever has been, and is, customary for there to be an intermed-

1 Ploughing—Cp. for the figure, I Cor. iii, 6-9 ; 9, 10.

iary in arranging a marriage. The Bible picture of this is in
Genesis xxiv, where Abraham's servant Eliezer, goes on a long
journey to find a wife for Isaac. He takes with him a good
report of his master's son, and tells how that his father has
made him heir of all his vast possessions, and he shows the
damsel and her friends samples of this wealth in camels and
jewelry, and gives them some of the latter. Thus allured,
Rebecca left her known circle and took a long, desert journey
to become Isaac's wife, though she had never seen him.

Thus did Paul speak to men of Christ, telling of His love and
His glory and how that God has appointed His Son the heir of
all things (Heb. i, 2). Thus did he bestow upon those who
heeded his words a foretaste of heaven's wealth, by the Spirit
of Christ giving them in present enjoyment both pardon, life,
and power for right living, as well as peace, joy, and other good
things spiritual, He—the Spirit—being thus the "earnest" (Eph.
i, 14 ; Rom. xiv, 17), of the full inheritance which will be
received when the betrothal is consummated at the marriage of
the Lamb.

Now on that return journey it was Eliezer's chief care that
Rebecca was preserved safe to be duly presented to Isaac ; and
thus Paul continues, "I espoused you . . . that I might
present you as a pure virgin to Christ." The word pure in this
connection presents the picture of a maiden who has never
had cross her mind thoughts concerning any other man than
the one to whom she is betrothed. Thus did Paul long that
their hearts should never dote on the world or its god, or
hanker after pleasures or persons with which Christ cannot
have fellowship. The apostle yearned that when the day comes
that the church shall be presented to Christ, to be eternally
with Him and for Him, these christians might be found to have
loved Him only and always, and not to have turned from their
"first love" to Christ to allow baser affections to captivate
their heart. There is real and constant danger of such
unhallowed intimacy; and if the believer does turn from Christ,
even in heart only, and coquets with the world, it is equivalent
to adultery against a husband, as says the Scripture (James iv, 4),

"Ye adulteressess, know ye not that the friendship of the world is enmity with God ? whosoever therefore is minded to be a friend of the world maketh himself (takes his place as) an enemy of God."

In this case how shall the intended bride be found at last fit for the embraces of the faithful bridegroom, seeing that she has become defiled and unchaste ? "But I fear," says Paul solemnly, I fear, I fear !—"I fear lest by any means, as the serpent beguiled Eve in his craftiness, your thoughts should be corrupted from the simplicity and the purity that is toward Christ." While Eve thought only pure and loving thoughts of her gracious Creator all was well. But the serpent to whom she listened, raised in her mind doubts as to God's goodness, and thus he "beguiled" her, that is, led her heart away from its virgin state of love to and confidence in God. This is still the object of his desire.

The word craftiness seems equivalent to the phrases that he, to secure his ends, is *equal to anything* and will *stop at nothing (panourgia—pas ergon : any work)*. By false teachings concerning the Person of the Lord, by denials of the accuracy and trustworthiness of His Word, by contempt for the teaching that the Bridegroom will come for His church, by fascinating the eyes and stupifying the mind and satiating the heart with things present, even lawful things, does he seek to make us faithless to our Beloved. And if so be that he can then cause the thus corrupted heart to advance to open worldliness or gross sin in practice, the more does he rejoice that he has alienated the affections from Christ and captivated them for himself or his things.

It is for the betrothed damsel to watch over her heart, guarding herself against thoughts that are evil, and from doting on others than her Lord. "Keep thy heart with all diligence ; for out of it are the issues of life" (Prov. iv, 23). Let her fill her mind with thoughts of Christ by frequently reading and pondering what He has written to her; let her constantly send Him messages of her affection ; let her seek from Him help at all times of danger and distress, nor ever turn to another for

aid ; let her daily delight in and be content with the gifts that
His love has already made her own[1] ; let her continually set her
hope perfectly on the grace that is being brought unto her at
His appearing ; and thus will her heart be occupied and satisfied
with Himself only, and she shall be kept safe, " kept for Jesus
Christ " (Jude 1). " But ye, beloved, building up yourselves on
your most holy faith, praying in the Holy Spirit, keep yourselves
in the love of God, looking for the mercy of our Lord Jesus
Christ unto eternal life " (Jude 20, 21).

But if one turn aside in heart how great is the immediate loss
of present joy in the Lord, and how incalculable the future and
ultimate loss if found unworthy to be part of the "bride," a
place in which company will be forfeited by spiritual fornication.[2]
It is purely the grace of God that has called sinners to such
fellowship with the Son of His love, and has given us such a
prospect ; and that same grace, in order to give effect to its plan,
has provided every possible and sufficient inducement to enable
us, by the Spirit, to reach the intended goal, the bridal day.
Only, if we neglect or spurn the proffered grace of God, and prefer
the present Christless pleasures of the world, we shall not lay
hold of that for which we were laid hold of by Christ Jesus
(Phil. iii., 12). Thus is the calling and the attaining wholly of
grace, and to the "praise of the glory of His grace" shall be
every glorified saint ; but we on our part must continually be
"looking carefully lest there be any man that falleth short of
the grace of God" (Heb. xii, 15).

The difficulty as to some believers not sharing in the first
resurrection that is found by some in I Cor. xv, 22-24 and 51,
52, is not so real as it may appear.

The statement in ver. 22 that "As in Adam all die, even so in
Christ shall all be made alive " applies to the whole human race.
This is evident in the first clause. The assertion is not concening

---

1 "Whosoever drinketh of (keeps on drinking of ; confines his drinking to) the water that I shall give
   him shall never thirst" (John iv, 14).

2 If Jer. iii, 1, is urged to the contrary, the reply is that the call is to Israel as a whole. The nation
   as such will turn to the Lord, but *those individuals who were personally ungodly*, and "were
   cut off from their people," have no promise of sharing the blessing of re-union with Jehovah. Thus
   also the church as a whole will reach the final afore-ordained position, but individuals may lose
   their portion therein.

the first resurrection, that of believers, but the thought is the same as that of the Lord in John v, 28, " all that are in the tombs shall hear His voice and shall come forth." But the apostle at once explains that this will not be all at the same time, but at different times. This subject he does not open up here, and its enlargement and details must be sought in other passages dealing with the theme.

The real point to be determined is the exact force of the expression in v. 23 " those of the Christ," as it reads exactly. We hope to examine this more thoroughly on another occasion. It would require a considerable paper. Critical study will, we think, show that it is not the same as the English expression " they that are Christ's." The latter is a wider phrase than the former.

As to the statement in v. 51 "we shall *all* be changed," it is not certain that this applies to the dead. It may apply only to the living at the hour the Lord will descend, for at the close of the statement they are distinguished, and of the former it is said that " *the dead* shall be raised incorruptible, and *we* (that is, the then living) shall be changed." If this is correct, then it is not here said that all the dead shall be raised, but only that all the then living shall be changed. Can the dead be " changed " seeing they have not a body to be changed? They will be clothed upon with the body that is from heaven (II Cor. v, 1, 2), and that will not need any change to pass over it to fit it for that heavenly world. This passage therefore seems to leave open the question as to which of the dead will be accounted worthy of the first resurrection, according to Luke xx, 34, 35.

But if it be that the two "alls" mean the same persons, "not all (of us) shall sleep, but all (of us) shall be changed," then, as to the word "all" it must be remembered that in Heb. ii, 15, R.V., it is said that the purpose of the death of Christ was that "He might bring to nought him that had the power of death, that is, the devil, and might deliver *all* them that through fear oᴋ death were all their lifetime subject to bondage." Yet other scriptures shew that not all, alas, will be delivered. Though the word translated "all" (*hosoi*) is not the same as that in Cor. xv., yet doubtless the R.V. gives the sense correctly, and the passage affords an example of an important feature of the Word of God, that when a matter is dealt with in general, and from the point of view of the divine purpose and willingness, wide universal terms are used. But these must ever be read in the light of more detail statements, such as open up the human side of the matter, which God allows to interact with His own workings, to the limiting of these latter. Another good instance will be seen later in Exodus xv, 13-17, where the entrance into Canaan of every person that had come out of Egypt is celebrated in advance as an event that had already happened. Notice the past tenses. Yet in fact a great number of those in question did not get to Canaan.

To take the surface sense of one solitary verse (as I Cor. xv, 51), and settle by it a question dealt with in many other passages also, is not the way to arrive at truth. Its harmony with all else upon the same theme must be sought, and not till all statements have been harmonized can there be hope that we truly understand the subject. This applies to some other important topics also.

THE HOPE.

"For by the Hope were we saved."—*Rom. viii, 24.*

"The crown .... to all who have loved His appearing."
—*II Tim. iv, 8.*

Psalm cvii, 23-32.

Safe home, safe home in port !
Rent cordage, shattered deck,
Torn sails, provisions short,
And only not a wreck :
But oh, the joy upon the shore
To tell our voyage perils o'er.

II Tim. iv, 8. Rev. ii, 10.

The prize, the prize secure !
The wrestler almost fell ;
Bare all he could endure,
And bare not always well :
But he may smile at troubles gone
Who has the victor garland on.

Rev. xvii, 14 ; ii, 25-28.

No more the foe can harm,
No more of leagured camp,
Or cry of night alarm,
And need of ready lamp :
And yet how nearly he had failed,
How nearly had the foe prevailed !

I Pet. ii, 25. Psalm xxiii, 6. Rev. vii, 16, 17.

The lamb is in the fold,
In perfect safety penned ;
The lion once had hold,
And thought to make an end :
But One came by with wounded side,
And for the sheep the Shepherd died.

I Cor. iv, 11. John xii, 26. Heb. xii, 1, 2.

The exile is at home !
O nights and days of tears !
O longings not to roam !
O sins and doubts and fears !
What matters now ? O joyful day !
The King has wiped all tears away !

Eph. v, 25 27. Rev. xix, 7, 8.

O happy, happy bride !
Thy widowed hours are past ;
The Bridegroom at thy side,
Thou all His own at last !
The sorrows of thy former cup
In full fruition swallowed up.

(S.S. and S. 719, old ed.)

"Brethren, I (Paul) count not myself yet to have laid hold (of the prize) . . . .

THE FEAR.

"But I fear, lest— ! "—*II Cor. xi*, 2, 3.
"Let us fear, lest—! "—*Heb. iv*, 1.

I Tim. i, 18-20.

The rocks ! men stood aghast !
  The voyage was almost done,
Such fearful perils past,
  The port so nearly won :
But oh, the grief to see the shore
With costliest wreckage littered o'er !

I Cor. ix, 24-27 ; x, 12, 13. Rev. iii, 11.

The crown he longed to gain
  Shall ne'er his brow adorn !
He stoutly strove, with pain,
  And yet the prize is gone :
O'er confident, he tripped, and lo,
He crippled lies before the foe.

Luke xxii, 45, 46, 62. Heb. x, 32-39.

So long and brave the fight,
  And yet the field is lost ;
The warrior, put to flight,
  Bewails the awful cost :
'Twas such a little hour of sleep,
But many a day his soul shall weep.

I Pet. v, 8.

The lamb is in the waste !
  How wild the wintry blast !
The Shepherd moves with haste,
  The silly sheep flees fast :
Oh, should the lion once get hold !
Oh, should the sheep succumb with cold !

Matt. xxiv, 24. II Cor' xi, 13-15. Heb. iv, 11.

Allured by falsest Guide
  In flower-strewn fields to stray,
The pilgrim turned aside,
  Nor held the narrow way :
O darksome wild ! O chilling fears !
O distant home ! O scalding tears !

II Cor. xi, 2, 3. Jas. iv, 4.

O grief for words too sore !
  The bridal day is nigh,
The virgin, *that* no more,
  Is left to weep and sigh :
All sullied by the foul embrace,
She lost for aye her queenly place.

(Wolkendorf, Roumania, 24th April, 1923).
G. H. L.

. . . . but one thing I do . . . . I PRESS ON toward the goal."—Phil. iii, 13, 14.

83

CHAPTER IX

FIRSTBORN SONS.

"Shimri the chief; for though he was not the firstborn,
yet his father made him chief."—(I Chron. xxvi, 10).

The section of Scripture a sentence of which has been before
quoted is another passage which demands the fullest consideration. It reads thus :

Heb. xii,   "Follow after peace with all men, and the sanctification
14-29   without which no man shall see the Lord : looking
carefully lest there be any man that falleth short of the grace of
God ; lest any root of bitterness springing up trouble you, and
thereby the many be defiled ; lest there be any fornicator, or
profane person,'as Esau, who for one mess of meat sold his own
birthright.

"For ye know that even when he afterward desired to inherit
the blessing, he was rejected (for he found no place of
repentance), though he sought it diligently with tears.

"For ye are not come unto a mount that might be touched,
and that burned with fire, and unto blackness, and darkness, and
tempest, and the sound of a trumpet, and the voice of words ;
which voice they that heard intreated that no word more should
be spoken unto them : for they could not endure that which
was enjoined, If even a beast touch the mountain, it shall be
stoned ; and so fearful was the appearance, that Moses said, I
exceedingly fear and quake : but ye are come unto mount Zion,
and unto the city of the living God, the heavenly Jerusalem,
and to innumerable hosts of angels, the general assembly,
and to the church of the firstborn who are enrolled in heaven,
and to God the Judge of all, and to the spirits of just men made
perfect, and to Jesus the mediator of a new covenant, and to
the blood of sprinkling that speaketh better than that of Abel.
See that ye refuse not him that speaketh.   For if they escaped
not, when they refused him that warned them on earth, much

" more shall not we escape, who turn away from him that warneth from heaven : whose voice then shook the earth : but now he hath promised, saying, Yet once more will I make to tremble not the earth only, but also the heaven. And this word, Yet once more, signifieth the removing of those things that are shaken, as of things that have been made, that those things which are not shaken may remain. Wherefore, receiving a kingdom that cannot be shaken, let us have grace, whereby we may offer service well-pleasing to God with reverence and awe : for our God is a consuming fire."

It is very plain that this portion of God's word has no reference to the unsaved. Months before they reached Sinai, Israel had experienced the redeeming power of the blood of atonement, and were freed from the authority of the destroying angel in Egypt. They had also left Egypt for ever as their sphere of life, and the Red Sea was rolling between them and its scenes of bondage or of pleasure. They are thus a picture of us who have accepted the eternal deliverance from wrath through the precious blood of Christ, and who have thereupon been cut off from the life of heart-association with the world by the power of the love of Him Whose death on the cross at the hands of the world implies our death with Him to that world. This union with Him is set forth in our immersion in the waters of baptism in His name ; and Israel crossing the Sea is declared in the New Testament (I Cor., x, 1), to be an old-time parallel to our baptism.

Thus redeemed, and thus separated to a walk of faith in God, Israel presently drew near to Mount Sinai, there to gain a fuller knowledge of the great Jehovah, the God with Whom they had to do. But how terrible was the aspect in which they there met Him ! With what dreadful accompaniments did he present Himself ! The exhibition was indeed suited to their condition, for their first need was to know that their God was infinitely greater and grander than all the gods of Egypt or the other nations, so that the dread of these latter might be broken from off their hearts.

They stand, then, beneath the mountain, which towers above
them some 7,000 or more feet, and gaze with terror at its cloud-
capped, lightning-lit, earthquake-rent summit; and even Moses,
the friend of God, says "I exceedingly fear and quake."

But how different is the prospect at which we are called to
look. From our present place as pilgrims in a world that affords
our hearts naught by which we can profit, we are brought to
gaze up to a height of privilege and glory which is as entrancing
and encouraging as Sinai seemed to Israel to be forbidding.

"Ye *have come*," says the Scripture: it is a perfect tense that
is used. As Israel had come to Sinai, so we "have drawn near"
to these higher, because heavenly and eternal, glories. Let us
then closely inspect what is spread before and above us.

1. "Ye have come unto the blood of sprinkling, that
speaketh better than that of Abel."

> "Abel's blood for vengeance
>   Pleaded to the skies;
> But the blood of Jesus
>   For our pardon cries."

No matter what is the privilege now known, or hereafter to be
gained, all our standing and hope is based upon the atonement
of Calvary. Had not the blood of Jesus put away our sin we had
been destroyed in Egypt, and had never drawn near to God,
nor had any prospect whatever to which to aspire. And if
that same blood does not keep us clean, then will continuous
communion be impossible; "but if we walk in the light, as God
is in the light, we (God and the saint) have fellowship one with
another, and the blood of Jesus His Son cleanseth us (keeps us
perpetually and wholly clean) from all sin " (I John i, 7). And
to all eternity, and in whatever height of glory we may reign on
Mount Zion, we shall still discover our security to stand in that
eternal redemption.

> "I stand upon His merit:
>   I know no other stand,
> Not e'en where glory dwelleth
>   In Immanuel's land."

2. "Ye have come unto Jesus the mediator of a new covenant." This theme is a chief part of the burden of the epistle. The Hebrew believers, cast out of the synagogue, unwelcome at the temple, deprived therefore of the sacrifices and priesthood, seemed to have lost all that made life great and safe for the Israelite. To comfort their heart they are instructed that there are heavenly realities of which Israel's earthly privileges were but shadows. The covenant made at Sinai gives place to the new covenant of which God had spoken through Jeremiah (xxxi, 31). This covenant has eternal force, being assured by a sacrifice which has eternal value; it carries promises which are far, far better than any limited to the earth could ever be; and it is guaranteed and administered by a Priest Who is none less than God's Son incarnate and glorified, and whose office does not pass from Himself to another, seeing that He ever liveth in the power of an indissoluble life (Heb. vii, 16).

Thus those who have come unto Jesus as the mediator of the new covenant gain heavenly and eternal privileges; and these they receive for the sake of what He is to God, and not out of regard to any merit of their own; even as God wrought for Israel in Egypt not because of ought that He saw in them, but because of His own unmerited love, and because of His covenant with their fathers, the heads of their family (Deut. vii. 7, 8). Christ is the Head of all the redeemed family of God, the Surety of this better covenant, in which all now share who accept Him as their sacrifice and mediator.

3. Ye have come unto "the spirits of just men made perfect." We understand this to mean that we have come unto a point of privilege entitling us to anticipate a share in the first resurrection of the just. Man as described in Scripture is a being composed of spirit and soul and body (Gen. ii, 7; I Thess. v, 23, etc). He is therefore not perfect except as his "spirit and soul and body be preserved entire." Hence the disembodied (unclothed) state the apostle did not desire (II Cor. v, 4), but longed to be "clothed upon with our habitation which is from heaven." Immediately before our chapter (Heb. xi, 40) we have been told that the saints of older days cannot be "made perfect"

apart from us of this age, and this in spite of their heavenly
attitude (vv. 9-16) and their noble faithfulness and sufferings.
All things await for their perfecting the manifestation of the
sons of God (Rom. viii, 19). But when clothed in bodies
immortal and mighty and glorious, then the saints will be perfect
in the highest and most absolute sense, and this will be at the
resurrection and rapture, when called to our Lord's presence,
and in His kingdom for ever. Personality in man attaches to
the soul, not to the spirit: "*man* became a living *soul*" (Gen.
ii, 7). It is therefore the *spirit* that returns at death to God
who gave it (Eccl. xii, 7; Luke xxiii, 46; Ac. vii, 59); but the
person, the soul, goes to paradise, the restful part of Hades, the
world of the dead in "the lower parts of the earth"—Thither
our Lord and the thief went at death (Lk xxiii, 43; Ac. ii, 27;
Eph. iv, 9, 10); there David still was later than the ascension of
Christ (Ac. ii, 34). The just therefore are not yet made perfect,
nor can be till resurrection. It is a prospect to which we aspire;
just as Israel did not reach the summit of Sinai, but gazed up at it.

4.   Therefore the next honour named is that we have come
unto "God the Judge of all." From the preceding clauses it
will be seen that the force of the words "ye have come" is that
we have come to *participate* in the privileges stated, and not
merely to view them. Even thus it was open to Israel to share
in the benefits of the sacrifices offered at Sinai, and in the
advantages of the covenant there enacted. Keeping therefore
to this sense, and thus interpreting the clauses with uniformity,
the present words will not mean that we have drawn near to
God to be judged, but rather to share with Him the honour of
the office indicated by the title. As the Judge of all we shall not
meet God, for Christ Himself declared this in the plain and
memorable words, "Verily, verily, I say unto you, He that
heareth my word, and believeth him that sent me, hath eternal
life, and cometh not into judgement, but hath passed out of
death into life." (John v, 24). And as regards the appearing of
the saints before the judgment seat of Christ (II Cor. v, 10),
that is indeed a solemn prospect to be ceaselessly reckoned upon,
but it is not the matter here in question. The saints are to

judge the world and even angels (I Cor. vi, 2, 3). The apostles are assured of this office in relation to Israel as a nation (Luke xxii, 28-30). The same thought is suggested by the promise of sitting upon the throne with Christ, the Judge (Rev. iii, 21); that is, by the dignity of kingship being conferred, for of old the king was the chief judge of his people; and by such a promise as that to the saints who overcome that they shall rule the nations (Rev. ii, 27).

In the administration of His mighty kingdom, and in the adjusting and rewarding of the affairs of the ages of human and angelic history, the glorified saints will be associated with the King of glory. Doubtless a large part of our training on earth is directed by our Father to capacitating us for such responsible and honourable office. If then a self-willed child refuses and nullifies the training, how shall he be found fit for the high but delicate position that he might have gained?

5. Being thus included in the company of the "kings and priests" of the future, we have come unto the "church of the firstborn (ones) who are enrolled in heaven." The law of primo-geniture is divinely recognized in both the sphere of the family and in that of the nations, and also in the heavenly regions as well as the earthly. God commanded to Israel that the first-born son should inherit twice as much of the father's estate as any other child (Deut. xxi, 17). To this son fell also the right of control in the family, subject to the father; and also, in the older eras at least, the first-born son acted as the family priest. An interesting instance is found in the excuse that David told Jonathan to offer to Saul for David's intended absence from the king's table on a festival day, when specially the royal house-hold should have gathered. Jonathan thus expressed himself; "David earnestly asked leave of me to go to Bethlehem: and he said, Let me go, I pray thee; for our family hath a sacrifice in the city; and my brother he hath commanded me to be there: and now, if I have found favour in thine eyes, let me get away I pray thee, and see my brethren. Therefore he is not come unto the king's table (I Sam. xx, 28, 29).

Thus on a day of family sacrifice the brother ("my brother";
necessarily suggesting one whom the younger must obey, that
is, the then eldest son) is seen both acting as priest and
"commanding" the attendance of the rest of the family. And
how obligatory obedience was is suggested by it being taken for
granted by both David and Jonathan that non-attendance upon
the king himself would be, or should be, condoned on such an
occasion. This honour is evidently the initial reason for the
kingship descending as a rule to the eldest son of a monarch.
The honouring of the eldest son is, indeed, founded in nature,
and is further enforced by divine sanction. It is still largely
acknowledged in the east, as in the case of a young lawyer in
Egypt remarking to the writer that his eldest brother had just
taken off a book, for, said my friend, he thinks that because he
is the eldest he can do as he likes with our things.

In this we may see the explanation of Pharoah's prompt and
dogged resistance to God's call that he should free Israel.
Egypt was then the chief of the nations in wisdom, wealth,
power, and glory. To the proud sovereign of this haughty
people a message comes from a God who claims to be the Lord
of heaven and earth, the eternal one, Jehovah. The Egyptians
though by that time worshipping many gods, still owned that
above all there was the great original Deity. From this over-
lord of heaven and earth the mandate comes to Pharoah,
"Israel is my son, my *first-born*" (Ex. iv, 22). No wonder if the
monarch starts at the words. To him they mean nothing less
than that Egypt's supremacy among the nations is to pass to
this race of miserable slaves. Greater humiliation could not be :
it were worse than the national foe, the Hittites, wresting this
glory from him in fair fight : and the foolish king will dare
anything rather than consent.

This word of God remains in force. Israel is still God's firstborn among the peoples of the earth, and must, as we have
seen, "possess the gate of his enemies" (Gen. xxii, 17), "and the
nation and kingdom that will not serve Israel shall perish"
(Isa. lx, 12). Referring to that coming period when this shall
be fulfilled, and speaking of Israel's King, "David My Servant,"

Jehovah has said "I will make him first-born, the most High to the kings of the earth" (Psalm 89, 27. Variorum Bible).

Thus our thought enlarges from the family to the state, and must now expand to the entire universe as the whole realm of God's kingdom. Amongst all the various orders of beings that God will have to His praise in eternal ages, one company is to be to the rest what the first-born has been shown to be. This company is the church of God : "ye have come unto," ye have membership in "the church (*ecclesia*, the selected, the called out) of the first-born ones,[1] who are enrolled in heaven." These will have a double share of the Father's inheritance, that is the glory of the spacious and magnificent heavenly regions and conditions, as contrasted with the great but limited glory of the earthly section of the kingdom of God. To them will be given with Christ authority over all other beings, creatures, and things ("*all things* are yours" I Cor. iii, 23) ; and so fully will God dwell in them that they will be intermediaries, "priests," between Him and His universe, " they shall be priests of God and of Christ, and shall reign with Him" (Rev. xx, 6). Well may the same scripture exclaim, "Blessed and holy is he that hath part in the first resurrection."

God keeps a full register of all His family, and therein the names of these blessed and holy ones are entered as being the firstborn. The reference is probably to the registers kept at the temple in Jerusalem, and which were of final authority as compared with local or family records. Who in a numerous family was the firstborn son could thus be settled beyond controversy, for each such had to be presented to God in the temple (Ex. xiii, 11 ; Lk ii, 22). And God has the names of His firstborn duly inserted as such in His heavenly register.

6. The next point in the panorama of privilege is the relationship of the church to the angelic hosts on a day of festivity to which these will come. The English versions do not rightly divide the clauses here. Commenting on this Dean Alford remarks that " it is difficult to see why the coupling

---

1 The noun is plural, and cannot refer to Christ personally, as is further shown by the plural verb following, "who *are* enrolled."

of clause to clause by 'and' (kai) which prevails through the sentence, should be broken through"; and Darby (*New Translation*; note) says, "The words 'and' (kai) give the division very clearly here," and he translates thus: "and to myriads of angels, the universal gathering"; whilst Alford seeks to give the full force of the words by rendering, "and to myriads, the festal hosts of angels." We may therefore read the clause thus, Ye have come unto "myriads of angels, the universal festal gathering."

And what a vista of splendour thus opens to view as the mind conceives as much as possible of the glory of the Son of God, in Whom "dwelleth all the fulness of the Godhead bodily," coming in His own glory and in the glory of the Father and that of the holy angels (Luke ix, 26). Such a monarch in such state and with such a retinue will eclipse all that the world ever thought grand and splendid. And in that glory the firstborn are to share, being the "bride, the wife of the Lamb," who with Christ will "be seen coming down out of heaven from God, having the glory of God" (Rev. xxi, 9-11). To her as to her Lord the angels will be attendants, for already they are "ministering spirits sent forth to do service for the sake of them that shall inherit salvation" (Heb. i, 14).

But this clause fixes the exact occasion when the church shall enter upon these supreme honours. For this gathering of angels is both "universal," that is, all the holy hosts will be present at once, and it is also "festal," that is, the gathering is on an occasion of joy and triumph. The Word of God elsewhere speaks of only one such day, and that the day of Messiah's appearing in Jerusalem to establish His kingdom on earth. Zechariah foresaw that event, and cried rapturously, "Jehovah my God shall come, and *all the holy ones* with Thee" (xiv, 5); and Christ Himself gathered up this and some other prophecies into the thrilling declaration, "when the Son of man shall come in His glory, and *all the angels* with Him, then shall He sit on the throne of His glory" (Matt. xxv, 31). Thus shall be fulfilled the promise of God summarized through the angel th a announced His birth: "the Lord God shall give unto Him the

throne of His father David : and He shall reign over the house
of Jacob for ever ; and of His kingdom there shall be no end "
(Luke i, 32, 33) : and then shall come to pass the word
concerning the church, "When Christ, our life, shall be
manifested (to men on earth), then shall ye also with Him be
manifested in glory " (Col. iii, 4).

> "Let that day come, O Lord,
>   And other days pass by ;
> Night is far spent, and dawning tells
>   That Thou art drawing nigh."

> "Hasten Thy coming, Lord !
>   Dawn, O Thou glorious day !
> Then shall the fairest days of earth
>   Pass into shade away."

7. But great as are the things thus enlarged upon, there are
greater and higher glories unto which we have drawn near. Ye
have come unto "the city of the living God, the heavenly
Jerusalem." During the reign of Christ on earth, Jerusalem, the
" city of the great King," will be His earthly metropolis, and the
world's centre. But in the heavenly regions there will be
another " city," of which that on earth is but a reflection. In
that upper realm where the substance of being is spirit, God
will have a spiritual metropolis, Himself being the architect that
designed and the builder that erected it (Heb. xi, 10). And the
persons of the church of the firstborn, perfected spirits
inhabiting incorruptible spiritual bodies, will form that dwelling
place of God.

During the panorama of the Revelation, John had heard a
great multitude in heaven rejoicing that the hour had come for
the long expected marriage of the Lamb, but he had not yet
seen the bride. And it may be that as the mighty visions
progressed, and the millenial age passed into the eternal state,
he inwardly wondered at this omission. But after all else had
been shown to him the Bride was unveiled to his enraptured
gaze, for, he says (Rev. xxi, 9, 10) : "And there came one of the
seven angels who had the seven bowls, who were laden with

"the seven last plagues; and he spake with me, saying, Come hither, I will shew thee the bride, the wife of the Lamb. And he carried me away in the Spirit to a mountain great and high, and shewed me," shewed me—what? a bride? no, a city, "the holy city, new Jerusalem." So, then, the "city" is the "bride," and the latter being a figure of a company of persons so must the former be. The assertion that the "city" is an *interpretation* of the figure of speech "bride" is not founded on the passage. The angel did not say to John, I will interpret, or explain, to thee the metaphor "bride," but he said, "I will *shew* thee the bride," that is, give thee a vision of her. Thus the "city" is a second vision in symbol of the same company of which the "bride" was the former symbol. Such oriental duplicating of metaphors is common in Scripture. The figure of the bride was no longer adequate to reveal the glory of the church, nor her most exalted office as the dwelling-place of God in a reconciled universe, from which all the wicked had been banished. Therefore the city comes into view; and nature and art and language are exhausted to portray her splendour.

In interpreting this vision one error is particularly common, namely, to speak of the city as a region into which the members of the church of God will enter and be blessed. This notion effectually forbids any right understanding of the matter. The bride, that is, the glorified heavenly church of the first-born ones, is the city. Others of the saved enter its gates: these compose it.

It may be hard to assign an exact meaning to each of the details given, but the main features described readily yield their teaching.

i. In the persons of His heavenly saints God will dwell so personally and be so actually present, that they will be to Him what a capital city is to a monarch—a place of residence, a scene for the display of His majesty, a spot to which His subjects may come to have dealings with Him, and a centre of government around which the corporate life of the empire may revolve.

ii. "And the wall of the city had twelve foundations, and on them twelve names of the twelve apostles of the Lamb" (xxi,14). To members of the church this was not a new thought, for it had been before taught that they, as a body corporate, were "built upon the foundation of the apostles and prophets" (Eph. ii, 20). Historically it is the preaching, teaching, labours, and sufferings of the apostles upon which the church is founded ; and of their teaching Christ Jesus Himself was the all-prominent theme (the "chief corner-stone"), binding together the foundation, and affording unity and stability to the building.

iii. "The nations shall walk by the light thereof; and the kings of the earth do bring their glory into it" (xxi, 24). It will be under the beneficent guidance of the heavenly saints that the nations, so long "alienated from the life of God because of the ignorance that is in them" (Eph. iv, 18), will learn to walk in His fear; and they in return will honour those who are thus the occasion of their eternal blessing.

iv. But as it will be by recognizing Israel as the chief nation on earth by God's will, that the Gentiles will own God's sovereignty, therefore through Israel mediately it is that they will enjoy the blessings dispensed through the church ; and hence on the portals of the city are written the names of the tribes of Israel. For the Gentiles the means of access into heavenly blessings will be by honouring Israel (Isa xiv, 2 ; xlix, 22, 23) ; lx, 12 ; lxvi, 20 ; Zeph. iii, 10, marg.; Zech. viii, 20-23). It would be as unreasonable to "spiritualize" the literal Israel out of this picture (ver. 12) as to "spiritualize" out of it the twelve apostles of the Lamb who are next mentioned (ver. 14).

v. The Holy Spirit of God will thus flow out through the church for the quickening of all, as pictured by the river of the water of life ; and it will be in response to obedience that the peoples will have the benefit of the River, for this proceeds out of the *throne* of God and of the Lamb.

Further into such fascinating details we may not give time to go ; but it is unto no less privileged service and glories that we have come. Such is the ravishing prospect unto which the

E

saints of this age are called, for " God hath called us into His
own kingdom and glory " (I Thes. ii, 12).

8. But we have anticipated the highest feature of all: "ye
have come unto Mount Zion." In the earthly Jerusalem two
mounts have been prominent, Mount Moriah and Mount Zion.
The former was presently crowned with Solomon's temple; but
in the heavenly Jerusalem there is no temple seen (21, 22), for
God no longer dwells hidden behind a veil, for Calvary has
made possible His manifest dwelling with men (xxi, 3). But
Mount Zion is found in His eternal realm. On that hill in the
earthly city David's palace stood (II Sam. v, 7-9), and it was the
supreme court of justice for the kingdom, for "there were set
thrones for judgment, the thrones of the house of David"
(Ps. cxxii, 5). Not a throne, but thrones, are mentioned. How
accurate a prophetic picture of the heavenly things yet to be;
for Christ, the Son of David, will associate with Himself in His
kingly office those who have been counted worthy of their
calling, and who have reached this pinnacle of honour to reign
with Him for ever and ever (Rev. xxii, 5). And as many dwelt
in Jerusalem, and but few comparatively on Mount Zion, is
there not here again the suggestion that many more may reach
the blessedness of the "city" than will reach the crowning
honour, and reign on a throne on Mount Zion? "One star,"
though truly a star, that is, a heavenly being, "differeth from
another star in glory" (I Cor. xv, 41).

Only one man, Moses, was permitted to climb to the top of
Sinai; the rest of God's people could but look from afar to
that height of glory, and in truth they had little enough desire
to draw near to those devouring fires. But many are the sons
now being brought unto glory in Christ Jesus, and such as walk
in the power of His fellowship may approach unto that same
God with boldness. Let us therefore "abide in Christ; that if
He shall be manifested, we may have boldness, and not be
ashamed from Him at His presence" (I John ii, 28). Let us
look to ourselves that we lose not the things that we have
wrought, but that we receive a full reward (II John 8).

Of that supremely and eternally glorious state a sevenfold
perfection is declared (Rev. xxii, 3-5). "There shall be no curse

any more"—perfect sinlessness and blessedness: "and the throne of God and of the Lamb shall be therein"—perfect government: "and His servants shall do Him service"—perfect service: "and they shall see His face"—perfect communion: "and His name shall be in their foreheads" perfect resemblance and identification: "and there shall be night no more"—perfect knowledge and strength: "and they shall reign unto the ages of the ages"—perfect glory.

"Oh, what a bright and blessed world
This groaning earth of ours will be,
When from its throne the tempter hurled
Shall leave it all, O Lord, to Thee.

"But brighter far that world above
Where we as we are known shall know;
And, in the sweet embrace of Love,
Reign o'er the ransomed earth below."

Truly is it said of the unspiritual that eye hath not seen, nor ear heard, neither have entered into the heart of man, whatsoever things God prepared for them that love Him. But unto those who, by faith in Christ, have received the Spirit of the Lord, God hath revealed these things so vast and deep and high, for "we received, not the spirit of the world, but the spirit which is of God; that we might know the things that are freely given to us by God" (I Cor. ii, 9-12). And therefore, both the knowledge of and the attaining to these things is possible through the Spirit.

* * * * *

But that same Revealer has very solemnly intimated that these heavenly glories are forfeitable on certain conditions. Let us turn back to examine closely the opening sentences of this great passage.

"Follow after peace with all men." Our God is the "God of peace" (Heb. xiii, 20). Strife of every sort is not of His promotion. Therefore they who aspire to deep and rich communion with Him must "seek peace and pursue it" (I Peter

iii, 11). "Blessed are the peacemakers : for they shall be called
the sons of God" (Matt. v, 9). They must *at every personal cost*
promote peace. God has made peace possible between man
and Himself, and this at the highest cost to Himself, the gift of
His own Son. Christ "made peace," and this at the greatest
cost to Himself, the shedding of His own blood on the cross.
Such as are of His Spirit will exercise their right to forego their
rights rather than provoke dissention by insistence upon these.
They will endure to the last extent, and will "as much as in
them lies"—that is, not merely to the utmost of their powers of
endurance, but rather that they, on their side of the matter,
"will be at peace with all men" seeing to it that the cause and
the continuance of the difficulty is on the other party wholly
(Rom. xii, 18).

But this, in its practical out-working in such a world as the
present, is necessarily a life of difficulty and of almost certain
loss ; for the wicked will readily take advantage of the meek.
Thus this opening exhortation calls for high attainment in daily
life. But we are steadily to pursue this path, for such a course
of life is quite indispensable to attaining to "the sanctification
without which no one shall see the Lord" (Heb. xiii, 14).

And who is the "Lord" in the sense of the term in this
place ? and what is "the sanctification" without which no
one shall see Him ? The answer to the first of these questions
is that it is certainly not Christ who is intended. It is distinctly
declared that "every eye shall see Him" and that so far from
an advanced state of holiness being requisite for this, His
enemies that pierced Him will see Him (Rev. i, 7). For God has
declared upon His oath that to Jesus every knee shall bow, and
that every tongue shall confess that Jesus Christ is Lord (Phil.
ii, 10, 11), which last clause must include even the finally lost.
The Father has committed all judgment unto the Son (John v,
22), and before His judgment seat, at one or other of its
sessions, every person must be made manifest.

It is therefore to some face to face vision of God the Father
that our clause refers. We ought not to conceive of the
Father of our Lord Jesus Christ as formless. The Son of God

speaks of Him as having form—"ye have neither heard His voice at any time, nor seen His form" (John v, 37). He said also that the angels of the little children "do always behold the face of My Father Who is in the heavens" (Matt, xviii, 10), and at that time the Son was absent from the heavens, so that it was not in the person of the Son that the Father was thus visible. It is certain that His voice is actual, for it has been heard three times by men on earth (Matt. iii, 17; xvii, 5: II Pet. i, 17; John xii, 28). So that the voice, form, and face are literal, and the two latter are visible. This seems to be involved distinctly in the Lord's further words: "Not that any man hath seen the Father, save He Who is from God, He hath seen the Father" (Jo. vi, 46). Christ Himself has "sat down on the right hand of the Majesty on high (Heb. i, 3, 13; x, 12). And forasmuch as angels are distinct and localized beings, and that the exalted Christ also is the same, it is evident that some localized, defined, and personal presence of the Father is here indicated. To the same effect speaks the great doxology that closes Jude's brief but pregnant letter. We there read of "the only God our Saviour" being "able to guard us from stumbling and to set us before the presence of His glory without blemish in exceeding joy"; and "God our Saviour" is here plainly the Father, for it is "through Jesus Christ our Lord" that the glory is ascribed to Him.

But this "blessed and only Potentate, the King of kings and Lord of lords, Who only hath immortality," "dwelleth in light unapproachable," and "no man hath seen nor can see" Him (I Tim. vi, 15, 16), not even though it be such a man as Moses the friend of God (Ex. xxxiii, 18-23). For man on earth is in no wise capacitated for bearing the blaze of the glory of that light. But man in Christ Jesus is "made capable" (Alford) for sharing the "inheritance of the saints *in the light*" (Col. i, 12); and this capacity of inward nature will be extended to the body itself at the "appearing of the glory of our great God and Saviour Jesus Christ" (Tit. ii, 13), "Who shall fashion anew the body of our humiliation. that it may be conformed to the body of His glory" (Phil. iii, 21). "It is not yet made manifest what we

shall be.   We know that if He shall be manifested we shall be
like Him ; for we shall see Him even as He is" (I John iii, 2).

The initial condition upon which man may aspire to this
beatific vision is the atoning work of the Redeemer. "Christ also
suffered for sins once for all that He might *conduct us to God*"
(I Peter iii, 18).   But the final condition for realizing in fact
that which the atonement has made possible, is set before us
in the clause under consideration ; "pursue the sanctification
without which no man shall see the Lord." And what is this but
a re-statement of Christ's searching beatitude, "Blessed are the
pure in heart for they shall see God " ? (Matt. v, 8).   How
many are satisfied with attaining to external propriety of life
whilst the heart continues to be complacently engaged with
things that are not of God.   Good is Tauler's definition : "A
pure heart is one to which all that is not of God is strange and
jarring." A heart that has no desires but for the glory of God,
whose affections all centre in Him, whose delight is in His good
and well-pleasing and perfect will, such an one, by the power of
the Spirit of grace, will make due progress in holiness—though
perhaps unconsciously to himself—and will reach the sanctification which will warrant the bestowing of the fullest and
highest bliss possible through the precious blood of Jesus, even
this supernal vision of the face and presence of Him Who
before was personally inaccessible to man.[1]

Thus the condition of the glorified saint is indefinitely
superior to that of Adam even in innocence ; and thus is
revealed the manifold wisdom of God in His power to make
the very fall of man the occasion, through Christ's mediation,
of the elevation of man to the absolutely highest degree of bliss
and glory that God Himself can ever offer to any of His creatures ;
for He purposes to exalt the "Bride " to sit *with* Christ, and He
cannot put her *above* Him.   "In Him the sons of Adam boast
more blessings than their father lost."

[1] It is remarkable that whereas the enjoyments of the Moslem Parrdise as pictured in the Koran are
grossly sensual and abominable, yet Mohammed had somewhere caught this conception of the seeing
of God being the supreme delight.   Lane (*Manners and Customs of the Modern Egyptians*
ch. iii), dealing with this aspect of the doctrines of Islam, says, "But all these enjoyments will be
lightly esteemed by those more blessed persons who are to be admitted to the highest of all honours—
that spiritual pleasure of beholding, morning and evening, the face of God."

And therefore how strenuous should be our watchful and trustful endeavours to progress in personal sanctification. Natural indeed was the deep paternal zeal of the apostles for the growth in holiness of their children in the faith, for they knew how great things were at stake. Natural too is the vigorous exhortation that follows, bidding us to be at all seasons " looking carefully lest there be any one that falleth short of the grace of God," that is, lest any, by carelessly neglecting to live in the power of the available grace of God, fail to reach that highest felicity to which grace would have brought them.

In that case, peace not being diligently pursued, it may be expected that contention will result, and some root of bitterness latent in the carnal nature, or some specific impulse to bitterness of spirit planted in the heart by our ever watchful spirit foes, will spring into activity, and a general state of strife result in the community of believers in question, by which means the more part of them may become defiled. These will thus be far other than sanctified, and will be risking becoming disqualified for that supreme vision of the Father. How serious therefore is the responsibility of the one through whom occasions of stumbling enter a circle of God's people. As Achan troubled the whole nation, so may a christian cause present injury, and final and most serious loss, to fellow-believers, a loss only less great than that of eternal life. And as Achan bore a due penalty, so shall a christian not pass unvisited. It was into the eyes of His chosen and beloved disciples that our Master and Judge looked as He uttered these terrible words : " Whoso shall cause one of these little ones that believe on me to stumble, it is profitable for him that a great millstone should be hanged about his neck, and that he should be sunk in the depth of the sea " (Matt. xviii, 6). What is the impending chastisement that shall result from stumbling a fellow saint, and what is the severity thereof, that an untimely and violent death were much to be preferred thereto ? Good therefore it is for each to give most earnest and constant heed to this exhortation, offered in view of "the day of redemption": and "grieve not the Holy Spirit of God, in whom ye were sealed unto the day of

" redemption. Let all bitternsss, and wrath, and anger, and clamour, and railing, be put away from you, with all malice : and be ye kind one to another, tenderhearted, forgiving each other, even as God also in Christ forgave you." (Eph. iv, 30-32). A heart that loves peace will guard against harbouring a single bitter feeling. By the power of the love of God, it will cast forth at its first uprising any such emotion ; and thus will be prevented the defilement of others, and thus will be promoted the purity of that heart itself, and its preparation for seeing the Lord will be advanced.

The Word now turns from such inward dangers to physical and open wickedness, of which fornication is specified, and then we are exhorted to be full of care " lest there be any profane person as Esau, who for one mess of meat sold his rights of the firstborn."

The story of Esau is found in Genesis xxv, 27-34, and ch. 27. It is pregnant with most solemn instruction, and no line of exposition which does not give due and full weight to its most powerful lessons can be correct. And yet we confess that after forty-five years of constant contact with Bible-loving christians and teachers, we have never once heard even an attempt to apply this passage in the Hebrews to any persons, believers or otherwise !

The points of his case to be noticed are :—

1. Esau, being the firstborn son, held by right of birth the privileges before described as belonging to the firstborn. He did not have to win or buy these rights ; they attached to him by birth according to the will of God. Yet it was incumbent upon him to retain them.

2. But he held them in such small esteem that he readily bartered them away in exchange for a passing gratification of the palate. It was not that other food could not easily have been obtained, for he had come into the encampment. The fact is, as recorded by God, that he " despised his birthright."

3. And though later in life he regretted his folly, he found it not possible to reverse his own act and deed, or to change

his father's mind, so as to secure the richer blessing which followed the possession of the birthright.[1]

We submit that it is simply impossible that Esau is here offered as a warning to a false professor of the faith who is not really in Christ Jesus. For (1) Esau was Isaac's legitimate son, not a bastard nor an alien. (2) He legally held the rights of the firstborn, and was not a false claimant thereto. (3) Even after his forfeiture of those rights, his father blessed him as fully as was possible, though he could not restore to him the priority he had thrown away. (4) He did not lose those things which would have made him a type possibly of one finally lost, namely, his life or his sonship, but he did lose his superior dignity and privileges.

None of these conditions is fulfilled in an unregenerate person, however plausible and long-continued be his profession of christianity. Such an one is (1) not God's child at all ; (2) has no rights that he can be warned not to forfeit; (3) and in the issue will be utterly unblessed and reprobate, not having, or ever having had, eternal life, but being "a child of wrath even as the rest." The two cases are utterly dissimilar ; but Esau's example does most accurately correspond to the case of us to whom it is here applied. "Take heed," says the Scripture, "lest there be any profane person as Esau, who for one mess of meat sold his rights of the firstborn" ; and then, in a paragraph directly connected by a particle with that warning, there is immediately added the statement "For ye (ye who are thus warned) have come unto the assembly of the firstborn ones." Thus it is to those who hold the analogous rights in the heavenly realm and family that the warning is held up, and to such only can it have any force. To warn one against losing what he does not possess is a futility that we dare not attribute to the Spirit of the Lord.

But real believers, being born of God and being called to His kingdom and glory, fulfil the facts of Esau's case. Such

---

1 The question of the exact construction of the clause " he found no place of repentance " is not vital to the main argument of the passage, and I do not enter upon it. It is theological rather than practical. That the results of his act were irreversible is the point of the matter. But I believe the meaning to be that the prophetic utterance of his father could not be altered.

persons are (1) really children of God by faith in Christ Jesus;
and (2) they are the firstborn of His family, and hold the rights of
primogeniture.   These rights they do not have to earn, or buy,
or win : they are wholly a birthright by the sovereign grace of
God.   *But they do have to value and to keep them,* and are warned
against forfeiting these privileges.   Their sonship is inalienable,
and their eternal life is unforfeitable, not being deposited in
them and held by them at their own risk, but being " hid with
Christ in God " (Col. iii, 3) ; but these higher personal dignities
and glories are forfeitable, and by as much as they are worth
retaining by so much is found in this teaching a salutory and
sanctifying power.   Let the believer be assured that all, all is
secure, and great is the danger of inducing a subtle carelessness
of heart; but with the retention of the highest privileges left
conditional upon our walk, strong is the inducement to press
on unto perfection.

The forfeitability of the birthright is further indicated and
emphasized in the case of Reuben.   Being Jacob's eldest son
this honour was his; but because of his yielding to an
unnatural sensual craving, it was taken from him (I Chron. v, 1),
and was given, as to the territory, to the sons of Joseph, the
latter thus, in his children, receiving the double portion ; and
as to sovereignty, to the tribe of Judah, in the person of David
and his sons, including Messiah ; and as to the priesthood, to
Levi.   Was this in the writer's mind when he specified in our
passage the sin of fornication ?

Yet Reuben remained of the family, and was blessed in
measure; but as showing that the rights in question if once
lost cannot be regained, it is to be remembered that in the days
of the future kingdom the status created by Reuben's misconduct
will still abide : the King will be of the house of Judah, the
priesthood in Israel will be in the family of Zadok the Levite
(Ezk. xlviii, 11), and Ephraim and Manasseh will hold their
double portion.   These things Reuben has lost for ever, though
for ever remaining of the house of Israel, and sharing a portion,
though this of ordinary and not special degree.   All this is seen
by comparing the final and prophetic announcements of Jacob

(Gen. xlix, 1-4) and Moses (Deut. xxxiii, 6); for Jacob declared that the dignity of the firstborn with its pre-eminence and power belonged to Reuben, yet should not be his, not even in the latter days; yet Moses guaranteed *life* to the tribe, but nothing more: " Let Reuben live, and not die; yet let his men be few."

The transferability of the birthright is also shown in I Chron. xxvi, 10, quoted at the head of this chapter; and the solitary circumstance given, that it occurred in a Levitical family, carries its lesson for us who are called to heavenly service, typified by the tabernacle service.

The chief theme of this passage in Hebrews, and indeed of the whole letter, is crystallized in the words of verse 28, which speak of "receiving a kingdom." This is the subject under discussion, *not* the question of securing salvation from eternal perdition. The epistle presupposes this latter benefit to have been secured, for it starts with the thought that the persons addressed are already "holy brethren, partakers of a *heavenly* calling" (iii, 1). Its call therefore is, that being thus privileged by God's grace in Christ, we should not "turn away from Him that warneth from heaven;" that is, who warns us by pointing to such a case as that of Esau, and of others of whom we shall proceed to write. For there is at hand a final shaking and removing of all things movable, so that only the immovable and therefore eternal may remain. It is to the glory of reigning in that kingdom, beginning in the millenial days and continuing eternally, that we are called. Let us therefore, by the grace of God, serve acceptably the God of grace, attending upon Him and doing all His will, and this not in carnal complacency, as if it mattered little how we live and serve, but "with reverence and awe, for *our* God is a consuming fire," as not a few of *His own people* have found.

Leader of faithful souls, and guide
  Of all that travel to the sky,
Come and with us, e'en us, abide,
  Who would on thee alone rely,
On thee alone our spirits stay,
While held in life's uneven way.

Strangers and pilgrims here below,
  This earth, we know, is not our place,
And hasten through the vale of woe;
  And, restless to behold thy face,
Swift to our heavenly country move,
Our everlasting home above.

We've no abiding city here,
  But seek a city out of sight;
Thither our steady course we steer,
  Aspiring to the plains of light,
Jerusalem, the saints' abode,
Whose founder is the living God.

Patient the appointed race to run,
  This weary world we cast behind;
From strength to strength we travel on,
  The new Jerusalem to find;
Our labour this, our only aim,
To find the new Jerusalem.

Through thee, who all our sins hast borne,
  Freely and graciously forgiven,
With songs to Zion we return,
  Contending for our native heaven;
That palace of our glorious King,
We find it nearer while we sing.

Raised by the breath of love divine,
  We urge our way with strength renewed;
The church of the firstborn to join,
  We travel to the mount of God,
With joy upon our heads arise,
And meet our Captain in the skies.

Wesley.

CHAPTER X.

INHERITING OR BEING DISINHERITED.

"He that overcometh shall inherit."—(Rev. xxi, 7).
"Wrong-doers shall not inherit."—(I Cor. vi, 8).

The Word of God, in the passage last studied, thus lifts into
relief two classes of sins, giving a signal example of each,
namely, strife and fornication—the one operating mainly in
the moral, and the other in the physical, realm of man's being.
These are set forth as jeopardizing our reaching the highest
privileges toward which God is leading onward His sons. And
it is impressive to discover that in other epistles also these
same classes of offences are set in the same connection, and are
reprobated as involving the same severe loss.

In the christian assembly at Corinth grave evils had developed
since Paul had left them. In writing to correct these he deals
first with the evil that is first dealt with in Hebrews xii, 14,
namely, *strife* : "Ye are yet carnal . . . . there is among
you jealousy and strife" (iii, 3). Then he proceeds to deal next
with that which is also next dealt with in the Hebrews' passage:
"It is actually reported that there is *fornication* among you" (v, 1);
and he names precisely the same henious sort of fornication as
we have seen cost Reuben his birthright. Later (xi, 21), he will
solemnly condemn their sins of appetite (gluttony and drunkenness) indulged in at their love feasts, and which entirely vitiated
their outward observance of the Lord's Supper. This corres-
ponds to Esau's carnal preference for a tempting meal.

Next he enlarges upon the serious loss which the unwise and
unskilled workman will incur in the day of Christ, even though
himself be saved, and yet this with pain and difficulty (iii, 10-
17) ; which answers to the essence of the warning in Hebrews
xii, 15, to "look carefully lest any man fall short of the grace of
God."

In chapter vi he has severely censured another evil, and one sadly common among God's people to-day—covetousness ; a sin often rather admired, in its results at least, than abhorred. A covetous man (pleonektees) is simply one who is *eager to have more* than at present. It may be right things that he desires, and he may not intend at the outset to acquire them by other than morally right methods : but he must have more—whether a little more or much more is not the question : he is not "content with such things as he hath" (Heb. xiii, 5), and therefore he is in God's sight one of the covetous. These Corinthian believers had turned to God from idols; they no longer bowed before blocks of precious metals or of stone. But, as God estimates, the covetous of them had reverted to idolatry, and this of a more specious and dangerous nature. For their heart had turned from Him as the only object of adoration, and they were setting their affection upon *something else*, it mattered not what; and thus covetousness is idolatry (Col. iii, 5), and the covetous man is an idolater (Eph. v, 5). Let the western christian or the convert from Islam, who thinks loftily of his life as compared with that of the "poor heathen," ponder this dictum of our God, and search and try his own heart, lest haply he too in the sight of God be nothing better than an idolater.

In a powerful sermon upon I Tim. vi, 9, John Wesley dwells upon the definition of " being rich " which is supplied by the context. "Having food and coverings," says the apostles, "we shall be therewith content. *But* they that desire to be rich "— they who, in contrast to this contentment, *will* to have more than these necessaries, are the covetous. That God should sometimes allow more than this to some of His people, whose hearts crave not for it, and who will therefore use it well, is one thing : that any should set the mind on the acquiring of treasure makes them to be of the covetous. Do we not well to give diligent heed to our Lord's urgent exhortation, " See to it, and be always guarding yourselves (φυλάσσεσθε *pres. imperative middle*) from every kind of covetousness (Lk xii, 15) ? And this was spoken to and concerning one who appears to have wanted only what was his by right.

The apostle has numerous and powerful weapons that he directs against these mal-practices.

He warns the contentious that if, by provoking dissension in the christian circle or assembly, they mar its peace and sanctity as God's house where He dwells, then God will similarly mar them as individuals. They destroy (mar $\phi\theta\epsilon\iota\rho\omega$ LXX. Jer. xiii, 9—E.V. mar.) the house of God (the assembly of His people), and God will mar them in the midst of it or destroy them out of it (iii, 17). To what this points is seen when he later declares that the fornicator is liable to " the destruction of the flesh " at the hands of Satan, that is, to present bodily death, though the spirit will be ultimately saved (v, 5), and again when he explains (xi, 29-32) that the abnormal weakness and sickness which were afflicting many of them, and the premature falling asleep in death of not a few, were the judicial chastisement of their God, Who suffers not His house and its sacred ordinances to be glaringly defiled and abused, not even by His own children. The solemn cases of Ananias and Sapphira are also illustrations.

It is worthy of remark, and the more so as the point seems usually unrecognized, that God, Who is the Father of them who are born of His Spirit, is also, and perpetually, the Supreme Governor of the universe. In this office He administers its affairs under the full scrutiny of the angelic hosts, many of these being hostile to His administration. It is not possible for God to indulge His children in sinful courses that He would severely punish in His enemies : " there is no respect of persons with Him." His own nature forbids partiality, and so does the impossibility of leaving His ways open to just criticism by His enemies. Indeed, He the rather makes His own family the special sphere of the exhibition of the perfection of His dealings. It is at His own sanctuary that judgment begins (Ezk. ix, 6), and this as a warning to the godless that they may not expect to escape (Jer. xxv, 29). And this principle holds good in the church to-day, as in Israel of old (I Pet. iv, 17, 18). Only for His children the chastisement is parental, corrective, and temporary, however severe, for Calvary has delivered them from the eternal punishment; whereas for His foes punishment is penal, and ultimately eternal.

But beyond the present consequences of their evil doings, the apostle foresees another and severer penalty, one which he plainly asserts involves the loss of their possible share in the coming kingdom.

" Or know ye not," he exclaims, " that the unrighteous shall not inherit the kingdom of God? Be not deceived : neither fornicators, nor idolaters, nor adulterers, nor effeminate, nor abusers of themselves with men, nor thieves, nor covetous, nor drunkards, nor revilers, nor extortioners, shall inherit the kingdom of God." (I Cor. vi, 9, 10).

It is certain that here again he has in view true children of God. The warning has no *possible* application to one who is not a child of God.

1.   Wherever inheriting is in question the relationship of a child to a parent is taken implicitly for granted : " if children, then heirs " is the universal rule (Rom. viii, 17). It were wholly idle to tell an unregenerate man that he will not inherit the portion of God's children. Of course he will not ; he never had any proper ground for thinking that he would ; and therefore the warning is powerless. The truth needed by such is that he will be for ever the subject of the eternal wrath of God, which is already hanging over him, and is his just portion.

2.   This warning is addressed to those of whom Paul could acknowledge, "Such *were* some of you, but ye washed your-selves, but ye were sanctified, but ye were justified in the name of the Lord Jesus Christ, and in the Spirit of our God" (I Cor. v, 11). But now he has to say, "Ye yourselves (the pronoun is emphatic : I am not talking of worldlings, but of you same individuals), ye yourselves *do wrong* (adikeite), and defraud" : "know ye not that *wrong-doers* (the noun of the same verb, adikoi) shall not inherit the kingdom of God ?" Thus he asserts (1) that those who had been justified, sanctified, and washed from their old sins, may *do wrong* and *were doing it* ; and (2) that *wrong-doers* (there is no article) shall not inherit the kingdom.

3. The covetous who were seeking to extort money by process of law he repeatedly calls " brethren," and sets them in distinct contrast from the " unbelievers " to whom they were appealing as judges.

4. The particulars of the incestuous man show him to have been a true believer. *(a)*. It were drastically unbiblical to suggest that the present death of an unregenerate man will operate to the saving of his spirit in the day of Jesus Christ. This would indeed be a new way of salvation for the godless. *(b)*. The danger of such sin as his infecting the whole assembly, if they continued to condone him therein, as leaven permeates the whole lump of dough, indicates that the peril of falling into such sins is upon all the church ; and hence the warning must apply to them each. Is it to be believed that they all were but false professors ? The missionary having experience of dealing with converts from heathenism or Islam will have no difficulty in allowing that sincere believers may be entrapped into these evil deeds and states. The confessions of terrible sins wrung from real christians at times of powerful revivings in heathen lands are evidence in point. And II Cor. xii, 21 shows plainly that " *many* of them " in Corinth had actually committed " uncleanness and fornication and lasciviousness," and had continued therein for some time, for when writing even this second letter Paul fears lest he might come and find some unrepentant. *(c)*. Upon his repentance he was immediately, and without question, restored to fellowship, as one to whom christian affection was due and to be confirmed (II Cor. ii, 5-11), *(d)*. That excommunication from christian fellowship, or the fear thereof, overwhelmed the brother with sorrow, and caused him to cease from his entangling sin, goes far to show that he had a new heart, one of flesh and not of stone, else he would not have valued so highly the privileges of the house of God, or have felt so immediately and keenly the horror of being ejected into the outer darkness of his old heathen standing. Perchance too, he having been taught by Paul concerning the kingdom of God, knew enough of its coming glories to be unready to risk forfeiting these, as Paul's letter assured him was his peril.

F

5. That Paul himself intended to address his words to all these individuals as brethren in Christ, is indicated by his sending his love to *all*, and desiring for *all* the grace and love and fellowship of the triune God (I Ep. xvi, 24, II Ep. xiii, 14).

But the question of the application of these warnings is surely settled, and their impressiveness greatly deepened, by their repetition in letters to other churches. Different indeed in spiritual condition and apprehension were the churches in Galatia to the church in Ephesus. Yet to them all, as to the saints in Corinth, the apostle gives in faithfulness the same warning.

The Galatian christians were shifting their standing before God from the sole ground of His grace working in Christ Jesus to the ground of ceremonial observances being meritorious for salvation. Knowing that this falling away from confidence in the grace of God would involve their forfeiting the moral energy which that grace alone supplies, and that consequently the flesh would soon assert its old supremacy, the apostle addresses them thus: "Now the works of the flesh are manifest, which are these, fornication, uncleanness, lasciviousness, idolatry, sorcery, enmities, strife, jealousies, wraths, factions, divisions, heresies, envyings, drunkenness, revellings, and such like: of the which I forewarn you, even as I did forewarn you, that they who practice such things shall not inherit the kingdom of God. (ch. v, 19-21)." Can anything be plainer than these repeated and emphatic words, "Of the which I forewarn *you* (not carnal unregenerate professors among you ; but " you," all of you who form the churches of Galatia), even as I did forewarn you" ? Yet some would have it mean, "I forewarn *you* that if an *unregenerate man* does these things *he* shall not inherit a portion that he never has had any real right to expect." But surely this is to emasculate the warning of its whole strength and value.

The passage is noteworthy inasmuch as it shows that this line of teaching formed part of Paul's oral instruction to the churches: "of the which I *did* forewarn you"; presumably when with them, since we know nothing of an earlier letter to them. And, secondly, it is to be observed that the stress is here laid upon the *practice* of such evils. A believer may be suddenly tempted, and may without premeditation commit one of these sins. He will be blameworthy, for by watchfulness and prayer we may ever find grace to help in such an hour of need. But in such an event immediate repentance secures, through the blood of Jesus, immediate pardon, for " if we (believers) confess our sins, God is faithful and righteous to forgive us our sins, and to cleanse us from all unrighteousness " (I John i, 9). But such as deliberately turn to these wickednesses and persist in the indulgence, how do they stand before God?

One great school of theology has asserted that these passages which we are considering declare the final perdition of such ; which involves the idea that really saved people, justified, possessors of eternal life, the children of God, may forfeit all this standing and relationship and be finally lost. But this teaching seems so obviously to conflict with numerous and explicit assertions of Scripture, such as declare the everlasting security from God's wrath of those who are in Christ Jesus, that not unnaturally many others have rejected it. Yet it must be confessed that this latter school of teachers does not know how to give due weight to these many and awful warnings. At the most these can but apply them to persons (unregenerate professors) to whom by no fair exegesis can the passages be made to apply.

The radical error in the matter has been to confound terms that differ. By both schools "inheriting the kingdom" has been wrongly taken to mean simply being saved from hell ; and so "not inheriting" has been wrongly deemed synonymous with everlasting perdition. But once it is seen that receiving salvation from wrath is one thing, and that rising to the glory of rule in the kingdom is another thing, and is an attainment that follows, then the Gordian knot is untied ; for it at once becomes a possibility to forfeit the kindom by personal misconduct,[1] whilst yet retaining eternal life by the pure grace of God, exercised on the ground of the merit of Christ alone.

1 And to incur in addition abundantly severe chastisement, proportionate to the offences, and sufficient, if apprehended, to deter from carnality. But this is not our present theme. and we do not pursue it (Luke xii, 45-48 ; *e.g.*)

And this contrast gives much force and clearness to the exhortation found in Ephesians v, 3-6, where we read: "But fornication, and all uncleanness, or covetousness, let it not even be named among you, as becometh saints; nor filthiness, nor foolish talking, or jesting, which are not befitting: but rather giving of thanks. For this ye know of a surety, that no fornicator, nor unclean person, nor covetous man, who is an idolator, hath any inheritance in the kingdom of Christ and God. Let no man deceive you with empty words: for because of these things cometh the wrath of God upon the sons of disobedience." This may be paraphrased thus: Ye "*once* lived " as "sons of disobedience," and "*were* by nature children of wrath, even as the rest" still are. "*But* God" quickened you, and "by grace ye have been saved" [1] (ii, 3-5). Now as touching this sensual manner of life, if ye were still the sons of disobedience (which however is not now your standing, "for ye *were once* darkness, but *are now* light in the Lord, (v. 8), the wrath of God would come upon you for so living. But think not that therefore you, the sons of light, may abuse God's grace, and indulge these evils with impunity. For though this eternal "wrath" will not be visited upon you, as if you were yet "children of wrath," yet a dire penalty shall be exacted from you; "for this ye know of a surety "—there is no vestige of uncertainty upon this point—that no one who thus lives " hath any inheritance in the kingdom of Christ and God." Therefore " have no fellowship with the unfruitful works of darkness, but rather even reprove them " (v. 11); and if perchance any person has been lulled into a carnal security, and is, as it were slumbering in the charnal house of the vicious, let such hear the call "Awake thou that sleepest, and arise from among the dead, and Christ shall shine upon thee" (v. 14).

This call is not addressed to the dead, that is, the unregenerate (ii, 1), but to the living but sleeping christian, one who has shut himself off from the present enjoyment of fellowship with Christ

1 "Notice the perfect '*are* saved,' not σώζεσθε, 'are being saved', because we have passed from death unto life: salvation is to the Christian not a future but a past thing, realized in the present by faith." Alford *in loco*.

by having gone among the godless as his sphere of interest, and who is thereby risking future fellowship with the Lord in His kingdom. To come out of the tomb is the only way for Lazarus to get into the sunshine.

In view of this mass of testimony that a christian can sin, and can do so after the fashion contemplated, and in view of sad corroberations in practical life, what exegetical violence must be employed to make I John iii, 9, declare that a child of God cannot sin, and so cannot bring himself within these solemn warnings. Yet we have heard the words used for that purpose. But thus is John thrown into conflict, not only with other apostles, but with himself; for he has but a little before pointed out what is the resource of a believer *if he should sin* (ch. ii, 1); while to such persons as "*are* forgiven," and who "know Him who is from the beginning," and "*are strong*" because "the word of God *abideth* in them," so that they "have overcome the evil one" (ii, 12-14), he gives the direct warnings that they must guard against such evils as a love of the world and compromise with idolatry (v, 21). It is not incumbent upon us to attempt here an exposition of the verse in question; but it is a duty to protest that it must not be forced into antagonism with other inspired writings, nor be misused to break the force of sorely needed warnings. For any such wrong use as we have indicated the words must be held to teach that a christian cannot sin at all; which would carry the consequent assertion that no person who ever commits a sin is born of God. Surely the words should be read in the light of and in harmony with Romans vii, 16-25.

Considering how almost universally these searching appeals have been neglected or misapplied it can be perceived why once and again the Spirit exclaims "be not deceived," "let no one deceive you." The gross liver is unfitting himself for a realm into which nothing unclean can enter (Rev. xxi, 27), and they are equally out of sympathy with the kingdom of righteousness, peace, and joy (Rom. xiv, 17) who give place to the subtler moral defilement of enmities, strifes, jealousies, and the like, enumerated in Galatians v, 20. And seeing how widely these conditions obtain in the house of God, were it not well that these deep-acting and vigorous correctives were freely administered to the Lord's people? Thus might some be moved to amend their ways and their doings, to the present good of all, and to their own ultimate advantage in the kingdom.

Thou hidden love of God, whose height,
 Whose depth unfathomed, no man knows,
I see from far thy beauteous light,
 And inly sigh for thy repose ;
My heart is pained, nor can it be
 At rest, till it finds rest in thee.

'Tis mercy all that though hast brought
 My mind to seek her peace in thee ;
Yet, while I seek but find thee not,
 No peace my wandering soul shall see ;
Oh, when shall all my wanderings end,
 And all my steps to thee-ward tend !

Is there a thing beneath the sun
 That strives with thee my heart to share ?
Ah, tear it thence, and reign alone,
 The Lord of every motion there !
Then shall my heart from earth be free,
 When it hath found repose in thee.

Oh, hide this self from me, that I
 No more, but Christ in me, may live !
My vile affections crucify,
 Nor let one darling lust survive !
In all things nothing may I see,
 Nothing desire or seek, but thee !

O Love, thy sovereign aid impart,
 To save me from low-thoughted care ;
Chase this self-will through all my heart,
 Through all its latent mazes there ;
Make me thy duteous child, that I
 Ceaseless may, " Abba, Father," cry.

       (Tersteegen).

CHAPTER XI.

FURTHER CONDITIONAL PASSAGES.

It is a fairly sure sign that a line of exposition is correct when it enables numerous passages to be taken in the simple natural meaning of the terms employed. So long as we cannot accept the obvious sense of words and phrases, but must suppose them to *mean* something other than they *say*, we do well to question whether we yet understand them. When Kepler found that the theory of the elliptical orbits of the planets fitted all the known facts of their movements, he felt positive that he had reached the truth upon that matter. The same kind of assurance is gained when a given exposition of Scripture enables numerous and hitherto difficult passages to be understood in their plainest sense, and causes them to give an accordant teaching.

We have seen that using this key (the possible forfeiture of the kingdom) such a phrase as "shall not inherit the kingdom" may be taken in its first and plain meaning. And thus can be taken numerous other statements of Holy Writ. There are, for example, several passages in which a conditional element is prominent, but to which element due force cannot be given save when interpreted in the light of what we are now studying.

1. Col. i, 21-23 reads as follows: "And you, being in time past alienated and enemies in your mind in your evil works, yet now hath he reconciled in the body of his flesh through death, to present you holy and without blemish and unreproveable before him: if so be that ye continue in the faith, grounded and stedfast, and not moved away from the hope of the gospel which ye heard."

It has been held that the main theme of this passage is expressed in the term "reconciled," and that therefore the "if so be" must be construed therewith, and be taken to imply

117

that unless the professor continues in the faith, grounded and stedfast and unmoved, he reveals that he never has been reconciled to God. This is a good sample of the straits to which we are reduced when maintaining that the sharing the kingdom is non-forfeitable.

(i) For this view makes reconciliation, according to this verse, to be partly dependent upon conduct after conversion, and forbids assurance of salvation until life on earth has been safely passed without wavering as a disciple. (ii) Or else it demands that no genuine believer *can* turn from the faith or be moved away from the hope of the gospel: which is contrary to Scripture and fact.

In I Corinthians xv, 58, the same writer uses the same two terms "stedfast and unmoveable" and this as part of an *exhortation*, showing that those christians needed such a word, and that therefore they *could* cease to be stedfast and might be moved away; and he is addressing his "beloved brethren." Considering how many in this day who did for years run well are being moved away by such influences as higher criticism, evolution, and other false teaching, or by worldly inducements or cares, it is a solemn thing so to deal with such a scripture as to require the assertion that all these (and all such of other days, past and future), are after all unbelievers, and so to consign them to perdition. The view which does no violence to the testimony of the former years to their true regeneration, and yet forwarns such that they are risking the highest of God's possibilities for them, is surely truer to all the facts of the case, to the terms of Scripture, and to the mercifulness and the justice of God. (iii) It is not the case that the reconciling is the main thought of these sentences. We are stated to be reconciled with a view to being *presented to the Lord* "holy, and without blemish, [1] and unreproveable," and it is this presentation which is the dominant theme of the verses. [2]

Comparison with the Ephesian letter written at the same

---

1. Upon the force of this term as applying to practical personal holiness of life see ch. 12.

2. This sense of the passage is taken by such scholars as Alford, Jamieson, Faussett and Brown, Beet, Westcott, and Moule.

time will show what was engaging the apostle's mind at this season. He there says (i, 4, 5) that " God chose us in Christ before the foundation of the world, that we should be holy and without blemish before Him in love: having foreordained us unto adoption as sons through Jesus Christ unto Himself." That we should be ultimately "before Him," sharing the "adoption of sons," and be found "holy and without blemish," is the goal of God's purpose concerning us. He is, through Christ, "bringing many sons *unto glory*" (Heb. ii. 10). To fulfil this end "Christ so loved the church, and gave himself up for it; that he might sanctify it, having cleansed it by the washing of water with the word, that he might present the church unto himself a glorious church, not having spot or wrinkle or any such thing; but that it should be holy and without blemish," (Eph. v, 25-27). This presentation of the bride to the King, and by him to His Father, is the burden of these passages, as it was the supreme theme of the apostles, and that which differentiated their message from earlier revelations, (Eph. iii, 4, 5 ; Rom. xvi, 25, 26) ; and this it is that is in view in Col. i, 23. Reconciliation by the blood of the cross is part of the work designed to issue in this glorious end. The reconciliation is past and complete—"; yet *now hath* He reconciled you"; the presentation is future and is conditional, [1] requiring continuance in the faith and hope of the gospel ; for apart from this continuance moral state will not advance to the high standard by which God will determine future reward— they will not arrive at "the sanctification without which no man shall see the Lord," (Heb. xii, 14).

2. II Thess. i, 11, is another passage which creates the presumtion that the kingdom may be missed. If it be not so, if, that is, the sharing in the kingdom be an absolutely guaranteed and unforfeitable privilege, how *could* the apostle have written these words ?—"To which end" ("to the end that ye may be *counted worthy* of the kingdom of God, for which ye

---

1 " The particle *eige* lays great stress upon the condition as absolutely assential to, and certainly to be followed by, the accomplishment of the divine purpose contingent upon it " (Beet). Alford's note to the verse is : " (condition of this presentation being realized : put in the form of an assumption of their firmness in the faith and hope of the gospel)—IF THAT IS, (*i.e.* assuming that, etc.)."

also suffer," ver. 5), " to which end we also pray always for you,
that our God may *count you worthy* of your calling."

In Christ these believers were already possessed of perfect
judicial righteousness, nor did their exemption from the eternal
wrath of God in the least depend upon themselves. But plainly
the arriving at the kingdom to which they had been called, did
depend upon their being counted personally worthy thereof.
To this end Paul's prayers would contribute by strengthening
their " goodness " and " work of faith," so that they and the
Lord Jesus should be mutually glorified each in the other. Any
worthiness of a *believer*, and such as can be furthered by the
prayers of a fellow-believer, and is connected with " goodness"
and " work," is emphatically not the righteousness imputed to
him upon first trusting in Christ. But unless words have no
meaning, *such* worthiness is required for *admittance to the kingdom*.

3. We have before remarked upon Phil. iii, 11, 12, where
the apostle proclaims the uncertainty of attaining to the
first resurrection—" if by any means (*ei pōs*) I may attain," and
again " I press on, *if so be (ei kai)* that I may lay hold." A Bible
teacher much honoured in his sphere, James Wright of Bristol,
being asked as to these sentences, frankly replied in my hearing
that it was a passage that he could not explain. Honest teacher !
But who can take them in the simple plain sense of the words
save such as admit the possibility of not attaining to the first
resurrection and the kingdom ?

4. Romans viii, 16, 17.—" The Spirit himself beareth witness
with our spirit, that we are children of God: and if children,
then heirs; heirs of God, and joint-heirs with Christ; if so be
that we suffer with him, that we may be also glorified with him."
The latter verse should read, " heirs indeed (*men*) of God, but
(*de*) joint heirs with Christ; if so be (*eiper*) that we suffer with
Him, etc."

How clearly this establishes a condition for being glorified
with Christ let a competent scholar say who showed no leaning
towards our use of the words. Alford thus translates and
comments : "IF AT LEAST (see above on verse 9, *eiper*,
provided that, not *since*, which would be *epeiper) we are suffering*

" *with Him, that we may also be glorified with Him*: *i.e.* 'if (provided that) we are found in that course of participation in Christ's sufferings, whose aim and end, as that of His sufferings, is to be glorified as He was, and with Him.' But the *eiper* does not regard the *subjective* aim, *q.d.* 'if at least our aim in suffering is to be glorified,'—but the *fact* of our being partakers of that course of sufferings with Him, *whose aim is, wherever it is found, to be glorified with Him*" (Alford's italics). The reader will note the italicized words "*wherever it is found,*" implying that there may be those who are not found suffering with Him. The learned Dean adds, "The connection of *suffering with Christ,* and *being glorified with Him* is elsewhere insisted on, see II Tim. ii, 11 ; I Pet. iv, 13 ; v, 1."

Jamieson, Faussett and Brown implicitly reject the rendering "since" by translating "provided we be suffering with Him." So also Darby (New Translation) renders "if indeed we suffer." Moule explicitly condemns it (Cambridge Bible for Schools), and so does Bloomfield, who quotes Crellius as follows: "it was but just that they who wished to be partakers with Christ in his *glory*, should be also partakers of his *sufferings*."

Robinson (Lexicon) accepts the sense "since," but even so it is not fair to quote him thus, as has been done: "The Greek work rendered, *if so be*, implies an acknowledged and recognized fact, or as Robinson says, 'assumes the supposition to be true'." For what Robinson says is that *eiper* "assumes the supposition to be true, *whether justly or not*" (my italics). For the sake of argument or illustration a supposition may be *assumed* to be true, but where *eiper* is used it is open to question whether the assumed fact is a fact or only an assumption.

The ordinary grammatical rule that "if" with the indicative of the verb does not create a condition does not hold regularly in New Testament Greek. In II Tim. ii, 11-13, are four parallel clauses, which must all be construed alike, and all have this construction :

If we died with him, we shall also live with him ;
If we endure, we shall also reign with him ;
If we shall deny him, he also will deny us ;
If we are faithless, he abideth faithful ; for he cannot deny himself.

Now it is plain that the two last clauses cannot mean *since* we deny him, and *since* we are faithless, for that is not the fact of all believers ; so here the "if" does carry a condition, and thus living *with* Christ (as contrasted with only having life *in* Him) and reigning with Christ are conditioned by dying *with* Him (which is more than believing that He died *for* me), and enduring a share of His sufferings. Thus in this place also, and dealing with the same theme as in Rom. viii, 17, the same thought is pressed, and the privilege is made conditional. Upon this passage we shall comment further. *(see p. 127).*

All children inherit something from their parent, such as his nature, life, love, care, and their daily necessaries. But how much of his *wealth* they will each receive a wise father will determine by their several capacities for profiting by possessions. Already this salutary principle operates with the Lord, for " unto one He gave (for use during His absence) five talents, to another two, to another one ; to each *according to his several* (*particular, Darby*) *ability*." (Mat. xxv, 15).

Is not this the force of Rev. xxi, 7 : "The one that over-cometh shall *inherit these* things ; and I will be his God, and *he* (emph.) shall be to me a *son*" (emph.) ? The whole passage mentions three classes in the eternal state (i)—The lost, whose part is the second death (ver. 8) : (ii)—saved peoples (ver. 3), with God dwelling among them, and who, because salvation must include possessing eternal life by the new birth, must be *children* of God and have entrance to His kingdom (John iii) : (iii)—*heirs* and *sons* (υἱός) ; *inheriting* being not collective but strictly individual, and consequent upon being a conqueror ; " the one that overcometh shall inherit " ; and the " son " being a full-grown, mature man, according to the well-known emphasis, and the distinction between " child " and " son," found elsewhere as carrying the very point of the argument. See Luke xx, 36, where the first resurrection unto a heavenly position (" equal unto the angels ") is the question ; and Gal. iii, 23—iv, 7, where the teaching hangs entirely upon the difference between " children " and " sons."

Thus here the *son* is the *heir* of the heavenly glories, " these things" just before described, not simply one of the large family; a standing carrying larger privilege, and greater responsibility and opportunity. It is for the " revealing of the *sons* of God " that creation waits (Rom. viii, 19). The Roman noble of N.T. times chose one of his boys to be his heir, whichever he thought most suitable, and declared before the magistrates that this was his son and heir. This was the *adoption* of that child as distinct from the others of the family, and made him the head of the house under the father. His relationship to the father was as theirs, his position in the family was superior. *Now* christians are the *children* of God (Rom. viii, 21—τέκνων) who expect to be glorified with Christ " if so be that we suffer with him that we may be also glorified with him " (ver, 17); but we groan as yet, expecting the *adoption,* the open acknowledgement by the Father of the whole family of the saved that we, who suffer with Christ, are the *sons* in the family (ver. 23, υἱοθεσίαν).

The sharing of Christ's sufferings now is our training and qualifying for sharing His glory hereafter ; as well as the glory being the compensation graciously promised for the sufferings. "The path of sorrow is not indeed the meriting, but the cap-acitating preparation" (Moule, *in loco*). Those who refuse the distinction between simple heirship to God and joint heir-ship with the Messiah, make the former as well as the latter to become conditional upon suffering with Christ; and thus would the loss of those who avoid suffering become vastly greater, their salvation itself being imperilled.

But the force of this passage (Rom. viii, 17) will become yet clearer if we remember that the Greek term "Christ" is the equivalent of the Hebrew term "Messiah" (John i, 41), which is the official title of the King to whose universal reign the prophets pointed Israel. "What think ye of the Messiah ? whose son is He?" illustrates this title (Matt xxii, 42). Consider now this conditional clause :

5. Hebrews iii, 14 : "For we are become companions of the Christ if indeed we hold the beginning of the assurance firm to

the end" (J. N. Darby, New Translation). Here is another example of how a critically accurate rendering leads to this present line of teaching, even though the scholar translating would repudiate altogether the plain force of his rendering. Mr. Darby adds, "I use the word 'companions' as being the same one as in chapter i, 9, *metochoi*, to which, I doubt not, it alludes; that is, to the passage quoted Ps. 45. 'Partakers of Christ' has indeed a quite different sense." Now this Psalm is unquestionably a picture, and a peculiarly brilliant picture, of the Messiah in the time of His millenial kingdom. And we are of those who are to be his "fellows" or "companions" or "partners" (Delitsch) in that day; "*if* we hold fast the beginning of our confidence firm to the end."

So plain is the condition, and so evident the reference to the coming kingdom, that Delitsch (another front-rank scholar, but having no notion of the exact bearing of the words, and wrongly supposing eternal life and salvation to be the matter at stake) says, "The εανπερ implies that the first proposition holds true in all its extent, provided only the second be added. What Christ possesses belongs also to them, and will continue theirs, now concealed, but to be made manifest hereafter, provided only they remain stedfast in their confidence of faith, and so the close of their Christian course correspond to its commencement." And so Westcott on this verse: "That which has been stated as a fact (γεγόναμεν) is now made conditional in its permanence on the maintenance of faith. This is the ever-present antithesis of religion. That which God has done is absolute; but man's appropriaition of the gift is by continuous effort. Comp. Col. iii, 3, 5 (ἀπεθάνατε . . . νεκρώσατε οὖν)."

6. Hebrews iii, 6. Strictly in agreement with the foregoing is the teaching, under the figure of a house and its Ruler, of earlier verses (5, 6) in the same chapter, where we read that " Moses indeed was faithful in all his house as a servant, for a testimony of those things which were afterward to be spoken; but Christ as a son, over his house; whose house are we, if we hold fast our boldness and the glorying of our hope firm unto the end." So unquestionable is the conditional element

in the words "if we hold fast" that Delitsch comments thus:
"if the New Testament church holds fast (κατέχειν=obtinere, to
maintain) the treasure of hope, notwithstanding all the
contradictions between the present and the promised future,
in the midst of all dangers of offence and falling away prepared
for her by the threatenings and allurements of the enemies of
the cross, then, and only then, does she continue the house of
God." And Westcott upon the "if" (ἐάν) says; "The
spiritual privileges of Christians depend upon their firm hold
upon that glorious hope which the Hebrews were on the point
of losing."

Here again it must be admitted that if being a part of the
"house of God" be only an equivalent statement to being
saved from perdition, then they are right who say that such a
passage teaches that saved people can be afterwards lost. But
in fact the phrase points to something that becomes true consequent upon deliverance from hell, and in no wise with a view
thereto. The Israelites, to whom the Scripture carries back our
thought, were for ever saved from Egyptian judgment and
bondage before God did, or could, offer to constitute them as a
nation His dwelling place. It is to be noted that not only was
the tabernacle (or later the temple) itself a material house of
God, but because He dwelt in the midst of them in *that* house,
therefore *they* as a people were a spiritual dwelling place of their
God. "I will set My tabernacle among you, ... and I will
walk among *you*" (Lev. xxvi, 11, 12), "*Judah* became His
sanctuary, *Israel* His dominion" (Ps. cxiv, 2; Ex. xxix, 45; II
Cor. vi, 16); and herein lay the principal reason why they
should be holy in all their ways (Num. xxxv, 34).

Thus the blessing of being "saved," that is, in its more limited
meaning of escaping from deserved wrath, is one thing, and
this typically all Israel shared through faith solely because of
the merit of the blood of the lamb sacrificed, and without any
pledges being exacted as to their future conduct. But the
forming together a residing place on earth for the God of
heaven, was an additional and greater privilege; and it is evident
that the latter was not essential to the former, though the

former was to the latter. God, had He so decided, could have delivered them from Egypt, and have led them through the wilderness as His people, and have given them the promised land, without having been pleased to dwell permanently among them personally and in a ray of visible glory. In that case they would as individuals have been "a people saved by Jehovah," but they would not have been honoured by being nationally His "house."

But the solemn fact is that whilst they continued as a nation to be God's house, yet from time to time many an individual Israelite was "cut off from among his people" in judgment, and in particular the six hundred thousand adult men of war who left Egypt but who never reached the land where especially God would dwell among His people.

Today we, redeemed by the precious blood of Jesus, are the house of God; and to us this exhortation is addressed, not to threaten us with eternal ruin if we become timid and ashamed to confess our hope, but to warn us that those further and higher privileges which attach to the "house of God," continue ours only if we continue bold and hold fast the hope of the gospel.

And do we declare anything that is not all too sadly obvious and frequent when we speak of some who did run well, and in whose lives God was very manifest, "dwelling in them and walking in them" (II Cor. vi, 16), but from whom "the glory has departed," and now they are "outside the camp" in the place and state of the leper? And is there not warning that at the close of this backsliding age it will be thus in the case of the church as a whole? Laodicea is recognized by the Lord, as a church, yet is it by the time intended so worldly in spirit and in ways that He will have ceased to dwell in it, and will be found outside its portals (Rev. iii, 20); only eager still, in discriminating pity and yearning, to grant His sweet fellowship and sustenance to any individual believer that may desire His presence and so to abide a part of His house.

This distinction between the corporate and individual aspect is clear in Scripture? as, for example, in the warning of I Cor.

iii, 16, 17 : "Know ye not that *ye* are a sanctuary of God, and that the Spirit of God dwelleth in *you*. If any *man* destroyeth the sanctuary of God, *him* shall God destroy"; and, as we have pointed out, thus it was in Corinth—the assembly continued corporately, but individuals were losing their place in it, under the judgment of God (xi, 30), or by excommunication (v, 9-13). And if it be urged that, in spite of such present loss, these will still be found sharing the glory of God's "house" in the heavens, we demand proof of such a mighty assertion, which involves that one unfit for the society of the saints on earth, faulty as they are, is by death fitted for the vastly higher honour of membership in the church when it shall have been perfected in the immediate presence of God. As has been said by another, "Death works no magic upon character." In the moral state in which one dies so does he appear at the judgment seat of Christ. If death perfected us, then the sooner we die the better ; and then also the judgment seat would cease to be a *judgment* seat, for the perfect cannot be dealt with judicially. But so far from the condition of one justly excommunicate being reversed in the heavens from what it was on earth, our Lord declares the exact opposite, assuring His church that their godly decisions on earth will be ratified in the heavens : " And if he refuse to hear them, tell it unto the church : and if he refuse to hear the church also, let him be unto thee as the Gentile and the publican. Verily I say unto you. What things soever ye shall bind on earth shall be bound in heaven : and what things soever ye shall loose on earth shall be loosed in heaven," (Matt. xviii, 17, 18 ; xvi, 19).

7. II Timothy, ii. 10-13, is another of such conditional statements, and one at which it behoves us to look further and carefully *(see. p. 121)*. It reads: "Therefore I endure all things for the elect's sake, that they also may obtain the salvation which is in Christ Jesus with eternal glory. Faithful is the saying : For if we died with him, we shall also live with him : If we endure, we shall also reign with him : if we shall deny him, he also will deny us : if we are faithless, he abideth faithful ; for he cannot deny himself."

These are among the last words of the greatest of the great soldiers of Christ Jesus. Paul is looking back on his life of loss, pain, and toil, covering some thirty years since he first espoused the cause of Christ. In it he had enjoyed the minimum of the things that the human heart prizes, and had endured the maximum of the trials that it dreads and shuns. With the past beyond recall, with a prison his cheerless present, and with death by the sword just ahead, the veteran is not in the least regretting his course, but, on the contrary, urges his younger fellow-soldier more strenuously to follow his steps, crying to him, " suffer hardship with me, as a good soldier of Christ Jesus." What mighty incentives must have gripped the apostle's heart to inspire, and to sustain for so long, his vast unwearied efforts. One such impulse he reveals in verse 10. It was his ambition that sinners might not merely obtain salvation, but obtain it " with eternal glory." Here once more is the distinction between being saved and being glorified eternally.

This " faithful saying " is judged by some to have been a terse statement of certain of the major points that christians held and taught. This is very probable. In times and places where books and readers are few, it becomes natural to embody vital tenets in crisp sentences, for ease in remembering and teaching the same. But what great force this lends to our exposition, for this " saying," which Paul endorses as worthy of all belief, declares that " if we died with Him (an aorist), we shall also (fut. indic.) live with Him." But why " if we died with Him " ? Because, surely, it is one thing to believe that He died for me, and another to go through the spiritual experience of dying with Him. By the former faith the sinner becomes possessed of pardon and life eternal : by the latter he knows the present saving power of Calvary in the realms of indwelling sin and of the seducing world. The one, we may say, is the truth of Romans iii ; and the other that of Romans vi and vii. The final glory is reached in ch. viii ; but between justification in chs iii-v and the glory in ch. viii lies the experience of practical sanctification set forth in chs. vi and vii.

So many seem to know Christ as the Redeemer from hell who know Him not as the Redeemer from slavery. Are all such to be lost? Is deliverance from the pit in the valley contingent upon climbing to the top of a distant mountain? Or rather is not the man safe from the pit as soon as his Rescuer lifts him to the surface and sets his feet upon the rock, and this though he never climb any further? The man has life through his Deliverer; but if he would go to live with Him on the mountain summit, where are glorious views and radiant pleasures, unbeclouded by mists and unbeset by the dangers of the forest beneath, then he must climb, and leave far below the scenes where he formerly lived and had his interests. If we died with Christ to sin, and to the alluring world in which we formerly had part, then we shall duly rise to live with Him.

No doubt these two parts of salvation—faith in the Lord dying for me, and my adopting His death as my attitude to all that which brought Him to death and to which He died—might and ought to commence together. But in fact they often do not, but are separated by an interval of sometimes years, or the latter experience may never be reached at all in this present world; and hence the "if we died with Him." But the living with Him (not the having life " in "—because of Him) is dependent upon dying with Him. The rescued man cannot live in the valley and reach the summit; but all who have resolutely and definitely turned the back on the old life and associations, and who are pressing upward with eager desire to know Christ fully, are assured that, by so continuing through His grace, the summit will be duly gained, and then not only shall they live, but they shall live with Him. If any man serve Me, let him follow Me; and where I am there shall also My servant be (John xii, 26); and the path he took lay through death.

> " A homeless Stranger amongst us came,
>   To this land of death and mourning;
> He walked in a path of sorrow and shame,
>   Through insult and hate and scorning.

A Man of sorrows, of toil and tears,
    An outcast Man, and a lonely;
But He looked on me—and through endless years
    Him must I love, Him only.

And I clave to Him as He turned His face
    From the land that was mine no longer—
The land I had loved in the ancient days,
    Ere I knew the love that was stronger.

And where He died would I also die;
    Far dearer a grave beside Him
Than a kingly place amongst living men,
    The place which they denied Him."

"If we endure," continues the great statement, "we shall
also reign with Him." "Therefore I endure," says Paul: I
desire to reach the highest to which my Lord desires to bring
me. I would not that He have the sorrow of ought of His
loving purpose for me being thwarted. Since He will find joy
in my reigning with Him, I will give him that joy, and by the
same means secure to myself the joy of being as near to Him
as may be possible. "I press on if so be that I may lay hold
of that for which also I was laid hold of by Christ Jesus" (Phil.
iii, 12). And also I endure, that He may have the same full joy
in others for whom also He suffered, and whom I may turn to
Him; and that they too may secure *all* that He offers. Thus
the name of our Lord Jesus shall be *glorified* in them, and they
in Him; and this is happily possible, "according to the grace
of our God and the Lord Jesus Christ" (II Thes. i, 12).

By faith Paul saw the degraded slaves of sin not merely
rescued from shameless vice and dire peril, but elevated to the
throne of their Redeemer, with no trace left of their former
vileness, but clothed in the glory of their Lord. Well worth
while it is to "endure" for securing such a result.

But what if we become weak, and faint? what if unbelief as
to the golden prospect displace the first faith? what if thus we

cease to press on, and turn back from the upward path because
it is steep and narrow and lonely?

"Does the road wind uphill all the way?

Yes, to the very end!

Will the journey take the whole long day?

From morning till night, my friend!"

What if growing weary, we sleep on the roadside? or what if we
are even allured from the way by enticing worldly prospects?
"If we shall deny Him, He also will deny us: if we are faithless,"
continues the reciter of this early summary, "He abideth faithful:
for He cannot deny Himself!" Is this comfort or warning?
Possibly both, but especially the latter. He has given the plain
promise, "Every one therefore who shall confess Me before
men, him will I also confess before My Father Who is in heaven"
(Matt. x, 32); and this promise He will completely fulfil. But
He added (ver. 33) this warning, (and He cannot go back on His
word), "But whosoever shall deny Me before men, him will I also
deny before My Father Who is in heaven." And be it noted
that when He so spake He was addressing disciples (ver. 24): it
was part of His commission to them as preachers; and he made
the terms universal, saying "Every one," so that to themselves
and all others do they apply.

It is difficult to think of a greater liberty being taken with the
words of Scripture than to read this passage as if it said no
more than that, if we have faith in the Redeemer to save us
from hell, we shall live with and reign with Him.

When Luke wrote his gospel, addressing a Gentile convert,
the Spirit guided him to repeat these teachings to him, so
forbidding any limiting thereof to Jewish disciples (Luke xii, 8,
9; ix, 26); but by Luke and Mark they are quoted as given by
our Lord on different occasions, which shows that Christ sought
to impress the warning on the mind of the disciples by declaring
it to them more than once.

Note also that the early church were so well instructed in
this powerful line of truth that they enshrined and repeated it
in this short statement, or possibly hymn, as being somewhat
of first importance. And finally, just ere the great apostle to

the Gentiles passes from the scene of christian conflict, the
same Spirit led him to leave behind a definite endorsement of
its stimulating message.   Yet it has been generally overlooked,
frequently misapplied, and is often resented, all greatly to
the spiritual loss of the people of God.

Here then in the Word stand these conditional clauses. It
is to our profit to allow them their full weight : it may be to
irretrievable loss to ignore or to weaken them, or complacently
to pass them on to the unbeliever. These promises and
warnings are good medicine : let such christians as are in ill-
health take the remedy to their quickening.

Certain it seems that no other explanation of them gives
such due weight to these "ifs" and "if so bes," consistently
with maintaining the eternal security of each that is, by faith,
"in Christ Jesus."

Must it not be felt that the line of exposition taken is based
broad and deep in Holy Scripture ? If a reader be not satisfied
with the treatment of this or that passage, can he better explain
them all ? Is there not a consensus of teaching not easily
to be refuted ?

O Blessed Lord, what hast thou done,
How vast a ransom given?
Thyself of God the eternal Son,
The Lord of earth and heaven.

Thy Father, in His gracious love,
Did spare Thee from His side:
And Thou didst stoop to bear above,
At such a cost, Thy Bride.

Lord, while our souls in faith repose
Upon Thy precious blood,
Peace like an even river flows,
And mercy, like a flood.

But boundless joy shall fill our hearts,
When, gazing on Thy face,
We fully see what faith imparts,
And glory crowns Thy grace.

Unseen, we love Thee; dear Thy name;
But when our eyes behold,
With joyful wonder we'll exclaim,
"The half had not been told!"

For Thou exceedest all the fame
Our ears have ever heard;
How happy we who know Thy name,
And trust Thy faithful word!

(Mrs. Peters.)

CHAPTER XII.

JUSTIFICATION, SANCTIFICATION, GLORY.

"Christ loved the church, and gave Himself up for it (her);
that He might sanctify it (her), having cleansed it (her) by the
laver of water in the word, that He might present the church
to Himself a glorious church, not having spot or wrinkle or any
such thing; but that it (she) should be holy and without
blemish" (Eph. v, 25-27).

"Christ loved the church"—here is the fountain out of
which all her blessings flow: "and gave Himself up for her"—
surrendering at Calvary to justice that He might for ever free
her from its fatal grip. It has been before remarked that the
picture suggests a slave girl, forlorn and unkempt, whom a
Prince sees and loves, and pays the ransom price, thus freeing
her from all bondage save to himself. But ere He can fulfil the
purpose of His love, and receive her to His palace, something
more is as requisite as was her redemption. She cannot pass
direct from the slave market to the throne, but must be
cleansed and educated and clothed suitably for such a mighty
change of sphere and station. And this is our Lord's present
work with His church.

The ransom work is finished, absolutely, legally, and eternally
finished; and thus is opened the possibility of the slave
becoming the queen. But redemption was with a view to
sanctification, and both were with a view to the presentation
of His beloved to Himself in heavenly glory. Now all those
who are found there in that day of the reception of the bride
are seen "without blemish," a term borrowed from the Old
Testament figures, and referring to *external* completeness and
actual, visible fitness—see, for example, Leviticus xxii, 17-25.
The priest having narrowly inspected the animal and finding it
"without blemish," declared it "unreproveable," that is, fit for
presentation to the Lord. The *title* of the slave girl to the throne

and the bridal joy was the ransom price offered by her Prince
according to His own will ; but her personal *fitness* for that day
He must otherwise secure.   And so Christ sanctifies His people
by "the laver of water in the Word."   (ἐν ῥήματι).

The laver was not required in order to secure the pardon of
a guilty Israelite and his exemption from deserved judgment.
The shedding of blood at the altar sufficed for this.   But if the
priest was to have dealings with God, and enter the holy places,
washing himself at the laver was as essential as the shedding of
blood at the altar (Ex. xxx, 17-21 ; Lev. viii, 6 ; xvi, 4 ; II Chron.
iv, 6) ; in fact, in the consecrating of the priest and in the
supreme sacrifice of the year, that of the great day of atonement,
when alone the high priest entered the actual presence of God,
it was the *first* act performed.

For the cleansing and restoring of the leper from his
banishment the order was first the sacrifice and then the
washing (Lev. xiv) ; for the drawing near of the priest to God
the order was reversed : and thus is signally emphasized the
imperativeness of personal sanctification for those close
dealings with the Holy One which the exercise of the priestly
office involves.   To this double process presumably David
referred when he cried " purge me with hyssop, and I shall be
clean ; wash me, and I shall be whiter than snow " (Ps. li, 7) ;
for the hyssop was used to sprinkle the blood, and the washing
followed ; David retained this order, he having by his gross
offences at that time become a moral leper, and also not being
a priest.   But in I Peter i, 2, the order is first sanctification and
then the sprinkling of blood, and this because the believer is
there looked upon as a member of a " royal priesthood " (ii, 9).

In the culpable neglect to aim at the utmost and highest daily
and practical holiness is surely the reason why the bulk of
God's people are not priests in fact and power.   How few are
the intercessors ; those who have a conscious and enjoyed
access to God, and who intercede prevailingly for themselves
and others ! How few attend the prayer meeting ; and of these
how few lead in prayer ; and of these how few pray mainly for
others, that is act as priests.   The number of those who are

verily God's people and receive His favours, and who know the
need of, and are thankful for the saving power of, the altar and
the blood, is vastly greater than the number who "*draw near*
with boldness to the throne" and there prevail in intercession.
And the reason is that the many approach the altar and the few
use the laver. The priest, as much as the victim he presented,
must be "without blemish" or he might not perform the
priestly service (Lev. xxi).

But if present privileges are thus certainly forfeited by
personal unholiness of life, how vain is the notion that the
higher and future privileges will be retained in spite of practical
defilement. Directly contrary to any such thought is the
solemn teaching of our Lord that, at His return, the unfaithful
servant, who had not used the opportunities that had already
been at his command, is deprived of them (Matt. xxv, 28, 29 ;
Luke xix, 24-26). Though being a servant, and not an enemy
of his lord, his life is not forfeited, yet his privileges are less
and not more than during his lord's absence.

The church must be sanctified by her Lord as surely as she
must be redeemed by Him. Blessed it is that it is *He* Who
sanctifies, even as it is He Who redeems. It is His grace that
provides out of His riches in glory the means of cleansing. The
laver was composed of two elements ; (1) the water, which was
(2) in the basin of the laver. Without a vessel the water were
not available: without water the vessel were unavailing. The
"Word" is the vessel in which we come in contact with the
water, the Spirit of God (John vii, 38, 39). "Sanctify them in
the truth : *Thy word* is truth" are the words of John xvii, 17 ;
whilst "sanctification in the *Spirit*" is the term in I Peter i, 2.
But in fact it is only as we draw near and utilize in practice the
Word of God, being obedient to its precepts, that we know the
cleansing energy of the Holy Spirit. He is *in* the Word, as the
water was in the laver : the Bible *is* inbreathed by the Spirit of
God ; He is in it perpetually, nor can there be any other
explanation of its universally purifying influence. Thus Christ
sanctifies His own by "the laver of water in the Word."

But surely there is such a thing as a disciple neglecting the Word of God, or habitually disobeying its commands, and so grieving the Spirit of the Lord, and thus preventing the washing which alone assures sanctification. And if this thwarting of the gracious present work of Christ be persistent, how shall such an one be found at last fit for the bridal communion ? It is wholly unjustifiable to read this passage as if it said only that Christ loved the church, and gave Himself up for her, that He might present her to Himself.

Sanctification is possible, yea, is provided; and it is gained by so simple a process as obedience to the precepts of the Lord ; and this obedience is rendered not out of any slavish or selfish fear, but from the joy-imparting motive of love to Him Who has loved us from the pit of corruption. A father seeing some unseemly act or habit of his son, speaks to him upon the point. If the boy obey the word of his father, that word will have acted as water that cleanses away defilement: and in obeying the lad will find cleansing. And this process is imperative daily. "He that is bathed needeth not save to wash his feet," but this he does so much need that to one who would have dispensed with it the Lord said, "If I wash thee not, thou hast no part with me" (John xiii, 10, 8,). Solemn words were these to fall on the ears of a disciple, and one who had just sat at table in personal fellowship with his Lord. Peter had followed Christ for some years, had loved Him ardently, and had shared much hardship for the joy of being with Him. He could say, what few can say, "We have left all and followed Thee " (Matt. xix, 27). He had so nobly confessed the Godhead of the Lord that a special blessing had been pronounced upon him as one taught of the Father (Matt. xvi, 17-19). And now he is assured that further participation with his Lord depends upon that Lord finding him humbly willing for personal cleansing from daily defilement. What was there in the Saviour's voice and manner when speaking these few words, or what of their intense purport flashed into Peter's heart, that his opposition to the washing collapsed instantly, and he at once professed eagerness for even more to be done than was needful ? Let the believer who neglects or disobeys the Word of his Lord ponder this short incident, and it may be that the Lord will again repeat these words, and their searching meaning be applied by His Spirit with recovering power.

Christ did not say, If I wash thee not, thou hast no part *in* Me. That would have been to declare to Peter the loss of all things, including eternal life and security; that would have made justification to be dependent upon sanctification, as if the superstructure of the house could carry the foundation. But He said, "If I wash thee not, thou hast no part *with Me*" (*met'emou*). This term has no New Testament reference to the saving of a sinner from perdition, but large and impressive reference to the privileges of disciples. It is used of being members of the same family (Luke xv, 31; xi, 7), and so of sharing the one inheritance (Luke xii, 13). Then of some being companions of another (Tit. iii, 15); of their being his helpers and not hinderers (Matt. xii, 30); of their sharing his social life (Mk. xiv, 18), his trials (John xv, 27; Lk. xxii, 28), his watchings (Matt. xxvi, 38), his company (John xvii, 24; Rev. iii, 20); and his glory (Rev. iii, 4, 21 : xxii, 12). This sharing with Christ (compare above; "we are become companions with the Messiah") requires our submitting to the continual cleansing which our most gracious Master stoops to perform by speaking to us by His Spirit in His Word. If we suffer Him not to wash us we shall find that we too have no part (elsewhere rendered *portion*—Luke xv, 12) *with* Him. And—returning to Ephesians v—thus will be wanting our fitness to share in the bridal portion of the saints; for though redeemed once and for ever from slavery and death, the purifying and preparatory work will not have been accomplished, and we shall not be found "without blemish" nor "unreproveable," and thus will be unfit to be presented to the Lord.

A clear confirmation of this is found in Revelation xix, where the marriage supper of the Lamb is proclaimed, to the exceeding joy of heaven. The circumstance which occasions the marriage and the feast is stated in the significant words, "His wife hath "*made herself* ready" (7). True it is that she, beggared and enslaved as she was, could not provide the costly material and precious jewels in which to be suitably attired for this supreme hour. Her Lover must give the dowry which shall make possible her arraying and adorning. And true it is that only by the grace of our Lord Jesus can we ever be found clothed in garments of glory and beauty. But equally true it is that we, on our part, are left to use, by grace, that which grace supplies : the *virgin must make the trousseau* which her royal Consort's bounty has made possible. This was typified of old in that the priestly garments, in which the priests appeared in the holy places, had to be made by the people themselves out of material and jewels with which the bounty of their God had enriched them. And how long, alas ! has the church been about this work. How slowly do we who are called to be saints become saints. Is this part of the reason, on the human side, for the so long delaying of the marriage supper ? Esther (c. ii) illustrates all this.

And therefore is it " *given* unto her " to " array *herself*"— the right and power to prepare for this glory are a gift : the duty to use the gift is her's—she must array herself. How exquisitely accurate and balanced are God's words ! Her garments, however, for that great event are not of the garish type that man often counts glorious, but she arrays herself in " fine linen, bright and pure." Here in symbol, and most distinctly, we see again how absolutely requisite is sanctification to the bridal state ; for it is added, and, oh, that we would weigh the tremendous significance of the words, " the fine linen is the righteous acts of the saints."

The rendering of the Authorized Version, "the fine linen is the righteousness of saints," has led some to suppose that here is intended that righteousness of God which is reckoned to belong to the sinner who has faith in Jesus. But this idea is unwarranted. (i). *That* righteousness the believer has already had put upon him. It was imputed to Abram as soon as he believed in God, which was nineteen centuries before Christ (Gen. xv, 6 ; Rom. iv, 3). It was enjoyed by David nearly three thousand years ago (Ps. xxxii, 1 ; Rom. iv, 7). It is reckoned today to belong already to all " who believe on Him Who raised Jesus our Lord from the dead," these "*being* therefore justified by faith " (Rom. iv, 23; v, 1). But in *this* righteousness now in question the bride does not attire herself until the marriage day. (ii). Even the A.V. rendering calls it " the righteousness of *saints*," not of God. (iii). But the term is unambiguous. It is a neuter plural (*ta dikaiomata*), and as a plural is found in six places. In four of these it is translated by the plural word "ordinances" Luke i, 6; Rom. ii, 26; Heb. ix, 1, 10). But as if to fix its meaning here it is employed in the Revelation once before (xv, 4), and is there rendered in the A.V. as a plural: " All the nations shall come and worship before Thee, for Thy judgments have been made manifest," but by the Revisers it is translated consistently " righteous acts."

Upon the loom of our daily doings each of us is weaving our garment, some working with the white threads of "righteous acts," and others marring the fabric by what they know to be acts that are not right in the sight of the Righteous One.

In this same book of the Revelation is a distinction worth observing. The saints who "come out of the tribulation, the great one," are said to "have washed their robes, and made them white in the blood of the Lamb" (Rev. vii, 14). So that their robes had formerly been defiled : they had not succeeded in keeping themselves "unspotted from the world " (Jas. i, 27). But the overcoming saints in Sardis had walked more circumspectly, and at such a moral distance from the world, that they "did not defile their garments"; and to these is given the prospect " they shall walk with me in white ; for they are worthy " (Rev. iii, 4, 5). It is therefore possible to walk with undefiled garments ; that is, doing in practice only "righteous acts." No believer on Him " Who saves His people from their sins " is bound to do what he knows is wrong, or that he even suspects may be so. By the Holy Spirit's strength, he can refrain from wrong-doing, if he be simply prepared to pay the small price of doing the right, and to trust his heavenly Father as to the present consequences. And how trifling is the highest present cost in comparison with the heavy loss to be faced in the day of Christ if we have done wrong.

And if it be urged that surely there is no saint that never fails, we answer that it is He Whose "eyes are as a flame of fire" that declares that the Sardian saints had not defiled their garments. But it will be helpful at this point to reflect that "all judgment is committed unto the Son" (John v, 22, 27). We are not competent to determine our own condition before God, much less that of others. Paul could indeed say, " I know nothing against myself" : there was *nothing* against which his own conscience and judgment were protesting. As far as he knew he was undefiled; "yet," he adds, "not in this am I justified; but He that judgeth me is the Lord," "yea, I judge not mine own self" (I Cor. iv, 3, 4). Perchance, then, the Lord may know something against Paul, though he himself knows not of it; and in that case the undefiled condition is maintained by the process indicated in the words, "if we walk in the light, as God is in the light, we (we and God) have fellowship one with another, and the blood of Jesus His Son cleanseth us from *all* sin " (I John i, 7).

Walking in the light means that one is conforming to the will of God as far as ever it is known; and be it not forgotten that part of His revealed will is that each should search out what is His will, and specially, where possible, by personal meditation in His Word, and by attending the opening up thereof by others, especially if one cannot oneself read. Concerning our great Example it is written: " Lo I am come; *in the roll of the book* it is written of Me (or, prescribed to Me): I delight to do Thy will, O my God ; yea, Thy law is within My heart" (Ps. xl, 7, 8), And another gives us this golden testimony: " I thought on my ways, and turned my feet *unto Thy testimonies.* I made haste, and delayed not, to observe Thy commandments " (Ps. cxix, 59, 60).

If we are thus walking, fellowship between God and us is maintained ; for He is far from being an overbearing tyrant eager to find occasion against his victims, but is a gracious Lord, " good and ready to forgive," and asking from us no more than it is possible for us to render. It is possible, for He has made it so, for us to walk in all the light of His known will ; and while we so continue, as regards what He may see to be sin, though as yet we recognize it not as such, He gives us the benefit of His own estimate of the blood of Jesus, and that blood keeps us perpetually clean from *all* sin, not only that which we may have known and confessed, but all that also which is sinful in *His* sight.

This is the plenary aspect of atonement as prefigured on the great day of atonement (Lev. xvi). But an Israelite dare not say to himself, I may safely go on in this disobedience, for the day of atonement covers all our transgressions. One not walking in the light derived no benefit from that general sacrifice. He had to confess and forsake his known sin if he would obtain mercy (Prov. xxviii, 13), and bring unto God his personal sacrifice. Neither can the christian presume on the cross cf Christ to enable him to be careless as to the commands of our Lord.

Thus do the atoning blood and the sanctifying Word and Spirit continue to effect the requisite sanctification. And let not any presume to neglect the water because of an alleged sufficiency in the blood. The laver is as indispensable for its purpose as is the altar for its office. The latter indeed *must* be approached first ; but the former *must* be then used, if more of God is to be known than His bare pardon for guilt What God hath joined together let us not put asunder.

Justification is the judge declaring that the law has nothing against the man before the court. That declaration does not need to be made more than once. Sanctification is that man studying carefully to walk in righteousness and holiness all the days of his life. And as to *this*,

> " Let no one think that sudden, in a minute,
>   All is accomplished, and the work is done :
> Though with thy earliest dawn thou shouldst begin it,
>   Scarce were it ended in thy setting sun."
>
> (*Myers*-" *St. Paul.*")

The place thus given to the Word of God, and to sanctification as produced by that Word, as the necessary preparation for the heavenly glory, is set forth with remarkable distinctness in the Lord's commission to the chiefest of His apostles (Acts xxvi, 17, 18). Indicating to Paul the sphere and nature of his life-work as including both Jews and Gentiles, Christ said, " I send thee, to open their eyes, that they may turn from darkness to light, and from the power of Satan unto God, that they may receive remission of sins and an inheritance among them that are sanctified by faith in Me." Thus Paul had two vast benefits to offer to mankind : (i) the remission of sins, and (ii) an inheritance. These two favours are similarly distinguished in Heb. ix, 15, where we are reminded of (i) the " redemption of the transgressions " with the object (ii) that those who are called " may receive the promise of the eternal inheritance." What this inheritance is, where reserved, and how glorious, has been already indicated, though all too inadequately.

Now it is to be observed that the risen Lord most definitely connects the receiving of the inheritance, not with the remission of sins, but with being *sanctified*. Many in the different ages will receive the former who are not among the called who will receive the eternal inheritance of the saints in the heavens. We of this age, are, by God's message, called to this honour : it is the most distinctive element in the apostolic teaching (I Thes. ii, 12 ; I Pet. v, 10). But our arriving thereat is contingent upon our being sanctified, as well as justified. Nor is this an unreasonable or impossible condition. For it is *by faith* in Christ that we are to be sanctified, just as it is by faith that we have been justified. And he who has trusted Christ for pardon for sin, can as readily trust Him for power over sin, and is without excuse if he does not do so.

That Paul thus understood the terms of the message given to him to deliver, seems evident from the fact that many years after, as he neared the end of his long ministry, he spoke thus to the elders of the church at Ephesus, whom he was not expecting to see again in the flesh : "And now I commend you

H

to God, and to the word of his grace, which is able to build up, and to give the inheritance among all them that are sanctified" (Acts xx, 32). These men had been justified long since, and by himself had been received to chief office in the christian assembly, as appointed thereto by the Holy Spirit. With this taken for granted, he impresses upon them the indispens- ableness and sufficiency of the Word which proclaims the grace of God as being His instrument for building up, for sanctifying, and so for securing the possession of the inheritance that awaits the sanctified.

He who puts his faith in Christ as Sanctifier will give diligent obedience to His word, just as a patient seeking health follows the instructions of the physician in whom he has faith. Thus the process of a holy life is simple, even obedience to the Word of God; and power therefor is available, by confidence in Christ the Lord. The preparing and wearing of the marriage robe is possible, the bridal glory and joy are attainable. Therefore, forgetting those things which are behind—as well our failures as our successes—let us press on unto perfection, keeping to the path of a restful, confiding obedience to the Word of Him Whose blood has redeemed us from all iniquity, and Whose delight is now to purify us unto Himself a people for His own possession, marked out as such by our being zealous of good works, as He was when here among us (Tit. ii, 14).

> Father of peace, and God of love,
>   We own Thy power to save;
> That power by which our Shepherd rose
>   Victorious o'er the grave.
>
> Him from the dead Thou brought'st again,
>   When, by His sacred blood,
> Confirmed and sealed for evermore
>   The Eternal Covenant stood.
>
> Oh, may Thy Spirit seal our souls,
>   And mould them to Thy will,
> That our weak hearts no more may stray,
>   But keep Thy precepts still.
>
> That to perfection's sacred height
>   We nearer still may rise,
> And all we think, and all we do,
>   Be pleasing in Thine eyes.
>
>   (Doddridge).

CHAPTER XIII.

THE BODY OF CHRIST AND THE PRIESTHOOD.

It has been urged that this presumed failure to be glorified with Christ is impossible because it would mean that some members of His "body" would be missing, and thus the perfect Head have but a maimed body.

To answer this difficulty it might be sufficient to remark that the same objection might be used to show that Christ has no complete "body" even now. For a proportion of those who are supposed to be members of the "body" are even now in a state of paralysis or other disordered condition, and the Head has no use of them or service from them. Thus the "body" is already diseased, and maimed, and largely unworthy of its Head.

But the real answer to the objection is not along this line at all, but is different, and is twofold.

1. The objection assumes that every believer of this age is *ipso facto* a member of the "body." It is admitted that this is the ideal and was the possible, but is it the actual in either Scripture or experience? That initial work of the Spirit which suffices for the regenerating of a sinner, so that he receives eternal life, is not all that is required to incorporate him into the body of Christ; else believers before Pentecost, and those of the next age, equally with those of this dispensation, would be members of the "body," which the Word of God does not suggest, but rather negatives. The apostles were not to Christ as a body until His Spirit *indwelt* them all at once, uniting them thus to Him and to one another. Is it the fact that every believer has *thus* received the Spirit? or is it not rather to be feared that some have been simply regenerated, and know nothing more of His working and nothing at all of His indwell-

ing and infilling? If we discard preconceived theories and candidly face facts, it would seem that there can be but one answer.

The decisive passage is I Cor. xii, 13 : "In one Spirit were we all baptized into one body . . . ; and were all made to drink of one Spirit." Now the " baptism " in the Spirit means Pentecost (in its essential features), not merely the new birth. The apostles were born of the Spirit years before Pentecost. Having believed on Jesus as the Son of God, they were therefore God's children (John i, 12), and possessors of eternal life (John iii, 36). But Pentecost stands not for the first quickening by the Spirit, but for the regenerated man receiving *power for effective witness to Christ* (Acts i, 8), by the Spirit entering into and so dwelling in him that He pervades the heart, filling it with divine wisdom, knowledge, love, and boldness; and controlling the body, using it in speech and other service; and empowering for suffering. It is not to be maintained from Scripture that the accidental features of Pentecost— a rushing wind, cloven, visible tongues of fire, and the use of previously unknown languages, are to be known in every case. The Lord may give these, or the like, if He so please ; but the power and courage to witness, and to do so with spiritual effect on hearers, is the essence of the baptism. It is the absence of *such* a connection with the Spirit of Christ that is the only adequate explanation of the timidity, powerlessness, and uselessness in service which are the undeniable and generally mourned facts concerning multitudes of persons who certainly acknowledge Christ as God's Son and their own Redeemer, who often can tell the circumstances of their conversion, and sometimes can even go on to give an account of what arrested their growth. "No more alarming sign exists in the church of God of today than this, that so small a number of our church members ever are used to turn a soul to Christ" *(A. T. Pierson).*

The term the " baptism " in the Spirit is strictly limited to a sharing in the Pentecostal type of experience. It is used in respect to the Spirit but thrice, in addition to 1 Cor. 12, 13 already mentioned. First by John the Baptist when declaring that Christ was He who should baptize men in the Holy Spirit (Mat. iii. 11, and parallel passages); then by our Lord, Who defined that which should shortly take place on the day of Pentecost as being that promised baptism (Acts i, 5); and again by Peter (Acts xi, 16), when asserting that the endowment granted to Gentiles in the house of Cornelius was a further fulfilment of the promise. Peter did not say that the fact that persons had believed on Jesus as the Saviour necessarily implied that they had received their share in the baptism, and need seek nothing more, as is sometimes taught to-day. On the contrary it appears to have been the earnest care of the apostles to see to it that their converts did have an unquestionable enduement of power by the Holy Spirit coming upon them, and this sometimes long after He had worked in them unto salvation (Acts ii, 38, "ye shall receive the gift of the Holy Spirit"; viii, 14-17; xix, 1-6). In view of this their care we can understand that Paul could remind the Corinthians that they had all been baptized in one Spirit, for this baptism was a fact of them, as it was also of the Ephesians (I Cor. i, 5-7; Acts xix, 1-6). His statements in both cases are in definite historic (aorist) tenses: "We were all baptized . . . ye were sealed with the Holy Spirit" (I Cor. xii, 13; Eph. i, 13); and so apply only to the persons addressed. They are not general assertions concerning all believers, such as are found in connection with eternal life; "the one believing has eternal life" (Jo. iii, 36). The baptism is not anywhere stated to be an inevitable accompaniment of saving faith, but rather the contrary is shown, as in the two places in Acts just mentioned. Alas, that wide later experience confirms this.

Many believers seem to be living in a pre-Pentecostal state, and it is at least open to question whether such are regarded by God as, or if in fact they are, members of the body of Christ, seeing that His Spirit does not appear to dwell in them, for He neither energizes, nor controls, nor uses them. And it is just such as these, or others who may have quenched the Spirit that once empowered them, who, having no energy for maintaining holiness and service, will prove unfaithful and unworthy of the glory. But if they never were members of the body, or have lapsed from their place therein, their absence in the final state would not involve any incompleteness thereof. After all, the term "body" is a figure of speech, not a statement of a material fact. It denotes a privileged relationship and service. The notion that Christ's "body" must be composed of just so many members, neither more nor less, is mechanical, and not founded in Scripture. The words "not holding fast the *Head*" (Col. ii, 18, 19) should be weighed. If a member ceases to be attached to the head it thereby ceases to be of the body.

2. But there is something more to be noticed. The figure of the body is not employed by the Spirit to teach ought as to the relationship of Christ and His people from the day of His appearing and onward, and the figure of the bride is not used to teach ought of our relationship to Him prior to that day. We are now a betrothed virgin but not a bride, for the former never becomes the latter until the actual day of the union. Hence the church is spoken of as the bride in those passages only which deal with the marriage day (Rev. xix, 7; xxi, 2, 9; xxii, 16, 17). This restricted employment of these two figures is seen strikingly in Eph. v, 22, 23, where the following points are to be noted: (a) that the church is to be presented to the Lord as a wife to the husband; but this will be on the marriage day, which is future, not present: (b) that the church is called also the "body," which shows that in the divine possibility every member of the called-out assembly might be, and therefore ought to be, a member of the body: (c) and therefore the membership of the "body" and of the "wife" might be co-extensive. But it is noticeable that the term "wife" is not used of the church with a present application, whilst the term "body" is so employed. In verse 23 Paul having said that "the husband is the head of the wife, as Christ also is the head of the church," might have been expected to maintain the figure and to have said "being Himself also the Saviour of the wife," but instead we have "of the body"; and somewhat similarly in v. 30.

Every attempt, therefore to argue from the figure of the body as to the circumstances of the marriage day and forward, will but lead to confusion of mind; for God's figures of speech must only be used strictly within the spheres and limits of His own use thereof; and He makes no use of the symbol of the Head and body in respect of the church glorified, but uses it only concerning our present relationships to Christ.

The figure of the Vine and its branches (John xv) is prior to and parallel to that of the Head and its members. Both are figures, and of present application, not future. As the fruitless branch can be cut out of the vine, so the unserviceable member can be removed from the body. But salvation is prior to and wholly independent of *such* relationship to Christ as these figures picture, and so is not lost if this relationship is forfeited.

It may be helpful to give another and rich example showing that not all to whom a given dignity belongs necessarily secure the enjoyment of the same.

The privilege of the priesthood, that is, of direct access to God, and of acting for others in things pertaining to God, was open to *every Israelite*, for they had no sooner left Egypt than God spoke thus to the nation: "Thus shalt thou say to the house of Jacob, and tell the children of Israel; Ye have seen what I did unto the Egyptians, and how I bare you on eagles' wings, and brought you unto myself. Now therefore, if ye will obey my voice indeed, and keep my covenant, then ye shall be a peculiar treasure unto me from among all peoples: for all the earth is mine: and ye shall be unto me a kingdom of priests, and an holy nation. These are the words which thou shalt speak unto the children of Israel" (Ex. xix, 3-6).

In the day of their national restoration this intention of God will be fulfilled (Is. lxi, 5, 6); but as yet only one family in Israel, that of Aaron, has ever enjoyed the honour. And, further; of that family some by misconduct forfeited their priesthood, as Nadab and Abihu (Lev. x, 1), and the house of Eli (I Sam. ii, 27-36; iii, 12-14). On the other hand, it was by reason of faithfulness to God that Phinehas obtained a guarantee of the priestly office to himself and his sons (Num. xxv, 10-13; Ps. cvi,

30, 31); and of the house of Phinehas certain of the family of
Zadok (I Chron. vi, 4-8) are promised this honour in the days
of Messiah's reign at Jerusalem, because, says God, they "kept
the charge of My sanctuary when the children of Israel went
astray from me" (Ezek. xliv, 15; xlviii, 11).

Referring to the same great time, the day when Jehovah of
hosts shall have removed the iniquity of the land of Canaan,
Joshua, the high priest in the era of the return of the people
from Babylon, five centuries B.C., is thus addressed and
promised by God: "Thus saith Jehovah of hosts: *if thou wilt
walk in My ways*, and *if thou wilt keep My charge*, then, thou also
shalt judge My house, and shalt also keep My courts, and I will
give thee a place of access among these that stand by" (Zech.
iii, 7). The last clause reads literally "free goings between
these"; and who the "these" are the context shows, for in the
vision none are standing around save angelic beings. Hence
that excellent expositor, Mr. David Baron, approves a Jewish
Targum which paraphrases thus; "In the resurrection of the
dead I will revive thee, and will give thee feet walking among
these seraphim."

It is evident that this matter of the priesthood being open to
all, but the retention of the same being contingent upon fidelity,
is strictly germane to our subject and of direct application to
the church of God; for Christ "loosed us from our sins in His
blood; and He made us to be a kingdom, priests unto his God
and Father" (Rev. i, 6). We are called to be in the higher, the
heavenly realm, an "elect race," as Israel was called; a "royal
priesthood," as they might have been, and as their sons will
yet be; "a holy nation" as they could and ought to have been,
but were not (I Pet. ii, 9).

Of the lamentable present failure of saved persons to exercise
today this holy and powerful office we have before spoken;
but if it be not now valued how shall it be granted hereafter?
Have not these keen words of our Lord (Luke xvi, 12) a pointed
message to us in this connection: "if ye have not been (now)
faithful in that which Another's (His office of the priesthood,
for example, entrusted to us as stewards, for His honour and
the good of men), who will give you (in the day of account and
settlement—see ver. 2) that which is your own" (reward for past
faithfulness, with permanent continuance in the privileged
position, and enlarged service)?

SOME IFS OF THE NEW TESTAMENT ADDRESSED TO BELIEVERS.

FAITH AND INWARD DISPOSITIONS.

1. We are Christ's household, *if* we hold fast to the end our joy in hope. Heb. iii, 6; John viii, 31.

2. We are His companions (Greek) *if* we hold fast to the end our first confidence. Heb. iii, 14.

3. Presented to Him blameless, *if at least* we continue fixed in the faith. Col. i, 23.

4. *If* any hear Christ's voice, and open the door, Christ will sup with him and he with Christ. Rev. iii, 20.

5. *If* you will hear His voice, harden not your heart. Heb. iii, 15.

If not.

6. *If* our heart condemn us *not* we are confident toward God. I John iii, 20, 21.

7. *If* any receive *not* the kingdom as a little child, he shall not enter it. Luke xviii, 17; Mark x, 15.

8. *If not* repentance for lost love, the candlestick removed. Rev. ii, 5.

9. *If not* watchful, Christ will arrive unexpected by us. Rev. iii, 3.

10. *If not* repentant for fornication, will be cast into great tribulation. Rev. ii, 22.

11. *If not* repentant for immoral doctrine, Christ will fight against such. Rev. ii, 15.

II. PRACTICE.

12. *If* we live after the flesh, we are about to die; if we mortify the deeds of the body, we are about to live. Rom. viii, 13.

13. *If* defilers of God's temple ourselves to be defiled, or marred (Greek). I Cor. iii, 17.

14. *If* evil-doers against the civil power, be afraid. Rom. xiii, 4.

15. *If* your eye cause you to stumble, pluck it out : else — Matt. v, 29, 30.

16. *If* any add to the Revelation, plagues added. *If* any take away, his name taken out of the holy city. Rev. xxii, 18, 19.

17. *If* we seek applause of men, no reward for us in the kingdom of heaven. Matt. v, 46 ; vi, 1-4.

18. *If* Paul's work done willingly, a reward to be given. I Cor. ix, 17.

19. *If* the righteous draw back, God will have no pleasure in him. Heb. x, 38 (Greek).

20. Paul strove, *if by any means* he might attain the first resurrection. Phil. iii, 11.

21. *If* we suffer with Christ, with Christ to reign, II Tim. ii, 12.

22. Joint heirs with Christ, *if indeed* we suffer with him. Rom. viii, 17.

23. *If* we abide in Christ, our prayers are heard. *If we do not*, we become withered, and shall be cast as a branch into the fire. John xv, 6, 7.

24. *If* we deny Christ, denied by Him. II Tim. ii, 12 ; Matt, x, 33.

If not

25. *If not* born out of water and spirit, no entrance into the kingdom of God. John iii, 5.

26. *If* we do *not* change and become like little children, no entrance for us into the kingdom (Greek). Matt. xviii, 3.

27. *If not* possessed of righteousness beyond the Pharisees, no entrance into the kingdom. Matt. v, 20.

28. *If not* obedient, no entrance into the kingdom (Greek) Heb. iii, 18 ; iv, 5, 6 ; Matt. vii, 21.

29. *If* we forgive *not men*, not forgiven of God. Matt. vi, 14, 15.

30. *If* we forgive *not* our *brethren* we shall be dealt with as the unmerciful servant. Matt. xviii, 34, 35.

31. *If* quarrels *not* settled, the offender to be delivered to the judge, and to be cast into prison. Matt. v, 25, 26.

32. *If not* striving lawfully, not crowned at last. II Tim. ii, 5.

33. *If not* faithful in the false riches, how can we obtain the true ? Luke xvi, 11, 12.

34. *If* on the true foundation be *not* built godly works, loss to be suffered and escape to be so as through fire. I Cor. iii, 12-15. If our character and works stand the trial, reward to be given.

35. We desire resurrection, *if at least,* on being clothed, we shall not be found naked. II Cor. v, 2, 3.

36. We will press on, *if God permit.* Heb. vi, 3.

Inference from previous dispensations.

37. If the breaking one of the commands at Sinai, entails just recompense, how much more shall disobedience to one of Christ's ? Heb. ii, 2, 3 ; Luke xii, 47, 48.

38. If those who turned away from the voice at Sinai, escaped not, much less we if we turn away from any of the commands of Christ ! Heb. xii, 25.

(From an old tract ; revised).

CHAPTER XIV.

KADESHBARNEA AND ITS LESSONS.

"These things were our examples." (I Cor. x, 6.)

Rise, my soul, thy God directs thee,
　　Stranger hands no more impede;
Pass thou on, His hand protects thee,
　　Strength that has the captive freed.

Is the wilderness before thee,
　　Desert lands where drought abides?
Heavenly springs shall there restore thee,
　　Fresh from God's exhaustless tides.

Light divine surrounds thy going,
　　God Himself shall mark thy way;
Secret blessings, richly flowing,
　　Lead to everlasting day.

God, thine everlasting portion,
　　Feeds thee with the mighty's meat;
Price of Egypt's hard extortion,
　　Egypt's food no more to eat.

Art thou weaned from Egypt's pleasures,
　　God in secret thee shall keep,
There unfold His hidden treasures,
　　There His love's exhaustless deep.

In the desert God will teach thee
　　What the God that thou hast found,
Patient, gracious, powerful, holy,
　　All His grace shall there abound.

On to Canaan's rest still wending,
   E'en thy wants and woes shall bring
Suited grace from high descending,
   Thou shalt taste of mercy's spring.

Though thy way be long and dreary,
   Eagle strength He'll still renew:
Garments fresh and foot unweary
   Tell how God hath brought thee through.

When to Canaan's long-loved dwelling
   Love divine thy foot shall bring,
There with shouts of triumph swelling,
   Zion's songs in rest to sing,

There no stranger God shall greet thee—
   Stranger thou in courts above—
He who to His rest shall greet thee,
   Greets thee with a well-known love.
               (J. N. Darby.)

No contrast can be greater than the view which the Lord and His apostles took of the earliest books of the Bible, and the use which He and they made thereof, and the view which certain modern hyper-critical theologians hold, and the consequent practical uselessness to them of these books.

To Christ a single sentence in the story of God meeting Moses at the bush was sufficient ground upon which to settle decisively the deepest of problems. "I *am* the God of Abraham, and the God of Isaac, and the God of Jacob" left no room for doubting the continued existence of the patriarchs centuries after their decease. This to the Son of God was most certainly a word spoken by God; and its message, as enshrined in the Scriptures, was to all generations following, and not only to Moses, the one directly addressed: "Have ye not read that which was spoken unto *you* by God?" He demanded of the Pharisees (Matt. xxii, 31, 32). And the continuity of existence amply demonstrated by this one sentence, if by no other, argued that God had some

future in store for those whose preservation in being He
maintained, and so a resurrection of the dead was certain. How
far removed from such use of the Word of God is that attitude
which speaks of these early records as being legend, myth, or
fable, or as being at the best but late and unreliable narratives
of some ancient events of comparatively small moment, and
these magnified and adapted by the fertile imagination of
unknown patriotic moralists having no great regard for strict
accuracy, or even honesty.

The apostles followed their divine Master in the most
reverential use of the early histories; and, taught by His Spirit,
they perceived in them the richest practical teaching for later
saints. "Whatsoever things were written aforetime were written
for our learning" (Rom. xv, 4): "Now these things happened
unto them by way of example; and they were written for our
admonition, upon whom the ends of the ages are come"
(I Cor. x, 11).

And of "these things" that God thus overruled and recorded
none has vaster import for us, as none has larger place
in the records, than the story of the exodus of the Jewish
people from Egypt to Canaan. Further, of this period of
Israel's history no event stands forth in the narrative with
more startling prominence or solemn significance than the
refusal of the whole body of the men of war to enter upon
possession of the good land that belonged to them by the
covenant of God with their fathers, unto which He had
promised to bring themselves, and the conquest of which by
them He guaranteed.

The record of this unbelieving disobedience is given with
great fulness in chapters xiii and xiv of the book of Numbers.
Thirty-eight years later, when the next generation stood in the
same position, with the same prospect before them, and the
same promises to strengthen their courage, Moses took occasion
to recite before the children the sinful failure of their fathers
and its dread consequences (Deut. i and ii). Some four and a
half centuries pass, and again the nation faces the possibility of
national advance to something like a full possessing of the

inheritance still but partially secured. The victories in war won by David open such prospect; at this juncture the Lord again warns the people by the great sin at Kadeshbarnea, charging them not to harden their heart as did their fathers. "Today," cried the inspired king,

"To-day, Oh that ye would hear his voice!
Harden not your heart, as at Meribah,
As in the day of Massah in the wilderness:
When your fathers tempted me,
Proved me, and saw my work.
Forty years long was I grieved with that generation,
And said, it is a people that do err in their heart,
And they have not known my ways:
Wherefore I sware in my wrath,
That they should not enter into my rest."

(Ps. xcv, 7-11)

Truly He is our God; truly we are the sheep of His pasture (ver. 7): but so were our forefathers; yet they failed to secure the best that God had for them, is the lesson enforced.

Once more the centuries roll away, until a whole millenium of years have flown. Israel nationally has proved as unbelieving and rebellious as aforetime, even to rejecting their Messiah when He visited them. And now, they being temporarily set aside by God till long and bitter chastisement shall have humbled them, the Lord is doing in the earth a new thing, even visiting the rest of the nations with offers of grace, designing to gather from among all these peoples a new and heavenly company. Before these He sets a nobler prospect than was ever opened to Israel nationally, even that glory in the heavens, in association with His exalted Son, at which we have before gazed. And addressing these most highly privileged of all His people, He again and again reverts to the disastrous doings at Kadeshbarnea.

There are three principal passages in this connection: I Cor. ix, 23—10, 13; Heb. iii and iv; v, 11—6, 12. The first of these most important scriptures reads thus: "And I do all things for the gospel's sake, that I may be a joint partaker

thereof. Know ye not that they which run in a race all run,
but one receiveth the prize? Even so run that ye may attain.
And every man that striveth in the games is temperate in all
things. Now they do it to receive a corruptible crown; but we
an incorruptible. I therefore so run, as not uncertainly; so
fight I, as not beating the air: but I buffet my body, and bring
it into bondage: lest by any means, after that I have preached
to others, I myself should be rejected.

"For I would not brethren, have you ignorant, how that our
fathers were all under the cloud, and all passed through the sea;
and were all baptized into Moses in the cloud and in the sea;
and did all eat the same spiritual food; and did all drink the
same spiritual drink: for they drank of a spiritual rock that
followed them: and the rock was Christ. Howbeit with most
of them God was not well pleased: for they were overthrown
in the wilderness. Now these things were our examples, to the
intent we should not lust after evil things, as they also lusted.
Neither be ye idolators, as were some of them; as it is written,
The people sat down to eat and drink, and rose up to play.
Neither let us commit fornication, as some of them committed,
and fell in one day three and twenty thousand. Neither let us
tempt the Lord, as some of them tempted, and perished by the
serpents. Neither murmer ye, as some of them murmered, and
perished by the destroyer. Now these things happened unto
them by way of example; and they were written for our
admonition, upon whom the ends of the ages are come.
Wherefore let him that thinketh he standeth take heed lest he
fall. There hath no temptation taken you but such as man
can bear: but God is faithful, who will not suffer you to be
tempted above that ye are able; but will with the temptation
make also the way of escape, that ye may be able to endure it."

We are thus invited to consider the christian life and service
as an athletic ground where racers and wrestlers contend for
coveted prizes. It is therefore necessary to decide exactly what
the Spirit intended by the term "prize." But before seeking
the answer to this question, this at least may be settled
without prejudice to the answer that may be reached, namely,

that the prize, because it is a *prize*, is somewhat that must be won, and that it may be lost. The word used *(brabeion)* is of rare occurrence, being found here and at Philippians iii, 14, only. But a cognate *(brabeuo)* is found at Colossians iii, 15, and another *(Katabrabeuo)* at chapter ii, 18, 19, in the passage reading "Let no one rob you of your prize by a voluntary humility and worshipping of the angels, dwelling in the things which he hath seen, vainly puffed up by his fleshly mind, and not holding fast the Head, from whom all the body, being supplied and knit together through the joints and bands, increaseth with the increase of God."

This does not, indeed, help to the deciding what is the prize, but it does most strongly accentuate the warning that a prize may be lost, and further and plainly shows that there are foes who will bring about the loss if possible, and this by inducing any state of heart, or any line of worship or of conduct, which may suffice to cause the christian to relax his hold on Christ, not necessarily as Redeemer, but as the Head of the body, the church.

But the passage in Philippians iii, affords clearer light as to what the prize is. Using the same figure as in I Corinthians ix, the apostle says, "I press on, if so be that I may lay hold of that for which also I was laid hold of by Christ Jesus"; and again, "I press on toward the goal unto the prize *(brabeion)* of the high calling (calling on high=heavenly) of God in Christ Jesus" (verse 14). He has immediately before said that he purposes continuing so to order his life if by any means he may attain unto the out-resurrection from the dead. Proceeding at once to disclaim distinctly any thought that he has obtained the certainty of this honour, he reveals this desire to lay hold of that for which his Lord has taken hold of him. And for what it is, in its ultimate purpose, that the Lord had seized him, and had so royally changed him from a proud rebel into a loyal slave, he himself tells us in the words of 2 Corinthians v, 5, "Now He that wrought us for *this very thing* is God, Who gave unto us the earnest of the Spirit." For what "very thing" has God wrought? The context shows that it is that we may

J

presently be "clothed upon with our habitation which is from heaven . . . a building from God, a house not made with hands, eternal in the heavens." Not the disembodied state did he desire, but rather the wondrous moment when " what is mortal (shall) be *swallowed up* of life."

He had already revealed to the Corinthians what this meant in detail, and at what season it would come to pass (I Ep. xv). In glowing, heart-stirring terms he had irradiated the darkness of death in which their pagan minds had lain, assuring them of the certainty of an event for which no pagan philosophy has any room, even a resurrection, when this corruptible shall put on incorruption, and this mortal immortality, and that *then* shall come to pass the saying, " death is *swallowed up* in victory," the same word being used in each case (*katapinō*.) And this is to be at the moment of the descent from heaven of the Lord Jesus Christ, as is determined by a comparison with the "word of the Lord " in I Thess. iv., 15-17. Thus it was for the very end that Paul might share in the glory to which the first resurrection is the doorway that the Lord had laid hold on him, and thenceforth it was with him a supreme concern that he should be accounted worthy to attain thereto.

There is great manuscript authority for the R.V. margin of I Cor. xv, 49, "And as we have borne the image of the earthy *let us* also bear the image of the heavenly," and it is adopted in the Nestle text, and by Lachmann, Tischendorf, Tregelles, Alford, and Westcott and Hort. Ellicott prefers the common rendering, but on internal and subjective grounds, and his remark on the external authority is emphatic: " It is impossible to deny that the subjunctive φορέσωμεν, is supported by very greatly preponderating authority." Alford on Rom. x, 5, says : "that no conjecture (*i.e.*, as to the true Greek text) arising from doctrinal difficulty is ever to be admitted in the face of the consensus of MSS. and versions." Weymouth, who also accepts the subjunctive, gives the force well by rendering, " *Let us see to it* that we also bear the image of the heavenly," and with this no doctrinal difficulty is connected upon the assumption that the first resurrection and the heavenly glory are not guaranteed absolutely, but must be sought after zealously, and not be taken for granted.

It has been pointed out earlier that in Phil. iii, 11, Paul repeats the words of our Lord, when declaring that, whereas justifying righteousness is verily received through faith in Christ, *not* by our own works, yet, in marked contrast, "the resurrection which is from among the dead" (*teen exanastasin teen ek nekrōn*) is a privilege at which one must arrive (*katanteeso*) by a given course of life, even the experimental knowledge of Christ, of the power of His resurrection, and of the fellowship of His sufferings, thereby becoming conformed unto His death (Phil. iii, 7-21). Surely the present participle "becoming confirmed" (*summorphizomenos*) is significant, and decisive in favour of the view that it is a process, a course of life that is contemplated.

It has been suggested that Paul here speaks of a present moral resurrection as he does in Romans vi. But in that chapter it is simply a reckoning of faith that is proposed, not a course of personal sufferings. The subject discussed is whether the believer is to continue in slavery to sin (*douleuein*), as in his unregenerate days, or is the mastery (*kurieuo*) of sin to be immediately and wholly broken? It should be remembered that when writing to the Philippians Paul was near the close of his life and service. Could a life so holy and powerful as his be lived without *first* knowing experimentally the truth taught in Romans vi? Did the Holy Spirit at any time use the apostles to urge others to seek experiences which the writer had not first known, and to which therefore he could be a *witness*? And again, if by the close of that long and wonderful career Paul was still only longing and striving to attain to death to the "old man" and victory over sin, when did he ever attain thereto? Such reflections upon the apostle are unworthy; and, as has been indicated, the experience set forth in Romans vi is not to be reached, or to be sought, by suffering, by attaining, by laying hold, by pressing on, or by any other such effort as is urged upon the Philippians, but by the simple acceptance by faith of what God says He did for us in Christ in relation to the "old man." [1]

1 See my "The Clean Heart," as advertized at end.

Thus this suggestion is neither sound experimental theology nor fair exegesis, Paul indicates as plainly as language can do that the first resurrection may be missed. His words are:—" *If by any means* I *may* arrive at the resurrection which is out from among the dead. "If by any means" (*ei pōs*) "I may"—"if" with the subjunctive of the verb—cannot but declare a condition; and so on this particle in this place Alford says, "It is used when an end is proposed, but failure is presumed to be possible": and so Lightfoot; "The apostle states not a positive assurance, but a modest hope": and Grimm-Thayer (Lexicon) give its meaning as, "If in any way, if by any means, if possible": and Ellicott to the same effect says, " the idea of an attempt is conveyed, which may or may not be successful." Both Alford and Lightfoot regard the passage as dealing with the resurrection of the godly from death, and Ellicott's note is worth giving in full, "The resurrection from the dead; *i.e.*, as the context suggests, the *first* resurrection (Rev. xx, 5), when, at the Lord's coming the dead in Him shall rise first (I Thes. iv, 16), and the quick be caught up to meet Him in the clouds (I Thes. v, 17); comp. Luke xx, 35. The first resurrection will include only true believers, and will apparently precede the second, that of non-believer, and disbelievers, in point of time. Any reference here to a merely ethical resurrection (Cocceius) is wholly out of the question." With the addition that the second resurrection will include believers not accounted worthy of the first, this note is excellent.

The sense and force of the phrase "if by any means I may arrive" are surely fixed beyond controversy by the use of the same words in Acts xxvii, 12: "the more part advised to put to sea from thence *if by any means* they could *reach* (arrive at) Phoenix, and winter there" (*ei pōs dunainto katanteesantes*), which goal they did *not* reach.

Further, speaking upon the very subject of the resurrection and the kingdom promised afore by God, Paul used the same verb, again preceded by conditional terms, saying (Acts xxiv, 6-8), "unto which promise our twelve tribes, earnestly serving God night and day, hope *to attain*." Here the force of *elpizei katanteesai*, "unto which they hope to attain," is the same as his words in Philippians *ei pōs kantanteeso*, "if by any means I may attain." This hope of the Israelite of sharing in Messiah's kingdom is plainly conditional (Dan. xii, 2, 3). It is assured to such an Israelite indeed as Daniel (xii, 13), and to such a faithful servant of God in a period of great difficulty as Zerubbabel (Hag. ii, 23). It was also offered to Joshua the high priest, but upon conditions of obedience and conduct. Joshua had been relieved of his filthy garments and arrayed in noble attire (Zech iii, 1-5), but immediately his symbolic justification before Jehovah had been thus completed, and his standing in the presence of God assured, the divine message to him is couched in conditional language. "And the Angel of Jehovah protested unto Joshua, saying, Thus saith Jehovah of hosts, If thou wilt walk in My ways, and if thou wilt keep My charge, then thou also shalt judge My house, and shall also keep My courts, and I will give thee places to walk among these that stand by" (ver. 6, 7). It is at this point that the "ifs" of the Word of God come in, and are so solemn and significant. Whenever the matter is that of the pardon of sin, the justifying of the guilty, the gift of eternal life, Scripture ever speaks positively and unconditionally. The sinner is "justified freely by God's grace," and the "free gift of God is eternal life" (Romans iii, 24; vi, 23), in which places the word "free" means free of conditions, not only of payment. Eternal life therefore is what is called in law an absolute gift, in contrast to a conditional gift. The latter may be forfeited if the condition be not fulfilled; the former is irrevocable. But as soon as the sinner has by faith entered into this standing before God, then the Word begins at once to speak to him with "Ifs." From this point and forward every privilege is conditional.

By virtue of their relationship to Abraham all Israelites are natural sons of the kingdom which is the goal of their national hopes according to the purpose and promise of the God of Abraham; but the King has told them plainly, first that Abraham, Isaac and Jacob, together with all the prophets—that is, all the men of faith and devotion—shall be in that kingdom, but, secondly, that it is very possible that some of the sons of the kingdom may forfeit their entrance thereinto (Mat. viii, 10-12 ; Lk. xiii, 28, 29); for there are those who may have been first in privilege and opportunity who shall be last in final attainment.

If, therefore, an Israelite attains to that kingdom it will be on the basis of a covenant made by God with his federal head, Abraham ; the source of which covenant is the grace of God in Christ, the working principle of which on man's side is faith proving itself by obedience.   Wherein now does this differ in basic principle from that new and better covenant which introduces to better, that is, to heavenly privileges, to sharing the heavenly sphere of that same kingdom, not only its earth-ward side ?   This new and higher order of things is also derived from a covenant made with our federal Head, its source is in that same grace of God, its working principle on our side is a faith that proves its quality in obedience.

Moreover, since the man of true faith in that earlier age could aspire to this same heavenly city and country as ourselves (Heb. xi, 9-16) there manifestly was no difference in his position and ours in this matter, though it may be he had only a more distant view and not so full a revelation of the purpose of God in all this project.   So that if they of old could miss their share, on what principle of righteousness shall we be exempted from their need of diligence and obedience ?   Such exemption not only would contain an invidious and inexplicable distinction, but it would prove highly dangerous to our moral fibre and our zeal for godliness.   And has not this been seen ?

Paul's exhortation that believers should at least walk fully up to the standard set by whatever measure of light has been already gained (Phil. iii, 15, 16) connects naturally with the Lord's urgent call from heaven to the church at Philadelphia, " I come quickly ; hold fast that which thou hast, that no one take thy crown " (Rev. iii, 11).   Here again there is plain intimation, first, that there is a crown to be won ; second, that for winning it no higher attainment is required than is possible to us, even holding fast that which we have, which the context shows to mean a measure of spiritual power, fidelity to the word of Christ, and the confession of Him before men, with patience under the trials which such faithfulness may bring upon us (ver. 8, 9) ; and third, that the reward pictured as a crown may be lost. This agrees with both Col. ii, 18 and the passage from I. Cor. 9, that principally we are now studying. Indeed it should require no proof that the unsuccessful racer receives no crown. Lethargy may cause him to run indolently : previous indulgence of the body may have rendered him incapable of strain and have drained him of staying power : or disregard of the rules governing the contest may disqualify one otherwise " in the running," as the sporting phrase is. These three states we have already observed to be those which jeopardize our heavenly prospects. Esau was indifferent to his privileges ; sins of the flesh are repeatedly warned against, and especially so here by Paul ; and thirdly we are warned as to not allowing any deliberate disobedience to the known will of God, such as the precepts that we should pursue peace with all men, and not give way to anger, malice, or the like evils.

A consideration of the typical meaning of the " crown " brings the same conclusion as every other figure and statement. For the crown is used in Scripture as a sign of royal rank, and so at once suggests the dignity unto which we are to aspire and the possibility of forfeiting the same. It cannot be argued that the word *stephanos* does not import royal estate. That it does not necessarily do so, but sometimes refers to the garland of leaves won in the public games is true. The words in our passage, " they do it to obtain a corruptible crown" exhibit that meaning ; and so in II Tim., ii, 5. But the apostle expressly asserts that that which is the crown to us is something other and more than the athlete strove for, being so much more valuable than that as the incorruptible is nobler than the corruptible. To what other kind of crown *can* this contrast point than to the *royal* coronet, composed, as such have always been, of imperishable materials ? And the word *stephanos* was definitely used in this regal sense. For example, it is employed to describe the crown of thorns with which the soldiers wreathed the head of the Redeemer, which unquestionably they did in mockery of His claim to be *king*. But it is enough to know that the glory and honour which he now wears, and which betoken His universal sovereignty over all the works of God, are thus described: "we behold Jesus, because of the suffering of death *crowned* with glory and honour " (Heb. ii, ix.) Similarly of Adam as God's appointed sovereign of the earth, it is said that he was crowned (Heb. ii, 7); and so of the last Adam as the Ruler of heaven and earth. By suffering it was that He won that crown, and so it is properly a *stephanos* : and it is in that same acquired kingly rule that we are offered a share, and for it are called to strive and suffer. Thus our kingly crown also is a *stephanos*, and must be won, and may be lost.[1] But if a king suffer the loss of his crown he is no more a king; and thus we too, if robbed of our crown, have no more part in that company who are "kings and priests unto God."

It needs not, we hope, to be said that Paul makes not here the slightest reference to the question of eternal salvation. How often would a strict and sensible regard to the figures of speech employed save from false and blundering exegesis. The sinner apart from Christ is declared by God to be "dead through his trespasses and sins " (Eph. ii, 1) ; dead, that is, to God's realm of existence ; which statement is only an accurate description of the fact. But it is solely within God's realm of things that this race and crown have any existence. Therefore no "dead " person can be viewed as running in this course or striving for this crown. The rewards of Satan's kingdom the unregenerate may seek and win, for within that realm he is alive enough ; but he is utterly out of touch of divine experience and rewards, for him they simply do not exist as realities. It is therefore here necessarily taken for granted that the one-time dead sinner has received the life of God, or he *could* not run or strive. Hence it is not for eternal life that he aspires ;

1—Grimm's Lex (Thayer's ed), *stephanos*. A. prop. as mark of royal or (in general) exalted rank [such pass. in the Sept. as 2 Sam. xii, 30; 1 Chr. xx, 2; Ps. xx, (xxi), 4; Ezk. xxi, 26; Zech. vi, 11, 14 . . . perhaps justify the doubt whether the distinction between *stephanos* and *diadeema* was strictly observed in Hellenistic Grk.]. See also Voc. of N.T., s.v. στεφανος.

that he *has*: and it is not his life that he loses if " disapproved,"
but the reward that he, as a living man, might have secured.

And now to enforce this lesson upon his " brethren," the
inspired writer carries back their thoughts to Israel journeying
from Egyptian bondage to to the land of promise.

i. He first emphasizes that the whole people started with
equal providential and spiritual pivileges. They were not
deluded or deceiving professors, falsely claiming experiences
which they knew not, but were actual partakers of the vast and
saving benefits mentioned: it is expressly declared that they knew
and partook of the *spiritual* food and drink (Christ) of which
manna and living water were material types: " they did all eat
the same *spiritual* food, and did all drink the same *spiritual* drink:
for they drank of a *spiritual* rock that went with them: and the
rock was Christ." Thus they stand forth as a type of the real
believer, identified with Christ and partaking of Him.

ii. Also, they all had a title to, and a promise of, the glorious
land, God's sworn possession to their fathers.

iii. They had only to persevere awhile through the intervening
difficulties, and they would duly reach their goal; and thus

iv. By faith in the fidelity and power of their God they
would certainly gain possesion of their inheritance.

Thus, as a number of racers, they all started together and
without handicap, being all equal in opportunity and resources,
and the prize so ample that all might find a rich share: and yet
most of them never attained to it, but were overthrown in the
wilderness. The desiring of things evil; worshipping something
other than Jehovah; sins of the flesh; provoking God by declaring
that they wished that they had never come out of Egyptian
bondage; and murmuring against God's judgments and God's
leaders: these caused vast numbers of them to fail of the
possessions and joys which awaited them in Canaan.

There was, therefore, positive chastisement: " they were
overthrown in the wilderness," " they fell," " they perished,"
they came under the power of " the destroyer." How many
believers of our age would indeed have done well to have given

earnest heed to these things. How many have passed their lives in a wilderness of spiritual dearth and misery, and have died there after long wanderings, and all because they never pressed on to the better things of which God speaks. How easy it is to murmur against trial, to hanker after the forbidden things of the godless world from which we separated, or to give way to the lusts of the flesh. Such could have overcome, for God makes this possible for every one of His people; but carnal security induced laxity, and they fell.

Nor let us overlook the danger of things morally right over-engrossing, things present and pleasant. True are A. B. Simpson's lines:

> God hath His best things for the few
> Who dare to stand the test:
> God hath His second choice for those
> Who will not have His best.
> It is not always open ill
> That risks the promised rest;
> The better often is the foe
> That keeps us from the best.

So that there was, further, an actual loss of better things that were to come. They who suffer the positive chastisement in this life, dying in their hardness of heart and unbelief, forfeit their share of that which Canaan in this sense typifies. For that goodly land has a double significance typically. (1). As known under Joshua and down to the time of David's full conquests, it pictures the present conflict which the eager aspirer after exalted spiritual benefits must confront and sustain. Satan and his hosts set themselves to frustrate the christian warrior from obtaining enjoyment of his heavenly privileges in Christ. Power for righteous living, peace in troubled circumstances, joy under affliction, power in intercession, these and other such good things spiritual, our heavenly enemies will hinder our acquiring, or if we gain them, they will seek to rob us of them. (2). But the years of battle past, the Jebusites driven at length from Mount Zion (Ezk. xxviii, 16; Rev. xii, 7-12), then Canaan in Solomon's earlier years pictures that millenial day when the true Prince of peace shall reign before His ancients gloriously.

This latter aspect it is that is mainly now before us; only it must again be remarked that such as never enter the land never will enjoy its delights and glory. The redeemed but earth-bound heart to-day, neither knowing nor seeking the things that are above, content to believe his soul to be safe from hell, will take no part in the conflicts under Joshua and David, and will have no share in the glories of Solomon's household and government. "Wherefore let him that thinketh he standeth take heed lest he fall." And this exclusion will become plain as we pass on to the second of these special scriptures, the third and fourth chapters of the letter to the Hebrew saints.

In approaching this epistle it is imperative to observe that the christians addressed are not viewed as Jews belonging to the earthly nation. They are early and distinctly recognized as "holy brethren, partakers of (the) heavenly calling" (iii, 1). They had "endured a great conflict of sufferings" for the faith, and the "better and abiding possession" was so real to their hearts that they took joyfully the spoiling of their earthly possessions (x, 32-36); they loved the name of God, and showed it by serving His saints (vi, 9-12). It is as such that they are instructed, encouraged, and warned; the very argument of the epistle is based upon the fact.

They had been Israelites; but they had accepted Jesus as the Messiah, whilst the nation had rejected Him. This cleavage was too thorough, and duly became too wide, for any individual to be on both sides at once. Consequently Jewish christians lost their national privileges, such as the temple and priesthood and sacrifices; and how great this loss must have seemed to a devout Jew we may guage from the sorrow it still is to such. We have heard them with grief explain that the reason why they do not now offer sacrifice is that they have, alas, neither temple nor priesthood. And for these advantages the sincere of the nation still yearn.

But also the orthodox leaders soon persecuted the christian Israelites, and that very bitterly and often. So that to follow Christ seemed mainly loss; and thus the temptation was severe to turn back to Judaism, or at least to espouse Christ and His cause less vigorously. To counteract this tendency, and to save his brethren from the peril and permanent loss thus threatening, the writer, taught of the Spirit, addresses to them this letter.

i. His principal theme is the superior dignity, offices, and glory of the Son of God over all others, even the angels, as well as over the great leaders of Israel's national life, Moses, Aaron, Abraham, Levi, and Joshua. It was to the one Who is altogether unique in Person, and pre-eminent in power and glory, they had joined themselves. Let them not turn their back on Him.

ii. Next the epistle emphasizes that there is an actual heavenly realm of existence, with its throne and sanctuary, its immediate presence of God, its royal priesthood and eternal sacrifice, and many vast heavenly advantages, which are as much richer than Israel's earthly blessing as heaven is higher than earth. Of these divine things the tabernacle was but a copy; and who need sorrow to have left the picture for the original, or to have lost the shadow and have gained the substance? Far, far more than all that the sacrifices of animals could provide was theirs through the blood of Jesus; much more than the Aaronic priesthood could secure the priesthood of Christ guaranteed. Let them not forego these heavenly benefits in hope of retaining the imperfect and transitory earthly good.

iii. Lastly, whatever gain it was to Israel of old to be in Canaan as compared with Egypt and the wilderness, is to be indefinitely transcended by the "rest of God" which yet remaineth for the enjoyment of the believer. But even as many of Israel failed to reach the earthly inheritance, so let us also beware lest we fail to enter into the heavenly rest (chs. 3 and 4, spec. 4, 9-11).

The use that is made of the ninety-fifth psalm is characteristic of the treatment of the Old Testament by the apostolic writers which has been before remarked. It is pointed out

that by the mouth of David God refers to a "rest" of His own
which He had offered to Israel 450 years or so before, but as to
which He had sworn that they who rebelled at Kadeshbarnea
should never enter.   It is argued further (ver. 8), that not even
the next generation under Joshua entered into *that* rest, though
the land of Canaan, it is said, "had rest from war" (Josh. xi, 23).
For had the promise been fulfilled then God would not be
heard, after a lapse of centuries, still speaking of His rest as
awaiting the entrance of the faithful.   It is further evident that
none in the years that had intervened since God thus spake
through David had attained to such a condition as is implied in
the term "My rest," "for he that is entered into his rest
hath himself also rested from his works, as God did from His."
But the people of God are still toiling and striving in this world
of labour and conflict.   It is therefore concluded that there
must yet remain a sabbath-rest for the enjoyment of the people
of God.   And that none should fail to reach that blissful
era is the urgent message of the epistle.

But let us pause, for here is a ray of light as to what the rest
is *not*.   It has not yet been entered upon, and therefore it
remains, is the argument : and this is urged by and to men who
knew the fulness of present christian blessings in heart-
experience wrought by the Holy Spirit.   So that it is not here
intended to point to that inward state of peace which is the
present privilege of the saint.   By grace, not a few have known
the blessedness of being in perfect peace of heart as promised
in Isaiah xxvi, 3.   "The peace of God which passeth all
understanding" has been the mighty garrison of many that
had cause enough to have grown prematurely old with anxiety.
But not peace but rest is spoken of in these scriptures ; not
freedom from anxiety, but rest from labour, is what is here in
view.   So that it is somewhat that is future that is in question,
somewhat that is connected with circumstances and
surroundings.

And this meaning is required by the very force of the term
"sabbath-rest" (*sabbatismos*); for a *sabbath* rest is repose *after
labour*.   Hence we may further negative any thought that it is

the *eternal* rest of God which is here intended. For that state
of calm and repose in which God was and is eternally (and to
which necessarily all the finally saved will enter in the eternal
state), that rest, because it is a necessary attribute or condition
of the Almighty, has never been broken nor ever can be
disturbed, and this just because it is eternal and therefore
changeless. But this rest of which God speaks to man is a
sabbath rest, and therefore is a state which will follow upon the
period in which God is working.

Now after He had refashioned the earth, and had put man
upon it, and had seen with satisfaction that all was "very good,"
then God "rested from all His work which God had created
and made" (Gen. ii, 3). Thus He commenced a *sabbath* rest.
But, alas, the irruption of sin out of the angelic world into the
earthly sphere marred God's works, and constrained Him again
to start working to recover the ruin and restore beauty, for He
was by no means content to leave this world to the Enemy.
Thus the rest of God after creation was broken, and the greater
labour of redemption commenced. The Son of God asserted
that even down to His own day His Father had been working,
and not resting, and that Himself, the Son, was joined with
His Father in those works: "My Father worketh even until
now, and I work" (John v, 17).

This work is not completed in either heaven or earth. God's
servants are still labourers, working together with him (II Cor.
vi, 1 ; I Cor. iii, 9). The sacrifice which is unto God as a savour
of rest (as the term "offering of a sweet savour" means) has
indeed been offered at Calvary, and is the basis and promise of
that "rest which remaineth"; but the work of establishing
righteousness upon that basis, and so of assuring rest to the sin-
destroyed earth, is far from being accomplished. Nor can it be
completed save by the casting out from the heavenly places of
the rebellious angels who have disturbed those sacred realms
(Rev. xii, 9), and the pouring forth of the foretold and mighty
judgments which shall destroy the wicked from the face of the
earth, so that God's Spirit may be poured out upon all of mankind that are spared. When the brightness of the out-shining

of the Messiah of Israel shall have driven to perdition His foe
(Rev. xix, 19-21), the Antichrist, the last king of Babylon, the
coming world-emperor, then " it shall come to pass in *that day*
that the Lord shall give thee rest from thy sorrow, and from
thy trouble, and from the hard service wherein thou wast made
to serve, that thou shalt take up this parable against the king
of Babylon, and say, How hath the oppressor ceased! the
golden city ceased! The Lord hath broken the staff of the
wicked, the sceptre of the rulers; that smote the peoples in
wrath with a continual stroke, that ruled the nations in anger,
with a persecution that none restrained," and then shall it be
said with joy, " The whole earth *is at rest*—is quiet: they break
forth into singing" (Isa. xiv, 3-7). And as touching, not Israel,
but the church of God now labouring and distressed, the
promise is, " to you that are afflicted *rest* with us, *at the revelation
of the Lord Jesus from heaven*" (II Thess. i, 7). Then shall
Jehovah himself return unto His rest so long interrupted, as it
is written, " Sing, O daughter of Zion ; shout O Israel ; be glad
and rejoice with all thy heart, O daughter of Jerusalem . . . . .
The Lord thy God is in the midst of thee, a mighty one who
will save: he will rejoice over thee with joy, *he will rest* in his
love, he will joy over thee with singing" (Zeph. iii, 14-17).

It is therefore to the millenial day that these passages specially
point; and hence it is in harmony with all other scriptures that
strong exhortations are given which imply the possibility of
missing that rest, a possibility which cannot exist for even one
justified soul in relation to *eternal* security and repose. Let *us
fear*, therefore, lest haply, a promise being left of entering into
His rest, any one of you should seem to have come short of it " ;
and again, "Let *us* therefore *give diligence* to enter into that
rest, that no man fall after the same example of disobedience "
(Heb. iv, 1, 11).

We have a great priest, and drawing near habitually to Him
we may find pardon for past coldness and slowness, and may
find also grace to help in running the race that may yet lie
before us. Putting in Him our faith, by fully accepting and
responding to His word of promise (iv. 2), and thus diligently

obeying His call to press on to the goal, we shall duly arrive at His rest and glory. But let none dream that, because of Calvary's cross, indolence of spirit, or rebellion and unbelief, in His people, pass unvisited by God. The cross where the Son of God died because of sin can never be perverted into a pretext for allowing sin. Nay ! God's word—such a word as Psalm 95 here quoted and re-quoted—is " living and active and sharper than any two-edged sword, and piercing even to the dividing of soul and spirit, of both joints and marrow, and quick to discern the thoughts and intents of the heart. And there is no creature that is not manifest in His sight: but all things are naked and laid open before the eyes of him with whom we have to do" (Heb. iv, 12, 13), that is, to reckon (πρὸς ὃν ἡμῖν ὁ λογος).

We cannot escape from His scrutiny, nor deceive Him, as we may our fellow-christians, into thinking us to be diligent in things heavenly when in truth our heart is set upon things earthly. And this unchangeable oath shall certainly operate effectually against any entering into that rest who are unbelieving and disobedient. " Today; today "; cries our God, " harden not your heart " against My call that you strive to live wholly for My glory. " Today "—be not faithless but believing ; " today," labour in the work of the Lord ; " today " obey all My holy will, and especially that you set your heart on the things that are above, not on the things that are upon the earth, even its lawful things (Col. iii, 1-4). Oh, " Take heed, brethren, lest haply there shall be in any one of you an evil heart of unbelief, in falling away from the living God : but exhort one another day by day, so long as it is called To-day ; lest any one of you be hardened by the deceitfulness of sin : for we are become partakers of Christ, if we hold fast the beginning of our confidence firm unto the end : while it is said,

> To-day if ye shall hear his voice,
> Harden not your hearts, as in the provocation."
>
> (Heb. iii, 12-15).

The comments of William Kelly upon this chapter 4 are important. They are the more striking in that he would not have supported our view of the forfeiture of the millenial kingdom, and yet his own statements lead inevitably towards this conclusion. We quote from p. 65 et seq. of his *Exposition of the Hebrews*:

"The all-important point for a just interpretation is that God's rest is here before us, His glory with Christ. It is not at all rest for the conscience or the heart, which the believer has or finds now in Christ. The 'rest of God' is exclusively future. . . . . Faith makes both our own now; but we are called also to exult in hope of the glory of God. This is His rest; and we are going on toward it, as Israel to Canaan. Such is the text here applied. It is God resting in what satisfies His love and holiness when righteousness reigns and sorrow flees away, κατάπαυσις being stronger than ἀνάπαυσις. The former is applied in Gen. 2 (Lxx) when sin and death had not entered the world. It is used here also for the scene and time of glory, when they will be manifestly vanquished. . . . . It is impossible to understand the entire context if we regard the rest here spoken of as any other than the future rest of God into which Christ will introduce us at His coming. Wrest it to the primary need of the soul as men are apt to do, and all is confusion . . . The rest then is God's rest, made by Him, and suited to Him, which He will enjoy in perfected glory with those who believe in Christ, who alone by His work could fit sinful men to share it, perfected as they are through His one offering . . . .

"The present tense of verse 3 ['*do* enter into that rest'] is not historical but absolute, a usage most frequent in Scripture and in ordinary speech too, especially as to principles of truth . . . . There is no thought of an actual entrance now; for the whole argument shows the rest here is future, whatever rest may be for faith to apprehend before God shares His rest with all that are His own. This Epistle always regards the believer as on the way. The 'sabbatism' here in view is not yet enjoyed by the saints, but 'remaineth' (verse 9) . . . . .

K

"Verse 10 is an added word very characteristic of the inspired writer. It asserts the general principle, by the case put, that we cannot be working and have rest in the same things and in the same sense. When one is entered into his rest, he also has rested from his works. It is not at all the common notion of resting from bad works when a man gets peace with God. However true this may be, it has nothing whatever to do with what is here written. And this is demonstrable, not only from the whole passage treating, not of the soul's spiritual rest by faith of Jesus but of God's future rest in glory, yet by the comparison that follows, as God from His own (works). Now assuredly His works were never bad, but always and perfectly good. Nevertheless He is to rest even from the activity of His love to enjoy the glorious results. Such is the case spoken of. He that is entered into his rest is no longer busied with his works. It is a necessary principle and a blessed application to the matter in hand, and in no way a moralising upon a sinner ceasing from his evil works and finding rest in Christ. Now is the time for the saint not to cease from his good works. Soon he will enter the eternal rest of God. The prevalence of sin and misery calls for unremitting labour while it is day ; in this too we have communion with the Father and the Son (John v, 17). When they rest so shall we ; and eternity, as the active Arnauld d'Andilly said to Nicole, will be long enough to rest in. The A.V. is very faulty in its mistaken emphasis, which helps on the popular misapprehension.

"The eleventh verse concludes the caution against present rest for the Christian, followed by a statement of the means grace supplies to safeguard us through the wilderness . . . We are exhorted to earnest striving now ; for there is much that invites us to ease and relaxation. The very mercy of God to our souls might so dispose us . . . Immense is the deliverance from bondage and doubt and dimness by the simple yet profound gospel of God. Yet the danger of re-action is not small. We are saved that we may diligently serve Him. We are put into fellowship with God's feelings "as to all that surrounds us as well as what surrounds Him. This is not our rest, but our scene of labour where people and things are estranged from God. We shall rest when we enter what is perfectly according to His nature and purpose. Hence now and here below is the strongest call to diligence, not to rest . . .

"Let us then be diligent to enter into that rest, refusing every other. Israel is the great example of falling through not hearkening to the Lord. This is the fatal disobedience here spoken of. They stumbled at the word, being disobedient. And such is the danger of all Christians now, as well as those immediately addressed. We stop short, grow weary, make difficulties, get preoccupied, distracted from God's objects, attracted by things that are seen and temporal. We are called now to the work of faith and labour of love, while we patiently wait for rest in glory at Christ's coming.

Unbelief may work in us as in Israel as to both the way and the end. They were weary of the one, and they despised the other. Let us take heed that none of us fall into the same example of disobedience."

Others who take the "rest" as future are Bengel, Bloomfield, Weymouth, Govett, Delitsch, Alford, the last saying: "the promise still remains unfulfilled; they who at the time of its fulfilment shall be found to have believed, shall enter into it."

> Who would share Abraham's blessing
>   Must Abraham's path pursue;
> A stranger and a pilgrim
>   Like him must journey through.
> The foes must be encountered,
>   The dangers must be passed;
> Only a faithful soldier
>   Receives the crown at last.
>   *Paul Gerhardt.*

The alternatives of the argument in Hebrews iii and iv are thus inevadible. A redeemed earthly people had the promise of an inheritance, but many failed to reach it. A redeemed heavenly people have the promise of an inheritance, and are warned lest they fall after the same example of disobedience and come short of the goal. If the " rest of God " set before the latter be the eternal state, then redeemed persons may after all be lost. If this be not possible, *as assuredly it is not,* then the " sabbath rest " can be only the millenial, not the eternal. In this case (1) only actually redeemed persons can be in question, for such alone have any promise of the first resurrection and the millenial kingdom ; (2) the millenial kingdom may be missed by such as are heirs of the promise, or the very argument of the passage is futile, for it depends wholly upon the point that the " rest that remaineth " is as forfeitable as Canaan was by Israelites. That the heirs of the promise may lose eternal life *or* the millenial kingdom seem the inexorable alternatives.

We are persuaded that this same lesson from the rebellion of Israel at Kadesh-barnea is before the mind of the Spirit in the celebrated and much controverted passage which opens the sixth chapter.

It is the same danger that is before the writer's mind, that of not advancing, and therefore of retrograding, in christian knowledge, experience, and usefulness : " ye are become dull of hearing. For when by reason of the time ye ought to be teachers, ye have need again that some one teach you the rudiments of the first principles of the oracles of God ; and are become such as have need of milk, and not of solid food. For every one that partaketh of milk is without experience of the word of righteousness ; for he is a babe. But solid food is for full-grown men, even those who by reason of use have their senses exercised to discern good and evil " (v, 11-14).

Therefore he urges them to " press on unto perfection (full growth) "—a vigorous exhortation and a high standard. The passage reads : "Wherefore let us cease to speak of the first principles of Christ, and press on unto perfection ; not laying again a foundation of repentance from dead works, and of faith toward God, of the teaching of baptisms, and of laying on of "hands, and of resurrection of the dead, and of eternal judgement. And this will we do, if God permit. For as touching those who were once enlightened and tasted of the heavenly gift, and were made partakers of the Holy Ghost, and tasted the good word of God, and the powers of the age to come, and then fell away, it is impossible to renew them again unto repentance ; seeing they crucify to themselves the Son of God afresh, and put him to an open shame. For the land which hath drunk the rain that cometh oft upon it, and bringeth forth herbs meet for them for whose sake it is also tilled, receiveth blessing from God : but if it beareth thorns and thistles, it is rejected and nigh unto a curse ; whose end is to be burned " (Heb. vi, 1-8).

The whole picture is, in truth, very arresting. He views them as "babes." Now a "babe" in Christ has a title to a share of the family inheritance ; but if one die a "babe," or if though life be prolonged, there be "arrested development" and its consequent immaturity, how shall that one be competent for receiving and using the inheritance ? Hence the urgent exhortation "let us press on unto *full growth.*" It is delightful to observe in how short a time some "babes" grow to spiritual manhood, revealed in knowledge of God their Father, in wisdom, in power in service, in strength for suffering.

And now, counting upon their sympathy being aroused, he further exclaims, "and this we will do *if God permit.*" Is there then some doubt as to whether God will permit His people to press on unto fulness of experience and privilege ? Alas, there is grave doubt in the cases of some. Israel's example is the signal proof and illustration that God's people, chosen, redeemed, and beloved, may reach a state of heart when God absolutely prohibits their going forward toward His best and their highest privileges. For nearly two years He had led them on and urged them on—they followed haltingly, reluctantly, and with much murmuring. And when after He had brought them to within actual sight of the land, and they had plain testimony and visible proof of its goodness, they definitely refused to go forward, then at length God was driven to say, You shall never again have the opportunity to do so ! (Num. xiv, 28-35).

And when the next day the foolish and fickle people said they were ready to go on, and assayed to do so, God would not permit it, nor would He save them from the defeat that they courted by going against His fiat. Indeed, their then going up was as plain a proof of the rebellious state of their heart as was their going back the day before ; in both instances they went contrary to God's commandment.

Through Moses going to them in Egypt with God's message they had been " enlightened " as to their true God, as to redemption from judgment, and as to God's great purposes for them. Feeding on the passover lamb, and afterward on the manna, they had " tasted of the heavenly gift." [1] Drinking of the water that flowed from the smitten rock, or was otherwise supernaturally supplied (which, as ever, is a type of Christ giving His Spirit to the child of God—John vii, 37,38), they " were made partakers of the Holy Spirit." Hearing at Sinai the very words of God, and thenceforth discovering in the practice of life the suitability of His precepts to their daily walk, and how blessed are all they that keep His commandments, they " tasted the good word of God," or, " tasted the word of God that is good." [2] And as to their knowing the " powers of the age to come " how abundant was their experience ! A ray of divine glory ever in their midst ; a cloud that moved or stood by the volition of an unseen Presence, that the unimpeded desert winds could not disturb, and that perfectly guided and shaded them year in and year out ; water miraculously given ; the daily eating of angels' food ; clothing which did not wear out with age, and this in spite of the hard life of the desert ; these and many other startling demonstrations they had that heavenly forces were working around, upon, and for them.

But in spite of all these advantages and inducements they rebelled, through an utterly unreasonable and inexcusable want

---

1—Alford : " *have tasted* (personally and consciously partaken of)." Grimm. Lex. " to feel, make trial of, experience." " γευσασθαι expresses a real and conscious enjoyment of the blessing apprehended in its true character " (Westcott) Such enjoyment today of spiritual things in Christ seems not possible to the unregenerate.

2—. . . . "those spoken of had not merely tasted, but recognized. the goodness of the word of God." G. Milligan, D.D., *The New Testament Documents,* 68.

of confidence in God; and at Kadesh-barnea they "fell away," and God saw and declared that "it was impossible to renew them to a change of mind," that is, to make them thereafter dutiful and trustful. What was their cry "Would God that we had died in the land of Egypt" (Num. xiv, 2) but a hasty regret that they had accepted redemption at all ? What was their resolve "Let us make a captain, and let us return into Egypt " but an impulse to reverse the salvation effected by the the blood of the lamb slain and a putting Moses to an open shame as, in their view, an unsafe leader ? In this they were a type of those today who so openly turn from Christ and return to a worldly life as to "crucify to themselves the Son of God afresh, and put him to an open shame."

Such cases we have known. In an eastern land it was our joy to lead to Christ a cultured Englishman of good family. From the first he gave a fine public witness and maintained it for several years. Then he fell into sin, never humbled himself, and presently lapsed into the darkness of theosophy and occultism where he wandered before his conversion. Today he openly repudiates the Son of God and His atonement. Now had he died before his lapse no one could have questioned the reality of his conversion. But as all those earlier years the evidence was adequate, some other explanation of his fall must be found than the suggestion that he was never born of God, for the facts prove the contrary. And he is but one of many cases.

Those who so readily offer this too easy explanation should reflect that some to whom it would apply have returned to faith after many years, thus showing the reality of the early faith. The celebrated Professor F. W. Newman is an instance. In early manhood he was an earnest, devoted disciple, a companion of Groves, Darby, and the first Brethren. Then, for perhaps thirty or forty years, he was a leading sceptic ; but at the close of his long life he returned to the faith of his youth, and it was stated over his grave, by his own request, that he died trusting to the precious blood of Christ for salvation.

No one therefore is justified in saying that any particular person is beyond the possibility of repenting; nevertheless there are such who die in this apostate state, and it is these who are in question in Hebrews vi. Their unchangeable condition is known to God in their life-time, though not to us.

The few men of war were like the land that gives due reponse to the heaven-sent blessings, and "bringeth forth herbs meet for them for whose sake also it is tilled"; the many were as the plot that bore only the thorns and the thistles of faithlessness and rebellion. These latter were "rejected" by God : "they shall not see the land which I sware unto their fathers" (Num. xiv, 23) : for they had rejected God's special gift. And how "nigh unto a curse" they were these awful words of their God tell : "I will smite them with pestilence, and disinherit them" (ver. 12). And just as the present end of weed-producing land is that it be "burned," so it was said to them "your carcases (shall) be *consumed* in the wilderness" (ver. 33), a word which is used once again of Israel when later on God was rejecting them nationally : "The bellows blow fiercely ; the lead is consumed of the fire ; in vain do they go on refining ; for the wicked are not plucked away. Refuse silver shall men call them, because the Lord hath rejected them" (Jer. vi, 29, 30).

It will be still asked, Can such apostasy be possible in a real child of God ? are we not in this place at least driven to suppose that here (Heb. vi,) it is only professors making a fair show in the flesh, but not knowing the reality of divine grace, who are described ? Let us notice :—

1. These were *born heirs* to the land, being children of the covenant, and they were those who had been actually redeemed and emancipated.

2 The partaking in the benefits described implies the truly regenerate person. (See footnotes on the word "tasted").

3. Though they were "nigh to a curse" they were not actually cursed. Their noble leader interceded for them, and God said, "I have pardoned according to thy word : but in very deed, as I live" these rebels shall not see the land. Our great

Priest delivers His own perpetually from the wrath to come
(see I Thes. i, 10: "delivereth"), but He cannot, and would not,
hinder the severest chastisement and loss where such are due.

4. God saw to it that they never did get back to Egypt!
They perished in the wilderness, as a backslider may die in his
apostate state; but to the place which pictured unalleviated
separation from God they were not permitted to get back.

5. Even though they had forfeited the fullest of the proffered
blessings yet did God in most wondrous grace still deal with
them as His people, and not as foes. "In all their affliction He
was afflicted, and the angel of His presence saved them : in His
love and His pity He redeemed them; and He bare them and
carried them all the days of old" (Isa. lxiii, 9). "For about the
time of forty years suffered He their manners in the wilderness "
(Acts xiii, 18), feeding, clothing, guiding and protecting them,
and in fact doing for them all that He could do short of
restoring to them the prospect of entering the land that they
had rejected. It was thus, as we have already noticed, that
Reuben and Esau were dealt with by their fathers.

6. That the writer regarded those he addressed as genuine
saints is abundantly clear in the next verses (9-12). He was
"pursuaded better things" of them, though he thus warned
them : it was not of salvation itself but of "things that *accompany* salvation " that he was writing, not of escaping judgment
and slavery in Egypt, but of the benefits and prospects which
accompanied that deliverance. Unlike the salvation, these
latter were not yet secured and might be missed.

It is to be conceded that here is a picture of the extremist
kind of rebellion possible, and not of what we may term
ordinary failure. Lot's conduct in deliberately consorting with
the sinners of Sodom was a very different offence to Abraham's
failure of faith and of courage when he saw, as he thought, his
wife in danger in Egypt, and it was very differently dealt with by
God. For Abraham, though humbled, was helped, and was
restored to the hill-top communion with God, whilst Lot was
left barely to escape, and finally to close his days in shame,
conscious that his course had desperately corrupted his own

daughters, and involved himself in lasting dishonour. Let us remember the teaching in Galatians v, 21, as to the *practising* of gross moral or physical sin resulting in a disinheriting from the kingdom.

As in Esau's case, so with these men of war, it was a deliberate turning from high advantages offered, and indeed desired in measure, and a choice of the lower state because it seemed easier and more immediate. And have there not been instances of disciples facing God's call and leading towards high and noble living and full concentration upon heavenly things, but who alas, have feared to cut loose from the things that bound to the world ? Do none ever set the heart on the things that are on the earth though pleaded with by the Spirit to set the mind on the things that are above ? The full record of this aspect of powerful spiritual meetings, of holiness conventions, and of private labours by men who walk with God, has yet to be made known. A sad chapter it will prove to be as its tale is told of how alluring business or professional prospects, or worldly but fashionable marriage offers, or social and political ambitions, yea, and even sheer carnality, not to speak of a hesitant timidity that grieves and insults our faithful God, have caused some of His own people to turn back from the heights of conflict and of glory to the low level of being saved from perdition, as is believed, and then " making the best of both worlds," as is the hideously deceptive phrase, whereas it is in reality a making the worst of both.

Workers of long experience in the gospel have known ungodly persons who seemed utterly callous to eternal solemnities and impervious to heavenly appeals, whilst yet admitting theoretically the truth of all that the Bible teaches. And not so infrequently as might be thought it is learned that once or oftener such had been brought by the Spirit to a crisis, when a decision for or against Christ had to be made, and that it was by deliberate rejection that the state of apathy was reached which seems, and often proves to be, unalterable. And let those who have long and adequate experience in seeking to serve the people of God reflect upon cases of such as gave a clear account of a good conversion and of walking with God for a time, but who seem immovable as regards aspiring to elevated present experience and future and heavenly prospects. These admit the desirability of such a life and future, but present no sign of any determination to attain thereto. Most certainly it is not for us to pronounce upon any individual case, but rather to exercise the love that " hopeth all things "; but it is impossible at times not to inquire in one's own mind whether certain have not passed the limit of forbearance and been turned back to spend their days in the wilderness: "we will press on, *if God permit*."

As the Spirit ceases to strive with the ungodly remarked upon, so it is written of Israel as the people of God: "He said, Surely, they are my people, children that will not deal falsely; so he was their saviour. In all their affliction he was afflicted, and the angel of his presence saved them: in his love and in his pity he redeemed them; and he bare them, and carried them all the days of old " (Isa. lxiii, 8-9). They were His people, His sons, whose afflications He shared, giving them divine love and pity.   Himself was their Redeemer, and those whom He redeemed He bare and carried as a father his child.   "*But they*" —they "rebelled and grieved His holy Spirit: therefore He was turned to be their enemy—Himself fought against them " (ver. 10). And similarly we christians are warned that it is possible, not merely to grieve, but to *quench* the Spirit. Do we sufficiently reflect upon the inevitable consequences, present and future, that must surely attend so grave sin?

Thus is given, and given expressly for *our* admonition, the supreme example of how individuals may lose their place in the body corporate and their share in the fullest blessings open to attainment. Of course, God will perform His covenants, however long be the delay occasioned by His people's waywardness. In the fourth generation Abraham's posterity duly returned to Canaan; but *not all did so who might have.* Thus, too, God will have in His glory His church, and Christ will have His bride, and the universe will have its executive government. But let us each give heed that we obtain a full reward, and let us in love "exhort one another day by day, as long as it is called Today"—that is, so long as the opportunity for attainment remains open.

It surely ought not to be needful to add that the words, "whose end is to be burned," do not import the endless perdition of those so treated.   If it means that the thorns and thistles are to be burned, that would benefit and not finally ruin the land, and this would be a picture of the finally sancti-fying effect upon the believer of even the severest chastisement. But taking the meaning that it is the land that is to be burned, it still remains a picture of temporary affliction, for in any case the land abides.   And though burning it is a last resource of the farmer, yet the ultimate design and issue is beneficial. "Our God is a consuming fire": but the same fire which destroys the alloy cleanses the gold, though the process is drastic and may need to be prolonged.   The destruction of the flesh contributes, in the case of a child of God, to the salvation of the spirit, not from eternal wrath—that is secured by the cross of Christ—but as regards what must be faced "in the day of the Lord Jesus" (I Cor. v, 5.)

> "Across the will of nature
>   Leads on the path of God;
> Not where the flesh delighteth
>   The feet of Jesus trod,
> If now the path be narrow
>   And steep and rough and lone,
> If crags and tangles cross it,
>   Praise God! WE WILL GO ON.
>
> O bliss to leave behind us
>   The fetters of the slave;
> To leave ourselves behind us,
>   The grave-clothes and the grave;
> To speed, unburdened pilgrims,
>   Glad, empty-handed, free;
> To cross the trackless deserts,
>   And walk upon the sea.
>   *   *   *
> Oh, dare and suffer all things!
>   Yet but a stretch of road,
> Then wondrous words of welcome,
>   And then—THE FACE OF GOD!"
>
>   (Ter Steegen).

CHAPTER XV.

PRESENTED AT COURT.

" Every one therefore who shall confess Me before men, him will
I also confess before my Father . . . . . and the angels of God."
—Mat. x, 32, 33 ; Lk. xii, 8, 9.

An important instance of two passages being adjacent, of which the one seems to make an absolute statement and the other to have a conditional element, is found in the first chapter of Colossians. In verse 12 we read of " giving thanks unto the Father Who made us meet to be partakers of the inheritance of the saints in light," and in verse 23, before considered, it is intimated that we shall be presented " holy and without blemish and unreprovable before Him : *if so be that we continue* in the faith, grounded and stedfast, and not moved away from the hope of the gospel."

So evident is the conditional force of this latter passage, that it is exhibited by a writer who set out to prove that the being glorified with Christ is most certainly not forfeitable. But though this was the very thesis that he proposed to maintain, he did not get out of even the second page only of his pamphlet without undermining his whole case by writing thus : " Those who have received the gospel and know 'the grace of God in truth' are made meet for ' the inheritance of the saints in light,' and will be presented holy and unblameable and unreprovable before God, *on the one condition* of their holding fast ' the hope of the gospel.' " (italics ours).

As regards the former verse, here must apply the rules that the context must be regarded, and that a conditional phrase must modify one that seems absolute ; for if the process be reversed, and an absolute statement rules a conditional, the latter is necessarily nullified entirely. But in truth Col. i, 12, is not so strongly unconditional as it seems in its English form. For the proper force of the term translated " meet " (*hikanoō*, with its cognate *hikanotees* and its root *hikanos*) is not that of

187

worthiness but rather *capacity* and *ability*, and hence these
words in such connections are rendered "sufficient" (II Cor.
ii, 6, 16; iii, 5, 6) and "able" (II Tim. ii, 2). [1]   Thus the
expression points not to the acceptability of our person in
Christ our righteousness, but to that capacity for sharing and
using the mighty heavenly portion which is created by the
indwelling of the Spirit.   If the former were the point then all
justified persons of every dispensation might expect a portion
in the heavens, which idea is not warranted by Scripture;
but by the enduement of the Spirit now given, and linking
the saints effectively with One Who is in heaven, such
are rendered fit for sharing the glory of the sphere where they
are thus united to Him.   When that glorified One returns to
the earth, and His Spirit is again poured on men, those then
endued will have association with Him, blessed indeed, but on
earth.   We whose faith, by the Spirit, now attaches us to Him
in heaven—a much greater effort of faith, seeing that He is not
visible—are granted the capacity for the higher heavenly scene
where He is and where we take hold of Him.

We may therefore accept Alford's rendering and notes as
follows:

"Giving thanks to the Father Who made us (historical—by
the gift of the Spirit through His Son) capable (not *worthy*) for the
share (participation) of the inheritance of the saints in the light
(the inheritance is begun here, and the meetness conferred, in
gradual sanctification: but completed hereafter. tō phōs (is) the
region in which the inheritance of the saints, and consequently
our share in it, is situated)."

While the Colossian letter is before us it will be profitable to
gather the central thoughts of the great paragraph which runs
from verse 24 of chapter 1 to verse 7 of chapter 2, and which
reads as follows:

"Now I rejoice in my sufferings for your sake, and fill up on
my part that which is lacking of the afflictions of Christ in my

---

1—Paul did once use *hikanos* in the sense of "worthy" (I Cor. xv. 9). But such an isolated
use, when writing some years previously, and to different persons, and on a different theme.
cannot rightly govern the word as here employed, or require its being taken in other than
its normal sense.

"flesh for his body's sake, which is the church, whereof I was made a minister, according to the dispensation of God which was given me to you-ward, to fulfil the word of God, even the mystery which hath been hid from all ages and generations : but now hath it been manifested to his saints, to whom God was pleased to make known what is the riches of the glory of this mystery among the Gentiles, which is Christ in you, the hope of glory : whom we proclaim, admonishing every man and teaching every man in all wisdom, that we may present every man perfect in Christ ; whereunto I labour also, striving according to his working, which worketh in me mightily.

" For I would have you know how greatly I strive for you, and for them at Laodicea,'and for as many as have not seen my face in the flesh ; that their hearts may be comforted, they being knit together in love, and unto all riches of the full assurance of understanding, that they may know the mystery of God, in which[1] are all the treasures of wisdom and know-ledge hidden. This I say, that no one may delude you with persuasiveness of speech.

" For though I am absent in the flesh, yet I am with you in the spirit, joying and beholding your order, and the stedfast-ness of your faith in Christ.

" As therefore ye received Christ Jesus the Lord, so walk in him, rooted and builded up in him, and stablished in your faith, even as ye were taught, abounding in thanksgiving."

It is to be noted :

1.   That the great secret (mystery), formerly reserved but now revealed, has to do with that presentation of the glorified church to the Lord which we have before observed to be the special theme of the apostolic message (i, 28), and that it includes and declares all that God, in His divine wisdom and knowledge, has treasured up for the blessing of the universe. This is in strict accord with the statement in Romans viii, 19-21, that the releasing of the whole creation from the present

---

1—Of the various readings of this passage to which the revised margin refers, we follow that adopted by Grotius, Bengel, Meyer, De Wette, Alford, and Darby, considering that as the *mystery* is the subject of the whole paragraph, it is the most appropriate subject of this sentence also.

bondage to pain and corruption awaits the revealing of the sons of God. Creation was formerly established with a degree of splendour suitable to the dignity of Adam as its appointed ruler. When he fell his kingdom fell with him. But when creation's new rulers, Christ and His glorified church, are manifested, their kingdom will be elevated again with them. Are they for ever free from all pain and sorrow ; then so will their realm be. And by as much as their estate will be vastly more glorious than was that of Adam at the first, by so much shall the condition of creation be higher than ever before. Thus it becomes a natural consequence to take literally those promises of God which foretell for the earth and its occupants a future of surpassing beauty, fruitfulness, and joy. (See chap. 1).

2. This hope is marvellously inspiring to devoted service. Unto the furthering of this purpose of God Paul suffered gladly (i, 24), and laboured strenuously (i, 29—ii, 1) ; and greatly he rejoiced when he saw the saints living in such wise as gave hope of their being counted worthy of this calling (ii, 5, 7).

3. The apostle deemed it highly important that disciples should have " full assurance of understanding " of this final purpose of God. If the highest of prospects be unknown the highest stimulus to christian living, serving, and suffering will be wanting. The fullest appreciation of the magnificence of God's grace is known by those who best appreciate the magnitude of the benefits which that grace offers. The highest estimate of the Person and the cross of the Redeemer will be that of those who perceive most of all that which is conferred in Him.

4. It is further to be observed that the practical proof and basis of this hope is the present indwelling of Christ in His people. At this last thought we shall look closely, for it is pregnant with power.

When any person ignorant of God's counsels, or sceptically disposed in regard to them, hears of the christian hope, it is calculated to arouse incredulity. For a man solemnly to declare that he is expecting an hour when, on a sudden, an innumerable number of the long deceased shall start into life, and that at the same moment another throng of persons living on earth shall, with the raised, instantly find themselves clothed in a body spiritual, immortal, and glorious, free from the limitations of this earth-bound, death-stamped frame, the hearer is apt to question the credibility of the asserter of such things. And when the latter proceeds to add that these wonders will be accompanied by the instantaneous transfer of these raised and changed beings from the earth to some realm in the heavens above, astonishment deepens to amazement, and sometimes to indignation.

The christian should be prepared for this, since this scheme is of all schemes the most improbable from the human point of view. It is without parallel, and it involves some serious super-cession of the ordinary laws of matter, such as that of gravity, for example. Cemeteries have never been known thus widely to surrender their contents, nor throngs of mortals to rise bodily heavenward. The writer will not readily forget a still and lovely evening when, amid the shadows of a grove in a remote hamlet in South India, he explained this hope to a company of keen and educated Hindus, speaking English fluently, some of whom had come miles to attend the lecture. After the climax of the matter, the transferring of the saints to the superior world, had been reached, the question was suddenly interjected, " I wonder what you gentlemen are thinking about this program ?" : whereupon an elderly Brahmin, forgetting for the moment the suave courtesy for which his race are famous, blurted out the single word, " Impossible ! "

Seeing then that we are expecting the impossible—and *we are*—what is our justification for indulging such a hope ? How many of us are " ready always to give answer to every man that asketh us a reason concerning the hope that is in us " ? (I Pet. iii, 15). Yea, how many, or how few, who trust in Christ, know what the " hope " is, let alone can give a reason for the same ?

i. The reasonable basis for indulging such expectations is mainly twofold. First, as to the possibility of such an event, the proof is that precisely such a resurrection from the dead,

accompanied by the described change of body, and followed by
the ascending to the upper world, *has actually taken place in one
case*, and can therefore do so in any number of other cases if the
power that wrought in that instance be put forth upon other
subjects.

The resurrection and ascension of Christ as a literal event
is as indispensable to the christian hope as it is to faith. If
Christ were not raised it were vain to trust to His death for
justification, and still more vain, if that be possible, to look for
His return from heaven to receive His people to Himself, since
on that assumption He is not in heaven. Paul was not such a
poor thinker as some superior moderns affect to think. This
at least he knew, that no philosophy of man's erecting—and
what philosophy has been floated upon the ocean of speculation
since his day which was not, in essence, involved in those
current in his day?—that no philosophy could build into its
foundation or superstructure such an event as the bodily
resurrection of the literal person who died. Therefore it was to
disciples living at the centre of worldly philosophy (Corinth)
that he addressed his irrefutable discussion and proof of the
resurrection of Christ and of that of His people. Satan, too,
knows well that the fact of Christ's resurrection and ascension
is vital, and so he never ceases from seeking to discredit this
truth.

Christ's ascension is thus the valid ground for holding the
possibility and the certainty of that of the church in general ;
and of the certainty, as well as of the possibility, because the
same God Who promised to raise His Son from the dead, and
did so, has promised to do the same for the saints, and may be
trusted to keep His word to Christ's people as to Christ.

ii. But what is the ground upon which any individual may
rightly base a hope that he in particular is one of those to whom
the promise applies? The answer to this must be found in the
individual himself, or rather in God's work in him. "Christ
in you" is the "hope of glory." Christ *for* us on the cross is
the basis of that peace with God which the believer has as
touching the pardon of sin, but it is not by itself the ground

of assurance to the individual that he will attain to the height of glory. It is, indeed, the basis upon which God is able to propose to the repentant that they should go on unto perfection and glory; but "Christ *in* you" is the rational ground of assurance of being glorified.

And this is so because the glory consists in conformity to the image of God's Son (Rom. viii, 29), and that conformity is already in process of development in those in whom Christ now dwells; and the carrying on of a process is the simple and satisfactory ground for expecting the perfecting of the designed work: "He Who began a good work in you will perfect it until the day of Jesus Christ" (Phil. i, 6). If there is no sign of the process there can be no hope of its completion; but where the inner man is even now being moulded so as to reveal more and more fully and clearly the character of the heavenly architype, Christ Jesus, there is in such case solid and rational ground for expecting the perfecting of that work, including the fashioning of the outer man like unto the glorified body of the Lord. For this has been promised by God, and it follows naturally, since the method of the Lord is ever to work from within to without, and to complete that which He commences.

The practical bearing of this is obvious and salutary. The first step towards that glorious consummation is that we be purged from sin in the precious blood of Jesus: the next is that we co-operate with our God unto the developing in us of the moral likeness of His Son. And there is no middle ground between our "continuing in the faith" and Jesus Christ being in us, on the one hand, and our being, on the other hand, "reprobate" (II Cor. xiii, 5-7), which last term Paul had before used to the Corinthians (I Ep. ix, 27) of being refused the crown, as we have seen.

It is to be much observed that Christ dwelling in a believer is not a present inevitable consequence of conversion. There are those who have turned to the Lord that He may be their Saviour from perdition, and who stedfastly maintain that it is in Him only that they trust for this, but who get little further. Such may manifest a new interest in spiritual exercises, attending meetings and the like, and may even show some earnestness in religious efforts. And yet it may be still evident that it is what the *man* is, in his inner nature, that is presented to the beholder of his ways and spirit, and not what *Christ* is that is exhibited. "Ye in Me, and I in you," said the Lord to the disciples, and this was to result from His resurrection life being theirs (John xiv, 19, 20). This double association constitutes the full-orbed Christian life. The former experience alone—"ye in Me"—is but a partial salvation, which guarantees deliverance from perdition, since one who is "in Christ" cannot also be under a condemnation from which Christ is secure ; but alone it is not the ground of the "hope of glory."

Writing to believers who were failing to hold tenaciously the true faith of the gospel, Paul protests his deep concern for them in these moving words : "My little children, of whom I am again in travail until Christ be formed in you" (Gal. iv, 19). The formation of Christ in a believer is therefore a work additional to the setting of that believer before God in Christ, and is a work of such supreme moment that the apostle's large heart was as full of intense and soul-paining longing for its perfecting, as formerly, in their unconverted days, he had been solicitous for their regeneration. The heart of the pastor needs to be as deeply desirous for the growth of saints as that of the evangelist for their birth from above. Not the mere securing of vast audiences, nor the conducting of delectable services, nor the maintaining of successful organizations, are the important matters ; but rather the converting of the lost and the perfecting of the saints are the momentous interests of the christian ministry; and where preachers and pastors know throes and pangs of heart for these results to appear, there is the true work of God sure to make progress.

Paul similarly wrote to such advanced and healthy christians as those at Ephesus that he prayed for them that the Father "would grant you, according to the riches of his glory, that ye may be strengthened with power through his Spirit in the inward man ; that Christ may dwell in your hearts through faith; to the end that ye, being rooted and grounded in love, may be strong to apprehend with all the saints what is the breadth and length and height and depth, and to know the love of Christ which passeth knowledge, that ye may be filled unto all the fulness of God.

"Now unto him that is able to do exceedingly abundantly above all that we ask or think, according to the power that worketh in us, unto him be the glory in the church and in Christ Jesus unto all generations for ever and ever. Amen." (Eph. iii, 16-21).

Here again it is plain that the indwelling of Christ in the heart may not always accompany conversion, for he desires that Christ *may* dwell in their hearts. And there is shown a distinction between the presence of the Spirit and that of Christ, and that the latter is consequent upon the former, the Holy Spirit being He by whose power (not by Whose presence merely) the indwelling of Christ is produced. Where the Spirit indwells Christ may be developed, providing that the Spirit's power is not hindered by carelessness or wilfulness ; for it is only " according to the power that worketh in us " that God " is able to do exceedingly abundantly above all that we ask or think." On the side of the Holy Spirit there is not, indeed, any limit to the possibilities, but we may limit the Holy One.

The Spirit is in the saint as a Person, but Christ personally is at the right hand of the Father, and it is therefore *morally* that He dwells in His people. The Spirit dwells more especially in the *body* of the believer (I Cor. vi, 19), and sheds abroad His grace through the whole man, and thus by Him Christ is formed in the heart of the saint. The term heart covers in Scripture the three regions of the thoughts, the feelings, and the will. This is seen, for instance, in the three first places where the word is used. In Gen. vi, 5, we read of " the imagination of the *thoughts* of the heart " : in verse 6 we are told that by man's wickedness the Lord was " *grieved* at His heart " : and in viii, 21, we are informed that " the Lord said in His heart, I *will* not." And the work which the Holy Spirit is ready and longing to do in each child of God is to inform the intellect with the wisdom and knowledge of our Head in heaven, so that we can say that in measure "we have the mind of Christ" (I Cor. ii, 16). He can stay the flow of vain, merely human, not to say carnal, thoughts, and fill the mind with the ideas and conceptions of the Lord. The chief means to this end is the reverent and believing study of the Scriptures that He wrote for our learning. Then the Spirit can suppress in us all emotions that are not of Christ—selfishness in all its hydra-headed workings; and can impart ceaselessly the love of God, so that no sentiments triumph in us save those that are gracious, pure and loving; and "hereby we know that He abideth in us, by the spirit which He gave us," that is the spirit of love (I John iii, 24, 18). And thus it comes to be that, where Christ dwells morally in us, we shall be "rooted and grounded in love," and " be strong to apprehend with all the saints what is the breadth and length and height and depth, and to know the love of Christ which passeth knowledge"; and thus necessarily we shall " be filled unto all the fulness of God," since "God is love."

Moreover, the Spirit can remove the crookedness of the disposition native to all men, and well exhibited, for instance, by a child who answered her mother's question " Why do you do these naughty things?" with the frank avowal, " Well, mother, I *like* doing naughty things!" He renews the impetuous will until we *will* to do God's will, and can in some true degree say with Christ, "I delight to do Thy will, O my God." One wrote thus:

> " Thy wonderful, grand will, my God,
>   With triumph now I make it mine;
> And faith shall cry a joyous, Yes!
>   To every dear command of Thine."

Many others also have truly reached that blissful state of heart, and have been able to use the words of another poet, and to sing from the outflowing of a contented spirit,

> "I worship Thee, sweet will of God,
>   And all Thy ways adore;
> And every day I live I seem
>   To love Thee more and more.

Ill that He blesses is our good,
And unblessed good is ill ;
And all is right that seems most wrong
If it be His sweet will."

Where thus the mind and the desires and the will are renewed by the Spirit of the Lord, so that Christ's thoughts and preferences and resolves are effectually inwrought in the saint, and become the guide and impulse of daily life, there Christ dwells in the heart, and there His beauteous character is being developed and revealed. This is the basis for such to indulge the hope of reaching and sharing perfectly His heavenly glory, and this enables them meekly, but confidently, to give to others a convincing reason concerning their hope. Therefore it is not our wisdom to rest in any complacent notion that the initial act of faith, by which we accepted Christ as our shelter from the wrath of God, is all that is requisite to warrant these highest of expectations. Equally great is the error of thinking, even if it be only in our most secret heart cogitations, that we are sufficiently like our adorable Lord to be beyond risk of falling short. Rather must we go on to put in Him a continuous faith, asking that He will cause His sanctifying work in our hearts to advance daily. Yea, it must be our determined desire and earnest prayer that He shall remove, and keep excluded, from our heart every thought, feeling, and resolve that is not of Himself, so that He may verily be sanctified in our heart as Lord (I Peter iii, 15).

It is to be observed that the cleansing of the heart is not the same as the changing of the nature, though often confused therewith, and especially by such as teach the present eradicating of sin from the christian. The tendency or bias or natuie of the " flesh " in man is unalterable, and not improvable. Hence God gives a new nature, the " divine nature," to such as accept and live by His promises (II Peter i, 4). We find not that He teaches the removing of the old *nature* during this life ; but we do find that the *heart* may cease to be fed from that nature, and, by the Spirit, may derive its thoughts, desires, and decisions from Christ through the new nature. And through maintaining by faith the fellowship of the Spirit, this purifying of the heart, and therefore of the daily life, may be continuous and complete. But the tendency to "revert to the type," the former life, will assert its presence in the saint if he cease at all to live by faith in the Son of God. Hence watching and praying are ceaselessly needful ; and whilst they are exercised faith in Christ will assure victory and growth in holiness. Such as say they have no sin, and such as say that they cannot help but sin, are both far from perfection, whilst they are nearest to the goal who ceaselessly press towards it.

And one word more should be added. Whilst a measure of self-examination is beneficial, and is called for by the Word (I Cor. xi, 28 ; II Cor. xiii, 5), yet a little thereof is sufficient. It is not by overmuch occupation with our own heart that Christ is produced there, but rather by ceaseless heart-occupation with Himself in glory. "We all with unveiled face reflecting as a mirror the glory of the Lord, are transfigured into the same image from glory to glory, even as from the Lord the Spirit" (II Cor. iii, 18). It is good occasionally to look at the mirror, and to dust it if necessary ; but it is by the turning of the mirror sunward that it glows with the glory to which it is exposed.

[This theme is more fully treated in the writer's pamphlet *The Clean Heart*, as advertized].

O for a heart to praise my God,
A heart from sin set free !
A heart that always feels thy blood
So freely spilt for me !

A heart resigned, submissive, meek,
My great Redeemer's throne,
Where only Christ is heard to speak,
Where Jesus reigns alone ;

An humble, lowly, contrite heart,
Believing, true, and clean ;
Which neither life nor death can part
From Him that dwells within ;

A heart in every thought renewed,
  And full of love divine ;
Perfect, and right, and pure, and good,
  A copy, Lord, of thine !

Thy nature, gracious Lord, impart !
  Come quickly from above,
Write thy new name upon my heart,
  Thy new, best name of love.

                (*Wesley*)

CHAPTER XVI.

FOREORDINATION AND FREE-WILL.

"I would. . . .Ye would not." —Matt xxiii, 37.

It will be asked, How does this heavy emphasis upon the christian attaining consist with the teaching concerning the divine foreordination?

The answer is that a truth so abundantly revealed and powerfully enforced throughout Scripture will certainly be in harmony with all that Scripture teaches along other lines. But it may be that it will not altogether agree with some humanly constructed theories and theological positions as touching the profound counsels of God.

The suggestion has already been offered (ch. v) that it is in the realm of the heavenly kingdom, rather than in that of simple salvation from hell, that the foreordaining authority of God is exercised. This of itself intimates how much of the controversy upon the topic has been beside the mark; for divines have disputed as to the precise application of the scriptures in question to a matter to which do not apply, save in the very least degree, if at all.

And it may be futher enquired whether the divine decrees have not sometimes been interpreted in a too absolutely fatalistic sense, that is, that God's fiat has been unduly pressed to the virtual exclusion, or suspension, of man's God-given part in the great transactions in question. What if it be, for example, that God's decision always was that man should arrive at His kingdom and glory by the road of suffering and sanctification, and not apart therefrom? Certainly it was not according to our works, but according to His own purpose and grace, and this given to us in Christ Jesus before times eternal, that God saved us and called us with this holy calling (II Tim. i, 9); but be it noted that it was a *holy* calling, and therefore a calling to holiness, that was the purpose of God. Similarly we are reminded in Ephesians i, 4, that God " chose us in Christ before the foundation of the world, that we should be *holy* and without blemish before Him." Now what proof can be brought from the Scriptures to show that holiness *can* be attained by man apart from his own will, and his conscious, intentional, albeit God-empowered activity? That we cannot wholly trace out the secret workings of God is certain; and this may be more readily conceded seeing that we cannot always perceive the deeper, subtler workings of our own being. It follows that the interacting of the two invisible factors will be beyond our comprehending and defining. But our very ignorance should make us hesitate to dogmatize, and should throw us back upon the facts which are known and unquestioned; and of these facts one is that God deals with man as having the power to will, and complains that he wills not to agree with God (*e.g.*, Matt. xvi, 24-25; xxii, 3; Luke xiii, 34; xix. 14; John v, 40; vii, 17; viii, 44; Rev. ii, 21) and another fact is that each of us is conscious that we have this power and are morally responsible for its right use.

We do not find it stated in the Word, wherein God reveals Himself and His ways, that He either foreordained men to share the glory of His Son irrespective of their moral conformity to Christ, or that He pushes through His plan, which demands holiness in its subjects, without regard to the co-operation of the believer in his own sanctification. A forced sanctity were no pleasure to the heart of God; and this were just as much so if the compulsion were secret as if it were recognized by us.

The passage mostly urged against the view that we are advocating is Romans viii, 28-30, which reads thus; "And we know that to them that love God all things work together for good, even to them that are called according to his purpose For whom he foreknew, he also foreordained to be conformed to the image of his Son, that he might be the firstborn among many brethren: and whom he foreordained, them he also called: and whom he called, them he also justified: and whom he justified them he also glorified."

1. It is significant that this noble statement opens by an emphasis upon *our love to God,* and not first upon His resolves

concerning us. Now the Biblical definition of our love to God
is that we keep His commandments (I John v, 3), and such loving
obedience is just true sanctification, and neither more nor less.
So that it is to the sanctified that the following clauses apply;
and we ask upon what ground any others than those who love
God, that is, who live in obedience to Him, are entitled to take
to themselves what follows ? That all who are justified might be
and ought to be of the sanctified is true ; but it is not fact that
every person who has known the peace of the justified abides
in a state of love to God, that is, of obedience to His
commandments. Our Lord explicitly warned the disciples
upon the possibility of ceasing to enjoy His love, by saying, " *If
ye keep* My commandments, ye shall abide in My love " (John
xv, 10) ; and the church at Ephesus is searchingly reproved for
having left its first love, the proof of which decay was that they
were no more doing the " first works." (Rev. ii, 2, 5).

2. The fact that God's foreordination was guided by His
foreknowledge shows that it was not merely arbitrary, but was
conditioned ; and this is declared, and must be allowed, even
though we may not be able to determine what it was that, being
foreknown by God, influenced His ordaining act.

3. It is plain that God's foreordination was not applied to
the matter of who should or should not go down to the pit,
but was concerned with what persons so delivered should be
finally, in the heavens, made like unto His Son in character and
glory. " To accomplish this transformation in us is the end, *as
regards us*, of our election by God ; not merely to rescue us from
wrath," and that Christ " might be shown, acknowledged to be,
and be glorified as THE SON OF GOD, pre-eminent among
those who are by adoption through Him the sons of God.
This is the further end of our election, *as regards Christ*: His
glorification in us " (Alford). How, *at the coming of Christ* to set
up His Kingdom, shall these ends be served in the cases of such
believers as may have thwarted His purifying work, and have
so died, in a backsliding state ?   At the judgment seat such
will appear morally as they were at their decease.

4.   As soon as one arrives at the point where God's purpose is to take effect, and, hearing the good news, is "called," immediately the human element enters as a condition upon which the divine ordination takes effect.   For the called may refuse to respond (Mat. xxii, 1-14).

5.   In the next step, that of justification, also, the faith of the sinner who is giving attention to the call is again the condition set forth by God Himself upon which the purpose of God advances.

It is thus evident, as was before said, that the foreordination was conditional: in advance it was conditioned by somewhat that God foreknew; and in development it requires as self-involved conditions the response and the faith of its object. If therefore we find from this and other scriptures that sanctification is also required with a view to the glorified state being reached, that will but be in harmony.

6.   And in this connection it is proper to add that the word justified is sometimes used by the Holy Spirit to include sanctification.   As regards the delivering of the guilty from justly deserved wrath, this is effected solely and perfectly by the imputing to faith of that which Christ is and has done; and the sinner is thus justified apart altogether from works of his own.   But there is a fuller sense of the word in which it is considered as including the changed life of which it is the commencement.   Thus in its first use in this same epistle we read that the "doers of law shall be justified"—accounted righteous (Rom. ii, 13).   And again we find in James that Abraham and Rahab were justified by works.   Not that the "doing" and the "working" are the meritorious ground of justification; but they are the occasion in the one case, and the proof in the other, of the sinner being justified.   But in both cases the works are included under the term justification.   Similarly, the two are blended in the words (I Cor. vi, 11), "but ye were sanctified, but ye were justified in the name of the Lord Jesus, and in the Spirit of our God."

At this late place in the apostle's exposition, after he has laboured the question of holy living as well as that of justification, we judge him thus to combine the two aspects in one, and to mean the term justified to cover the sanctity of life that it makes possible and therefore demands, but which the justified may largely fail to produce, or cease to produce after having long brought it forth by the Spirit.

7. But we may further urge that this passage must not be read apart from its preceding context. (a) The sense that those would give to it who differ from our view practically ignores the fact that chapters six and seven intervene between chapters three to five and chapter eight of the letter. They as good as say that sanctification has no indispensable place in the glorifying of the child of God ; and so the orderly development of the exposition is set aside. This is like taking out the middle floor of a building and expecting the upper storey to remain in its place. (b) These sentences must be construed in harmony with the teaching immediately before given, even that our being glorified with Christ is dependent upon our suffering with Him (ver. 17). A preceding passage must not be ignored in dealing with one that follows upon the same subject, nor the latter be forced into conflict with that which goes before. These two verses are strikingly parallel with those before dealt with from Colossians i, in the proximity of a seemingly absolute statement to one plainly conditional.

Our passage must therefore (1) be read in the light of its context; and (2) of its late place in a consecutive exposition which has included a heavy emphasis upon practical holiness ; and (3) of the fact that the word "justified" may include the practice of holiness ; and (4) of the overwhelming consensus of the rest of Scripture : and we conclude that it cannot be made the basis of teaching that every justified person is unconditionally guaranteed a share in the heavenly glory of the Lord Jesus Christ. Thus Tindale wrote on this passage (see Wescott's *A General View of the History of the English Bible*, 1905 ed., 141), " God choseth of his awne goodnes and mercye : calleth thorow ye gospell: justifieth thorow faith and glorifieth thorow good workes."

They who would make it teach the opposite of this are obligated to show that their view is in harmony with all the rest of God's Word upon the subject ; that is, it is incumbent upon them to give as straightforward and harmonious an explanation as we have sought here to offer of all the large array of Scripture which is now before us.

But it is urged that the series of past tenses used in this passage shows that from God's point of view He sees the believer as already glorified as much as justified.   True, He does ; but this does not forbid that some for whom He prepared that destiny may forfeit it.   So heavy is the possibility of failure that we have from our Lord's lips this solemn word concerning those for whom a feast was provided and to whom the invitation was first sent, "I say unto you that *none of those* men which were bidden shall taste of My supper " (Luke xiv, 24); although it was expressly for them that the provision was in the first instance made.   The guests invited to the bridal supper may have their place taken by others, if they be found unworthy (Matt. xxii, 8).   Closer yet ; the special virgins that should attend upon the bride at the supper, may lose the opportunity (Matt. xxv, 1-13).   Finally, it becomes strictly a matter of proof from Scripture as to whether individuals who might have been of the comany that form the " bride " may not have a similar experience.   Or rather, considering how uniformly the principle applies in other circles of the redeemed, as well as to the perishing, the duty of proving that the company that will form the bride is exempt from this principle is upon those who allege the exemption.

It is the assumption that God's foreordination is absolute and irreversible *as touching the individual* that is not proven and that would throw this passage into conflict with the consensus of Holy Scripture.   In His purpose God did glorify all in question ; but equally in His purpose does He see every justified one as already seated "with Him in the heavenly places, in Christ Jesus" (Eph. ii, 6), and equally true it is that the Holy Spirit is ready to make this an operative reality to faith ; yet very many by carnality or ignorance are forfeiting this elevated experience, in spite of it being part of God's plan for them !

Again, it was God's *sworn covenant* to Abraham that his seed should return to Canaan, and He was ready to take there every child of Abraham ; yet six hundred thousand individuals missed the covenanted grace, and, later, some of the tribes were warned that they might occasion that second generation also to miss the promised land (Num. xxxii, 14, 15). No purpose of God can be more absolute than a covenant to which he binds Himself by an oath which involves His very existence, and such was His bond graciously given to Abraham (Gen. xxii, 16). This has been partly performed, and will be completely so in the yet coming restoration of Israel; but that oath did not hinder God taking'oath again in this dread utterance against those individual children of Abraham who proved faithless and rebellious ; "I have pardoned," He said to Moses, "I have pardoned"—they are forgiven " according to thy word ; but in very deed, *as I live* and as all the earth shall be filled with the glory of the Lord ; because all those men who have seen My glory, and My signs, which I wrought in Egypt and in the wilderness, yet have tempted Me these ten times, and have not hearkened to My voice surely *they* shall not see the land which I sware unto their fathers neither shall *any of them* that despised Me see it : but My servant Caleb, because he had another spirit with him, and hath followed Me fully, *him* will I bring into the land " (Num. xiv, 20-24). Surely nothing can be clearer than the way in which individuals, being all equally, by birth and standing, within a general purpose and covenant of God, are thus discriminated for or against the obtaining the offered benefits.

As justifying this exposition of these past tenses we draw special attention to certain words of Moses in the song the people sang at the Red Sea, wherein the passing of the nation through the desert in safety, and their entrance into the land, are spoken of as already as much accomplished as was redemption and freedom from Egypt. Verses 13 and 17 of Exodus xv are in this respect strikingly parallel to Romans viii, 30 :—

" Thou in Thy mercy *hast led* the people which Thou
    hast redeemed :
Thou *hast guided* them in Thy strength to Thy holy
    habitation.
The peoples *have* heard, they tremble . . . . . .
Thou *shalt* bring them in, and plant them in the
    mountain of Thine inheritance."

Yet of those whose entrance into the land was thus celebrated
in advance, the whole adult manhood of the nation, save two
men only, never arrived there.   The nation *corporately* arrived,
and the song found its fulfilment ; but all those *individuals* who
disobeyed dropped out of their place and prospects.

God's covenants will most assuredly be fulfilled ; but we are
wrong if we suppose that they are so phrased or so operate as
to condone sin in His children ; and we are failing to grasp one
most momentous fact concerning them if we overlook or make
void the truth that, *as against the individual*, they are revocable.
"Ye shall know My alienation," said God ; the force of which the
margin gives in the words, " Ye shall know the revoking of My
promise " (Num. xiv, 34).   Very solemnly is this emphasized
by a comparison of Ex. vi, 8 and Ps. cvi, 26 : "I will bring you
in unto the land, concerning which *I lifted up My hand* to give it,"
said their God, " and I will give it you for an heritage : I am
Jehovah."   But the people were found despising the land, and
murmuring and rebellious.   " Therefore He (the same Jehovah)
lifted up His hand unto them that He would make them fall in
the wilderness."   The repetition of the same phrase to indicate
His revocation of His promise is striking.   The uplifted hand
is, of course, a reference to the posture of the person taking oath.

As we have before shown, even after this nothing separated
them from the *love* of their God, but " in His love and in His
pity He redeemed them ; and He bare them and carried them
all the days of old " (Isa. lxiii, 9), for that love was toward them
not for their own sake, but out of God's regard to their fathers
(Deut. vii, 7, 8).   And thus nothing that we are urging
invalidates the mighty conclusion of the apostle that our God
and our Intercessor stand up at all times for our *justification*
(Rom. viii, 33), and that nothing shall be able to separate us

M

from the *love* of God, for that love is toward us not because of what we are but is upon us "in Christ Jesus our Lord." But we individually, as Israel, may cause an inevitable and irreversible withholding of somewhat that that love was ready to bestow, and in its own plan had bestowed.

Be it remembered that it is God Himself Who again and again takes up this page from Israel's history, and demands our repeated attention to its pregnant lessons and warnings (I Cor. x ; Heb. iii, iv.). The Corinthian passage shows the certainty of application to members of the church of God, and this forbids the attempt to limit the warnings in Hebrews to "Jewish" believers. And thus saith Jehovah, "To this man will I look, even to him that is poor and of a contrite spirit, and that *trembleth at My word*" (Isa. lxvi, 2).

It is surely consistent with this view of the electing will of God that we find another apostle most insistently exhorting saints to "give the more diligence to make your calling and election sure " (II Pet. i, 10).

Here once again is a brilliant example of how words which are perplexing to those who hold to the final salvation of the once justified, can on our present basis be accepted in their simple and cogent force.

If words teach anything these teach that our "calling and election " is only "sure " if we by much diligence make it so. If, therefore, the calling and electing are unto deliverance from eternal wrath, it would seem that they are right who assert that this deliverance may be forfeited by such as had formerly accepted the same. But Peter himself shall correct this erroneous thought by his earlier statement that it is " unto *His eternal glory in Christ*" that "the God of all grace " has "called" us (I Ep. v, 10). Here God's own glory, "His eternal glory," [1] and not merely some degree of blessedness of a lesser order, is that unto which His calling invites the church. And this is to be realized "in Christ," in union with Him ; and this at once allies

---

1—The pronoun and adjective have definite meaning and force εἰς τὴν αἰώνιον αὐτοῦ δόξαν: *eis tēn aiōnion autou doxan.*

the prospect with His own words in John xvii. 22 ; " the glory which Thou hast given Me, I have given unto them." It is all a question of the glorifying of the believer, and not of the sinner being rescued from the pit of darkness and eternal abhorrence. It was " by His own glory and virtue " that God called us, and it was "into His marvellous light " that we were called ; that is into the light of the prospect of sharing the glory of Him Who is Light, and in which glorious light the inheritance of the saints is located (Col. i, 12).

What bright illumination the knowledge of this calling and prospect throws upon all questions they know well who walk in its light. Numerous problems of present moment to the christian are easily settled when viewed in the light of the " calling wherewith we are called " ; for many things are seen to be unbecoming those who have such expectations as these, which things might have passed unquestioned but for this hope. Conduct that ordinary folk might indulge unquestioned will not be thought fitting in princes of the royal house ; and such as are seeking to qualify for such rank and service will abstain from all that does not contribute to the desired fitness.

Harmonious is the mind of Peter with that of the other inspired writers. With the Caller and the calling before his vision he, as they, earnestly exhorts believers unto holiness, saying, "like as He Who called you is holy, be ye yourselves also holy in all manner of living ; because it is written, Ye shall be holy, for I am holy " (I Pet. i, 15, 16). He too reminds us that an inevitable element in this calling is that it involves us, as it did Christ, in suffering, and this often the peculiarly painful sort of suffering of being persecuted for well-doing (I Pet. ii, 20, 21). He teaches that it is along the line of patient endurance and holy living that we shall inherit blessing (I Pet. iii, 9), and that, after we have thus suffered a little while, we shall be perfected in the eternal glory (I Pet. v, 10). So that the connection between the daily holiness and patience in suffering of the saints with their calling and glory is as plain in Peter's writings as in the rest of the Scriptures.

And to his heart, as to that of Paul, there was ever present a
sense of the constant danger of saints becoming indolent.
Therefore he thought it right to stir them up—a process that
the sleepy resent until sufficiently awake to perceive the
approaching danger and the kindliness of their disturber. Yea,
he was so solicitous for their progress as christians that he
would give diligence that not even after his decease should they
be able easily to forget their call of God to the eternal kingdom
(II Pet. i, 13, 15).

God on His side has most graciously done all that is necessary.
He has called us to set our hearts away from this world, and to
journey as pilgrims here to our home in His glory (I Pet. ii, 11);
and He has granted all things needful for our welfare by the
way (II Pet. i, 3, 4). We by faith have responded to the call,
and have started on the upward journey; but, oh, the danger
of turning again to the beggarly elements of humanly invented
beliefs or hopes, and of thus becoming slothful as pilgrims.
"Give diligence . . . give the more diligence," earnestly cries
the apostle. Even the proper and divinely allowed engagements
of your pilgrim days are but temporary and incidental; much
more be not overcome by things carnal and unlawful. Your
urgent care must be that out of the faith that is in you should
develop all that is virtuous and excellent (arete). Out of this
will spring more knowledge (gnōsis) of things heavenly, and
thus will you become strong to control all your being and its
cravings (enkrateia), and be equal to the strain of persevering in
your toilsome journey. The heart being thus godly in its condition shall manifest a love of your fellow-pilgrims (philadelphia);
yea, fed from the heart of Him at Whose call and to Whose
presence you journey, you shall have a wide and general love
(agapē) for those who do not travel with you, and for even
those who persecute you for being not like themselves, earth-
bound and ungodly. Such an active, vigorous condition of
soul obtaining, you shall not be as those whose inner man has
become stultified, and whose education and development are
arrested, as a tree, though living, may cease to increase and may
become unfruitful, but you shall advance unto the perfect
knowledge (epignōsis) of our Lord Jesus Christ.

But where, we now ask, can perfect knowlege of Him be reached save in His actual presence, when we shall see Him as He is, and shall know fully even as we have been known fully by Him ? (I Cor. xiii, 12). Until we see His glory there must needs remain some definite imperfectness in our knowledge of Him. Therefore the apostle has now led our thought to the goal to which all apostolic thinking ever travelled, the face to face vision of the Lord ; and it is along the path of persevering conformity to Him in the present that Peter has caused our minds to travel forward to reach that consummation. It is at this point that, with tremendous emphasis, he then beseeches the saints to give diligence to make their calling and election sure, adding, " for if ye do *these things* ye shall never *stumble.*" He does not say that they shall in themselves be perfect whilst on the journey, but he does say that so they shall continue journeying without stumbling, and therefore without falling, and therefore without risk of some injury by the way hindering them from reaching the desired goal.

That a pilgrim should make mistakes and commit faults is indeed to be deplored, but that is not the same thing as his " stumbling." Viewing us as men on earth the Scripture says that we all stumble, and especially in word (James iii, 2) ; which divine dictum should forbid any thought that we are already made perfect. But viewed as men *on a journey* to stumble means something more, even so to trip as to cease to journey. Israel has stumbled at Christ Jesus because He came in humble guise and not in glory, and because faith in Him was set forth as nullifying any hope of their becoming righteous toward God by self-effort (Rom. xi, 11). Thus for nineteen centuries the nation has made no progress toward the grand end God appointed for them nationally. From any such stumbling God is able to guard us, so as to set us at length before the presence of His glory (Jude 24), the intended goal of our pilgrimage as christians.

But if His guardianship is to be profitable to us, it must be taken advantage of by us, for we are guarded by Him "*through faith*" with a view to that salvation which is ready to be revealed in the last time (I Pet. i, 5). Picture a desert caravan, so common in the east, attended by a military escort. Clearly each individual member of the party must exercise personal diligence to stay under the care of the escort, if safety is to be assured. Rebecca must remain with Abraham's men (Gen. xxiv). It is imperative, therefore, that we give on our part all diligence, and ceaseless diligence, to provoke our faith into that activity which issues in virtue and the other graces named, for it is only "*if ye do these things* (that) ye shall never stumble," and that "*thus* shall be richly supplied unto you the entrance into the eternal kingdom of our Lord and Saviour Jesus Christ" (II Peter i, 10, 11).

It is to be observed that it is of the eternal, and not the millenial, kingdom that the writer speaks, and hence his distinction between the degrees of honour that will attach to the entrance thereinto. Into the eternal kingdom *every* saved person *must* at last enter, for to be outside that kingdom is to be eternally lost ; but some will pass in by the gateway of the first resurrection, and reach the glory of sovereignty in the kingdom (Rev. xx, 4), and some will reach that eternal age by the second resurrection, saved because of their names being written in the book of life, but not elevated to the glory of royal estate.[1]

That there will be degrees of honour among those who share the first resurrection is sure ; one servant was appointed over ten cities, and another over but two, and each according to his fidelity and proved capacity. But as to the heartiness of their welcome into the joy of their Lord He made no distinction, but used the same words of welcome to both alike, saying, " Well done, good and faithful servant ; enter thou into the joy of thy Lord " (Matt. xxv, 21-23) ; whilst the unfaithful servant had no entrance at all into that joy, nor any place of authority in his Lord's service, albeit his *life* was spared, as is clear from

1—That there will be saved persons at the great white throne judgment is obvious from the phrase used in Rev. xx, 15, "*if* any (man's name) was *not* found written in the book of life, he was cast into the lake of fire." If this indefinite, negative mode of expression was not intended to show that the name might be found in the book of life, it is, to say the least, singularly calculated to mislead, a fault which may not be imputed to Holy Scripture. What would be the force of the statement that—a great crowd was at the barrier, and if anyone was found *not* to have a ticket he was not allowed to pass ? Would not this imply at least that some there had a ticket?

Luke xix, 27 : "*But* (in contrast to the treatment of the unfaithful servant just detailed) those Mine *enemies* . . . . slay them." Exactly so does the Revelation pronounce each and all to be alike "blessed and holy that hath part in the first resurrection" (xx, 6), and this whether they were of the company of the " first-fruits," who escape the great tribulation period (xiv, 1-5), or of the multitude that come victoriously through that persecution (vii, 9-17), or of the prophets and saints that are raised at its close (xi, 18). Though doubtless some will have greater glory and fuller authority than others, yet as to their entrance these are all grouped together as sharing the reign of Christ (xx, 4), and it is this matter of freeness of entrance, not of more or less honour, that Peter raises. All who were ready for the marriage feast, though differing possibly in the splendour of their apparel, as in their rank, went in as freely, and by the same door, as each other ; though once within some would be preferred to couches nearer to the king than would be allotted to others less worthy.

It would therefore seem to be inapplicable to draw a distinction where Scripture appears not to draw one, namely, in the liberty of entrance of those who reach the kingdom at its opening day. And hence the distinction that remains is that the " richly supplied" entrance is that which ushers into the eternal kingdon via the millenial kingdom, as contrasted with the general entrance into the eternal kingdom of all ultimately saved from perdition.

"Let us therefore give diligence to enter into that (millenial) rest," so that no man fall out of the company on the road thither (Heb. iv, 11); and thus shall we, by His grace, make sure our calling and election to God's own glory, and be for ever "to the praise of His glory" as it will thus and then and there be put upon us through Jesus Christ our Lord.

CHAPTER XVII.

TIMELY TRUTH.

" Who bringeth forth out of his treasure things NEW and old."
—Mat. xiii, 52.

Those who have moved longest in the christian circles where the topics connected with the heavenly kingdom have been more habitually expounded, will, upon reflection, feel that the most intensely solemn of the passages here considered have been but seldom mentioned, and then almost always to be robbed of nearly all message and power to the saint by being applied to the sinner.

A singular fact of nineteenth century spiritual history is worthy of note.

It was by means of His enlightening a small group of very godly, and distinctly competent and independent, students of Scripture, that God, about the year 1828 and onward, restored to prominence the truths of the oneness of the church of God and its heavenly calling and prospects. The whole of the churches are under a heavier spiritual debt to the labours and teaching of these men than has been generally acknowledged. And yet the body of believers that gathered around them, and who were, in those earliest days, perhaps the greatest force in England for spirituality and godliness, *very quickly* failed to maintain the high experience to which the truths named lifted them as christians. For " Brethrenism," as the movement came to be called, within only twenty years of its rise entered upon and continued in a course of faction and division. Why this striking failure to correspond in life and practice to the heavenly pattern ?

Doubtless many influences combined to serve Satan's purpose to spoil this, from his point of view, eminently dangerous upward movement. But we cannot but enquire, even though no definite answer be possible, whether the teaching that the very highest of all God-given prospects, those, namely, which

214

we have been considering, are secure irrespective entirely of the tone and quality of daily living, may not have been a subtle, indefinable influence, inducing unconsciously a laxity in practical life, which showed itself in the guilt and danger of strife, jealousy, and the like heart evils, not being appreciated, the prominent and powerful warnings against these sins having been emasculated.   Certain it is that two of the noblest and earliest leaders of that movement, men worthy to be classed with the rarest saints of the centuries, did hold that the first resurrection is a privilege that may be missed.   They were A. N. Groves and R. C. Chapman.   It was so with another prominent person of those days, Lady Powerscourt (*Letters*, 143-147).

The great teachers of that period restored the proper emphasis to the truth that God is calling the saved of this age to a place in the heavens as the bride of His Son.   But they attached to this privilege that certainty of possession which the Word attaches to the possession of eternal life only.   How different might their and their followers' history have been had they seen and set forth the salutary and warning truth with which these pages are engaged, and which is complementary and balancing to that which they so ably expounded !   Is it too much to hope that God will grant their descendants grace to accept that to which He has of late years been specially drawing attention? Certainly those mighty leaders would have been the first emphatically to repudiate the sentiment which many of their later followers have virtually adopted concerning them, even the tacit assumption that they discovered all that remained unrecognized in the Scriptures.   They would have gladly endorsed Robinson's famous saying, " I am persuaded that God hath yet much light to break forth from His Word."   We pray that all God's beloved people of today may have the humility and candour of mind patiently to search the Scriptures and see whether these things are so, and to accept and spread all that which they see to be in the Word and profitable to the church in these evil and perilous days.

It has been God's gracious method to direct His people from time to time to those truths most signally adapted to the general state.   In Luther's day the church needed firstly and mostly to return to the blessed foundation doctrine of justification by faith in Christ apart from human works. But when the Reformed churches had lapsed into a Sardian contentment with dead externalism and lifeless orthodoxy, then Pietists and Quakers were used to call attention to the need and privilege of inward communion with God in spirit. Later, when the churches were widely paying the penalty of never having cast out the sacerdotal error of regeneration being effected by a priestly ceremony, and clergy and people alike were almost wholly dead in and sunk in sin of every sort, then God mercifully sent to England and America the mighty revivalists of the eighteenth century, and the Wesleys, Whitfield and their co-workers proclaimed the true teaching of the new birth through the Spirit by faith in Christ, and the life of daily holiness that was thus made possible and imperative. And somewhat after, to give a more permanent, exalted and heaven-ward tendency to this most notable advance, the " Brethren " leaders were sent of God, and great was His grace upon them, and indirectly upon the churches through them.

But none of the leaders of these various movings of God perfectly stated the truth of the time. Luther vitiated his own testimony by adhering to infant baptism, to the doctrine of a change of elements in the Lord's supper, and to state-ruled church systems. The Pietist school overstated the doctrine of the inner light, as Wesley seems to us to have done in his *theory* of sanctification. It is therefore in no carping spirit, but rather praying to be ourselves kept from this known tendency, that we think of the great teachers of whom we have first spoken as also being not infallible. And we are increasingly hopeful that the correlative teaching to theirs now coming to the fore, and which is a part of the message of these pages, may prove to be a portion of that which our gracious God will use as a suitable corrective to the insidious dangers which beset His people today.

Instructed from his earliest years in the truth of the heavenly calling of the church, the writer had always known, and thanked God for, the attracting and purifying power of this great

prospect. But for the very reason that he valued exceedingly
highly all that was thus before his heart, he the more
responded by grace to the additional stimulus afforded by the
possibility of losing those privileges. He will not readily forget
how powerful was the effect in stirring him to renewed and
increased service for Christ, and willingness to suffer for Him,
when first he saw that a low state of life might imperil his
sharing with his Lord in His kingdom. No other equal stimulus
had ever acted upon him. The light broke on his mind when
studying for quite another purpose the passage in Hebrews xii
where Esau's case is cited, to which scripture no one had ever
drawn his attention in this connection. From that hour to
become wholly the Lord's, at whatever cost, became life's fixed
determination. And the like positive effect has been produced
in more than one earnest missionary of the cross of the writer's
acquaintance. It is therefore with personal, and, as we believe,
God-wrought conviction that we write, and only after years of
reflection upon these subjects, and with that conviction inten-
sified by long and abiding blessing in our case and those of
others known to us.

But for the securing of these happy and Christ-glorifying results
it is needful that the scheme of thought be understood with
some fulness and accuracy. That is, it must be thoroughly appreciated that while, on the one hand, the heavenly glory is a prize
to be won because it is a privilege that may be lost, yet it is, on
the other hand, equally a birthright, given by the Father to His
firstborn sons upon their new birth in Christ Jesus ! Therefore it being ours by birth, no merit of our own is our title to
it. Neither will the retaining of it, that is the winning of our
prize, be to our own praise, since the strength and wisdom and
perseverance by the exercise of which we may retain the title
and attain at last, are as wholly the gift of God's grace, by His
Spirit through faith, as is our title wholly of His grace in Christ
Jesus. But as the sinner, by rejecting the grace of God in
relation to salvation, may miss eternal life, so the believer,
secure of eternal life, yet rejecting the grace of God for the
purpose of holy living, may forfeit the heavenly glory and
kingdom.

Thus the humble believer is not robbed of any certainty as
to the future which it is good for the pilgrim to enjoy.

1. It remains unchanged that he that is in Christ Jesus is
justified before God, is for ever free from liability to the eternal
wrath of God, possesses in Christ eternal life, and is sure of a
place in the eternal kingdom.

2. It remains certain that there is an inheritance, incorruptible and undefiled and that fadeth not away, reserved in
heaven.

3. It remains unquestionable that whosoever perseveringly
presses on to the end of life's race will certainly reach the goal
and win the prize and share the inheritance.

Uncertainty enters in three particulars only :

1. In the case of such as attain to the first resurrection there
is no guarantee as to the grandeur of the prize in each case, or
the greatness of any individual's share in the inheritance.
Christ uttered the parable of the labourers in the vineyard each
receiving a penny a day (Matt. xix, 27 ; xx, 16), to reprove any
spirit of bargaining in advance (ver. 27), to encourage us to
leave such matters to His unfettered discretion (ver. 14), to
assert His absolute sovereignty in the disposing of His own
property (ver. 15), and to prepare us for some severe surprises
when the day of reward shall come (vers. 30 and 16). He did
not hereby mean that in the coming reality each servant's
reward would be identical. The later parable of the servants
being given more or less authority according to their trading
shows this. The uncertainty in this particular has always been
recognized, and is allowed to be salutary as being a true and
wise stimulus to christian living. Equally salutary is the
remaining element of insecurity, which, indeed, differs from
this other in degree only, not in nature.

2. The uncertainty of whether a given racer or pilgrim may
ever reach the goal arises only if he stand still in indolence, or
turn aside to secure some passing trifle, or lie down in carnal
indulgence, or turn back in sheer rebellion. *But so long as he
presses on this uncertainty does not arise.* He may not be satisfied
with the speed of his running or his advance as a pilgrim ; and

this is a satisfactory state of mind, as prompting more strenuous endeavour: but the runner can and does know whether it be that his eye is on the goal, and the pilgrim whether his heart is already dwelling in his home, or whether it is not so.

3. The remaining possibility is that one who is going forward today may cease to do so tomorrow. Israel moved on for nearly two years, and then turned back. This is the peril that Paul contemplated in his own case (I Cor. ix, 26, 27). But if we watch and pray always we shall not enter into this temptation. Wisdom daily cries: Leave tomorrow alone, and steadily press on today. The grace that kept, and keeps, will keep: it is only he who forgets or doubts this that will fall short of that grace and will stumble.

Thus stated we find nothing in this teaching which in the least detracts from the grace of our God, but much that shows that it is truly "in all *wisdom and prudence*" that He has made the riches of that grace to abound towards us (Eph. i, 7, 8): so that the prospects held out strongly allure and sanctify the heart, while the accompanying warnings mightily promote care and zeal and holiness, together with a humble and constant dependence upon the grace of our Lord Jesus Christ.

It is perhaps well that the majority of minds are not too logical, so that practice is often better than creed, for the logical outcome of some popular views is disastrous. Dr. Bullinger did but carry through logically the earlier view that the three first Gospels are "Jewish," and the just issue was that all the New Testament was declared "Jewish" save only Paul's prison epistles. For him these are the only properly "christian" books. Again, it was but the proper and logical outcome of the popular teaching which a speaker made in my hearing when he said, and said with vigour, " no *matter how you live as a christian*, you are certain to be part of the bride of Christ and to reign with Him." Another, a veteran of eighty years, and a christian teacher of sixty years, declared in a conference I attended in 1935, "I could give you a hundred scriptures to show that every believer will be raised when Christ comes, *no matter how worldly you may be*. If you were in a cinema He would take you. If you were reading a novel—well, you would be ashamed that He should find you thus, but He would not leave you behind."

If these were perversions of the common view it would be unfair to plead them against it, but they are strictly legitimate applications of it. To us, who once ourselves would have made them, they now appear the most regrettable antinomianism, direct incentives to worldliness, and distinctly contrary to both the tenour and the terms of Holy Scripture. Concerning the hope of being like unto our Lord in glory we there read that " every one that hath this hope set on Him *purifieth himself*, even as He is pure " ; also " And now, children, abide in Him, that if He be manifested we may have boldness, and not be put to shame from before Him at His coming " (I Jo. iii, 3 ; ii, 28). The last rendering is Darby's, whose German is even stronger, and closer to the Greek *ap'autou* : "*nicht von ihm hinweg*[1] *beschämt werden*," that is, " not be shamed away from Him " (from His presence) at His coming." Comp. Matt. xxv, 24-30, the picture of the unfaithful servant, for the basis and illustration of these words of John from the lips of Christ himself.

A friend of the writer explained the views here advocated to a keen and spiritual north countryman. Their powerful moral bearing gripped him, and, contrasting them with the general opinion of the guaranteed security of the heavenly privileges, he said : " Look ye, mon, if it's wrung (wrong) it's rit (right), and if t'other's rit it's wrung ! "

Seeing how vast and varied are the themes that have been treated it cannot but be that some phases and questions have not been considered. The principal of these centre round two main matters : First, the nature and details of the judicial proceedings before the judgment seat of Christ in relation to His own servants : and then the resulting state and place of those of His people who shall be accounted unworthy of the heavenly kingdom and glory.

We designedly leave these points at this time. They are plainly but subordinate to the main question, that of the

1—A German might use this word in bidding another to leave his presence at once : Hinweg ! Be off !

forfeiting of the kingdom itself. And the settlement of what God teaches concerning this last matter does not at all depend upon our understanding the details of the consequences involved in such forfeiture. Adam does not appear to have been enlightened as to all that lay wrapped up in the death that was to follow disobedience : it was enough that he knew the main element of the attached penalty, without God enlarging at that time upon such matters as the temporary and the eternal states and places of the dead.

Similarly, for the purposes of the warnings given us, it is not necessary that we know where or how Esau lived after losing his birthright ; nor are we bound to determine precisely what is meant by the " outer darkness " into which the unfaithful servant will be cast, though it is clear to us that it cannot be the lake of fire ; nor to settle a fixed meaning upon the solemn threat that the servant who knew His Lord's will and did it not shall be " beaten with many stripes." Doubtless all these state-ments have a precise value and are of the deepest interest ; and the more we know of their exact force the deeper will be the impression left upon the heart. But at present we refrain from entering upon these topics, for (1), It is better to leave the main theme to stand upon its own testimony, unencumbered by the discussion of what are but subsidiary questions, so that it be not obscured, and that the weight of Scripture evidence for the same be appreciated. (2), The adequate discussion of these details cannot be as brief as space now demands, and a largely incomplete treatment were prejudicial rather than beneficial. It may please God that we shall deal with them later.

We have here sought to show that God most positively and repeatedly forewarns His firstborn sons that their heavenly privileges may be lost and the share in the inheritance in the kingdom be forfeited. To be less to Christ than one might have been, and to be further from Him in His kingdom than one need have been, this will be sad enough to any to whom He is even now the altogether lovely One. But to have lost entirely the gladness of sharing with Him in that kingdom, and to have forfeited eternally the sweetness and glory of reigning with Him as His bride—what heart that loves Him will risk such penalty merely to enjoy this world's poor and fleeting indulgences?

Pregnant is the following question : Who is the one conquering the world but the one believing that Jesus is the SON OF GOD? (I John v, 5). To every problem Christ is God's answer ; for every evil He is the remedy ; from every peril He is the Saviour. Really to *know* Him is all that is required. The deserved penalty of sin no more alarms him who knows Jesus as the propitiation ; the tyranny of sin is broken from off him who knows the risen Christ as his indwelling life ; the powers of darkness no more affright the one who is seated with Christ in the place of authority in the heavenlies ; and equally so the fascinations of this world cease to hold him upon whom has shined the glory of the SON OF GOD. "Ye therefore, beloved, knowing beforehand, beware lest, being carrried away with the error of the wicked, ye fall from your own stedfastness. *But grow in the grace and knowledge of our Lord and Saviour Jesus Christ.* To HIM be the glory both now and for ever. Amen." (II Peter iii, 17, 18).

> Marvel not that Christ in glory
>   All my inmost heart hath won ;
> Not a star to cheer my darkness,
>   But a light beyond the sun.
> All below lies dark and shadowed,
>   Nothing there to claim my heart,
> Save the lonely track of sorrow
>   Where of old He walked apart.
> I have seen the face of Jesus—
>   Tell me not of ought beside ;
> I have heard the voice of Jesus—
>   All my soul is satisfied.
> In the radiance of the glory
>   First I saw His blessed Face,
> And for ever shall that glory
>   Be my home, my dwelling place.
>   *T.P.*

Chapter XVIII

CONCLUSION.

" This is the end of the matter "—(Eccles. xii, 13).
" The end of the charge is—"—(I Tim. i, 5).

Although yet more might be advanced in explanation of these glorious prospects and in enforcement of these wholesome warnings, enough has been now put forward, and we will proceed to state briefly some general lessons which arise.

1. And first, let the truth sink into our heart that GOD HAS A PROGRAM. He is not an opportunist, driven to His wit's end by clever enemies, and just doing the best He can as occasion offers. Let the notion be for ever dismissed that He is as an unskilful chess player painfully watching for chances to outmanoeuvre an expert opponent. The great Architect of the ages drew out His plan before ever He began the work of construction, and those plans were complete, in both principles and details, before He commenced operations. The ends to be served, and the methods and measures for reaching those ends, were settled in advance : and the Lord God the Almighty is equal to the completing of the work that He has commenced, and He is not to be thwarted. Yea, in His infinite wisdom, He causes even the by Him undesigned, though foreseen, opposition of His foes to contribute to the accomplishing of His purposes.

If we His people are to co-operate with our God to further His designs we must have some understanding of what His plan is. *God has a program* : it is our necessity, wisdom, duty, and delight to grasp His plan and work in harmony therewith.

2. THE BIBLE IS GOD'S REVELATION OF HIS PROGRAM. The goal toward which God is working is not discernible in His creative works, nor is it discoverable from even His providences; but in His Word it is set before the diligent and spiritual student.

Hence arises the indispensableness of prayerful and habitual meditation upon Holy Scripture, and upon *all* parts thereof.

The New Testament *cannot* be thoroughly mastered apart from a knowledge of the earlier inspired writings, even as a house cannot be secure without foundations. A knowledge of how to be saved from the wrath of God may, happily, be learned from almost any part of the Word of God, but to comprehend God's program for the ages there must be a diligent searching of the whole Book. Nor will this divine Library ever be comprehended apart from a constant *consecutive* reading of it from beginning to end being the foundation of all study therein. Such study will reveal that the Bible is truly *one Book*, and evidently the product of one Mind, the mind of God. Of this the unity of its teachings, from its opening history to its closing prophecy, is irrefutable proof, and our present survey surely exhibits this feature in some marked degree.[1]

3. That THE PROGRAM AND THE BOOK ARE OF DIVINE ORIGIN is evident, self-evident in fact.

The scheme that has been here drawn out from the Scriptures is neither the product of any one writer nor the collaboration of any or all of them. They lived in different ages, and for the most part had no intercourse with each other. The topics which cohere to form the whole program are often of a specially hidden order, such as the persons and movements of the invisible world, and the facts of a prehistoric character, such as the rebellion of angels prior to man's creation. These matters they commonly do not elaborate, nor even claim any full acquaintance therewith, and yet their touch upon the same is firm and precise, as that of a master when he deals in passing with some one point of an abstruse subject with the whole of which he is entirely conversant. Of this feature no adequate explanation is forthcoming except that it is God Who was the real Writer, guiding His agents in what they declared.

And if any become sufficiently taught by the Spirit of God to gain some thorough grasp of God's program, the vastness and

1—The writer would add his personal recommendation that the Bible in English be studied in the Revised Version. No version is or will be perfect; but after some forty years' close study of the R.V. he is satisfied that it far exceeds earlier versions as a means of gaining the mind of God. As regards the accurate study and grasp of *prophetic* Scripture in particular, this is *simply not possible* from the A.V.; for its underlying text is imperfect. and also there is so great and studied a variety in its renderings of the same words and phrases.

majesty thereof will be its own witness that this plan of the ages is no invention of man, for *it is beyond invention*, and must have been conceived and revealed by God. What theological romancer or philosophical speculator, having the least design that his fellows should adopt his views, could or would have invented the notion of an innumerable multitude of the dead and the living being instantaneously transported to the clouds, being radically changed as to the nature of their bodies, and of their then returning with an incarnate God-Man to superintend the affairs of a rapidly regenerated heavens and earth? And even if such a scheme could have been invented, who would be expected to give credence thereto? and if any did adopt it, what human power could make belief in such ideas a purifying force in degraded human lives? Both the inherent greatness and the moral energy of this program proclaim it to be of God.

4. That THE OUTGATHERING OF THE CHURCH OF GOD FROM EVERY PEOPLE is the portion of the program at present being fulfilled is another lesson, and the one of perhaps the most practical moment.

By every possible device the prince of this world has striven to turn the minds of God's people from this work. To hinder the conversion and frustrate the after-training of those who are to take the places of authority that he and his angels would fain retain is plainly much to his advantage. To lead to general neglect of the work of spreading the gospel message, or to suggest concentration upon a few small fields to the neglect of the world at large; to divert the earnest to such good but premature work as the betterment of society and the elevation of the masses; to further his ends by fostering worldy-mindedness; to bring into contempt the teaching of the coming again of the Lord, or to postpone that hope to some indefinitely remote era; to cause the calling of the church to the heavenly kingdom to be overlooked or even derided, and this not seldom by those who do preach truly the way of salvation from hell, so that the atonement is set forth while the "mystery" is hidden: these and the like methods has Satan employed, and with all too marked success, to frustrate the church in her one supreme business of calling men to repentance and faith and offering them a share in God's kingdom and glory.

He who would work effectively with God is called upon to account that the longsuffering of our God, His not having sooner visited the wicked with condign judgment, is in order that the perishing may have opportunity of repentance (II Pet. iii, 9, 15), and he is therefore to make it his life work to explain the way of salvation to every person that he can reach, so that the company of the firstborn sons of God may be completed.

5. Our studies have made this also to be clear—that the PERSONAL COMING TO EARTH AND REIGN OF THE LORD JESUS CHRIST are absolutely indispensable to. the fulfilment of God's program. The accomplishment of the divine purposes without this intervention of God's Son in the affairs of the earth is simply not possible. It is upon this earth that the age-long battle between God and His foes is to be fought to the finish, and hither must God's Champion come to complete His victory. Nowhere else can the crisis be reached, and no One else is competent to meet it. " The appearing of the glory of our great God and Saviour Jesus Christ " is therefore the hope of the future for God and man, for the heavens and the earth, for the church, for Israel, and for the nations, even as it will be the despair and death-knell of God's foes whether angels, demons, or men.

6. GOD'S PROGRAM IS THE REVELATION OF GOD HIMSELF. What truly unsearchable wisdom is therein exhibited ; what inexhaustible resources are revealed ; what infallible judgment is displayed ; what irresistible power is exerted ! How infinite are the love, the grace, and the tender mercy lavished upon the wholly unworthy ; and how equally godlike is the inflexible justice that shines in the exhibition of that mercy through Jesus Christ, as well as in the final overthrow and eternal punishment of the finally impenitent !

The longer that God's purposes are devoutly pondered the more perfect is seen to be His provision for dealing with the conditions existing in heaven and earth, causing the humble heart to bow in deepest adoration. When the mystery of the church is properly grasped it is seen to contain "all the treasures of wisdom and knowledge" not formerly revealed, and to be a scheme as entirely worthy of God in all its parts as it will be proved to be by its blessed results. Thus, in the midst of present distresses and perplexities, faith can quietly rest in the assurance that the end will justify God in all His ways. Its triumphant declaration is that "As for God His way is *perfect*," and "He maketh my way *perfect*" (Ps. xviii, 30, 32). What faith does not know now it expects to get to know hereafter: and reasoning from what it does know of God and His dealings to what it waits to know, it confidently anticipates that that unknown portion of His ways will be entirely right and well-pleasing.

And when the consummation shall have been reached, and the victorious sit with Christ on His throne, in the fullest enjoyment of His love, in the highest possible degree of glory and happiness, with immeasurable possibilities of perfect service and usefulness, and all this to endure for evermore, there will then be but one answer to our opening question, even that it certainly was abundantly well worth while to have followed Christ, yea, to have been among those who followed the Lamb whithersoever He went, though the path to the kingdom led through many tribulations. For in divinely royal measure shall be fulfilled these words of the Son of God: "If any man serve Me, let him follow Me; and where I am, there shall also My servant be: if any man serve Me, him will the Father honour" (John xii, 26).

"Now unto Him that is able to guard you from stumbling, and to set you before the presence of His glory without blemish in exceeding joy, to the only God our Saviour, through Jesus Christ our Lord, be glory, majesty, dominion and power, before all time, and now, and unto all the ages. Amen." (Jude, ver. 24, 25).

INDEX OF SCRIPTURE PASSAGES.

OLD TESTAMENT.

NEW TESTAMENT.

MONUMENTAL WORKS

BY DILLOW, DODSON, GOVETT, LANG, MAURO, NEIGHBOUR, PANTON, PEMBER, RADMACHER, STANTON, WHIPPLE, AND WILSON

JOSEPH C. DILLOW
THE REIGN OF THE SERVANT KINGS

KENNETH F. DODSON
THE PRIZE OF THE UP-CALLING

ROBERT GOVETT
GOVETT ON ISAIAH
GOVETT ON THE PARABLES
GOVETT ON JOHN (2 vols. in 1)
GOVETT ON ROMANS
GOVETT ON GALATIANS
GOVETT ON EPHESIANS
GOVETT ON PHILIPPIANS
GOVETT ON COLOSSIANS
GOVETT ON THESSALONIANS
GOVETT ON II TIMOTHY
GOVETT ON HEBREWS
GOVETT ON I JOHN
GOVETT ON REVELATION (4 vols. in 2)
CALVINISM BY CALVIN
CHRIST'S JUDGMENT OF HIS SAINTS
CHRIST'S RESURRECTION AND OURS
ENTRANCE INTO THE KINGDOM
ESAU'S CHOICE
ETERNAL SUFFERING OF THE WICKED AND
    HADES
GOSPEL ANALOGIES
HOW INTERPRET THE APOCALYPSE?
IS SANCTIFICATION PERFECT HERE BELOW?
KINGDOM OF GOD FUTURE
KINGDOM STUDIES
LEADING THOUGHTS ON THE APOCALYPSE
REWARD ACCORDING TO WORKS
SINS BEFORE FAITH AND SINS AFTER FAITH
SOWING AND REAPING
THE BEST MODE OF PRESENTING THE GOSPEL
THE CHURCH OF OLD: 1 CORINTHIANS 12,13,14
THE FUTURE APOSTASY
THE JEWS, THE GENTILES, AND THE CHURCH
    OF GOD IN THE GOSPEL OF MATTHEW
THE NEW JERUSALEM
THE PROPHECY ON OLIVET
THE SAINTS RAPTURE
THE SERMON ON THE MOUNT
THE THREE EATINGS: EDEN, PASSOVER & THE
    LORD'S SUPPER
THE TWO WITNESSES
TWO VIEWS OF THE SUPPER OF THE LORD

G. H. LANG
AN ORDERED LIFE
ANTHONY NORRIS GROVES
ATONING BLOOD
BALANCED CHRISTIANITY
COMING EVENTS
DEPARTURE
DIVINE GUIDANCE
FIRSTBORN SONS
FIRSTFRUITS AND HARVEST
GOD AT WORK ON HIS OWN LINES

GOD'S PLAN, CHRIST'S SUFFERING, AND THE
    SPIRIT'S POWER
IDEALS AND REALITIES
ISRAEL'S NATIONAL FUTURE
PICTURES AND PARABLES
PRAYER: FOCUSED AND FIGHTING
PRAYING IS WORKING
THE CHURCHES OF GOD
THE CLEAN HEART
THE DISCIPLE
THE EARLIER YEARS OF THE MODERN
    TONGUES MOVEMENT
THE EPISTLE TO THE HEBREWS
THE FIRST RESURRECTION
THE GOSPEL OF THE KINGDOM
THE HISTORY & DIARIES OF AN INDIAN
    CHRISTIAN
THE HISTORIES AND PROPHECIES OF DANIEL
THE LAST ASSIZE
THE LOCAL ASSEMBLY
THE MODERN GIFT OF TONGUES
THE NEW BIRTH
THE REVELATION OF JESUS CHRIST
THE SINNER'S FUTURE
THE UNEQUAL YOKE
WORLD CHAOS

PHILIP MAURO
GOD'S APOSTLE AND HIGH PRIEST
GOD'S PILGRIMS

R. E. NEIGHBOUR
IF BY ANY MEANS
IF THEY SHALL FALL AWAY

D. M. PANTON
RAPTURE
THE JUDGMENT SEAT OF CHRIST
THE PANTON PAPERS

G. H. PEMBER
MYSTERY BABYLON THE GREAT
THE ANTICHRIST BABYLON AND THE
    COMING OF THE KINGDOM
THE GREAT PROPHECIES Vol. I
THE GREAT PROPHECIES Vol. II
THE GREAT PROPHECIES Vol. III
THE GREAT PROPHECIES Vol. IV
THE LORD'S COMMAND

EARL RADMACHER
THE NATURE OF THE CHURCH

GERALD B. STANTON
KEPT FROM THE HOUR

GARY T. WHIPPLE
SHOCK & SURPRISE BEYOND THE RAPTURE
THE MATTHEW MYSTERIES

A. EDWIN WILSON
SELECTED WRITINGS

Available Through Your
Local Christian Book Store or Consult Publisher